Under a M

'*Under a Mushroom Cloud* considers Europe as the primary power vis-à-vis Iran's nuclear ambitions. How Europe will use this unaccustomed power is the big question at the heart of this timely book.'

– *François Heisbourg, Special Adviser, Fondation pour la Recherche Stratégique, Paris*

'This is an important contribution to the debate about Europe's approach to Iran. As one would expect, Dr Ottolenghi has written a well-informed, perceptive and sobering book. I hope our European leaders, and those who study this potential flashpoint, will read what he has to say.'

– *General The Lord Charles Guthrie, Chief of the British Defence Staff (1997–2001), Colonel Commandant of the Life Guards and the Special Air Service*

'How to deal with Iran is one of the most pressing foreign policy issues of the day. Dr Ottolenghi provides a useful guide to the challenge and thoughtful suggestions on how to meet it.'

– *Professor Sir Lawrence Freedman, Professor of War Studies and Vice-Principal, King's College London*

'For almost three decades, conventional wisdom has presented Iran as a problem for the United States. In this seminal study, Dr Ottolenghi shows that a nuclear-armed Islamic Republic could be more of a threat to Europe, which, in one of those bitter ironies of history, has helped the Khomeinist regime not only to survive but also to build its arsenal of deadly weapons. A work of impeccable scholarship, this book is also a political wake-up call to European democracies.'

– *Amir Taheri, syndicated columnist, former Executive Editor of Kayhan, Iran's largest daily paper*

Under a Mushroom Cloud

Europe, Iran and the Bomb

Emanuele Ottolenghi

P

PROFILE BOOKS

First published in Great Britain in 2009 by
PROFILE BOOKS LTD
3A Exmouth House
Pine Street
Exmouth Market
London EC1R oJH
www.profilebooks.com

10 9 8 7 6 5 4 3 2 1

Typeset in Palatino by MacGuru Ltd
info@macguru.org.uk

Printed and bound in Great Britain by
CPI Bookmarque, Croydon, Surrey

A CIP catalogue record for this book is available from the British Library.

ISBN 978 1 84668 282 7

Mixed Sources
Product group from well-managed
forests and other controlled sources
www.fsc.org Cert no. TT-COC-002227
© 1996 Forest Stewardship Council

'All warfare is based on deception. When able to attack, we must seem unable; when using our forces, we must seem inactive; when we are near, we must make the enemy believe we are far away.'

– Sun Tsu, *The Art of War*

'All our nuclear activities have been completely peaceful and transparent.'

– Mahmoud Ahmadinejad, speech to the General Assembly of the UN, 26 September 2007

About the author

Emanuele Ottolenghi was born in Bologna, Italy. A Political Science graduate of the University of Bologna, he obtained his Ph.D. at the Hebrew University of Jerusalem and taught Israel Studies at Oxford from 1999 to 2006. Since 2006, he has been the director of the Brussels-based Transatlantic Institute. A frequent commentator on Middle East affairs and transatlantic relations for many English-language and Italian publications, he is the author, most recently, of *Autodafé: L'Europa, gli Ebrei e l'Antisemitismo* (Lindau, 2007, in Italian).

Contents

Acknowledgements   ix

Introduction   1
1   How we got here   17
2   In the shadow of Iran's bomb   59
3   Human rights and the illusion of 'Iranian democracy'   123
4   Iran's deceptive practices   152
5   What is to be done?   199

Conclusion   243
Bibliography   248
Index   269

Acknowledgements

This book is the result of more than a year of research, interviews and conversations held in Europe, the United States and Israel with senior government officials, intelligence and security officials, academics and elected leaders. To all those who agreed to speak to me and share their views on the subject of Iran and its nuclear programme, I wish to extend my deepest gratitude. I cannot mention their names – often our conversations were held off the record or under Chatham House rules. I did my best to take their comments, criticism and thoughtful observations into due account and sometimes report them faithfully without revealing their identity. I hope they will recognise themselves and the immense help they provided me without feeling in any way that our trust was broken.

This work could not have been completed had it not been for the valiant help of so many interns and research assistants at the Transatlantic Institute. I wish to thank Jonathan Feldman, Joshua Hantman, Max Kienzerle, Nate Miller, Margherita Sacerdoti, Benjamin Tankel and Rachel Weinberger for their invaluable support in finding, verifying and corroborating so much of the sometimes hard-to-assess evidence available in open sources.

Many other people contributed to this book – first and foremost Helen and Douglas Davis, who are both dear friends and colleagues. Their dedication in all phases of this work was a labour of love – and I could not have done it without them. Helen made this project possible from its very early stages and worked tirelessly to promote it. Douglas endured many editing rounds, ensuring that the final product was much better than its first draft. Needless to say, I alone am responsible for what's written in the coming pages. But their help was vital in ensuring that this book would come to light. It was an honour to work together and I am grateful and indebted to them for all that they have done. My thanks also to Paul Forty, for Profile Books, who patiently and thoroughly managed the editing of the final manuscript, always in good spirits and with a skilful touch.

This project could not have come to fruition had it not been for the generous contribution of two benefactors, who wish to remain anonymous. Their unwavering support made the publication of this book possible. I wish to thank them from the bottom of my heart for their invaluable assistance. Thanks also go to the Henry Jackson Society and its director, Alan Mendoza, who chose to co-sponsor this project alongside my own Transatlantic Institute.

Last, but not least, a special thanks to my family – my wife Nicole, first and foremost – who stood by me through the long and arduous journey that writing this work came to be. She helped me, assisted me and kept her smile coming when I needed it most.

This book is dedicated to her.

Brussels
January 2009

Introduction

Since Iran's illicit nuclear programme was exposed in 2002, Tehran has defied the international community and doggedly continued pursuing its nuclear goals. It has turned down tantalising economic incentives, borne the brunt of increasing diplomatic isolation and incurred a high price in sanctions. What, then, is impelling Tehran's nuclear quest? Is it the hope of 'wiping Israel off the map'? Is it the dream of finally establishing Shi'a predominance over Sunni Islam? Or is this a search for a trigger to usher in a millenarian Shi'a vision – the final eschatological act in the war between the City of God and the City of Man?

Is Iran maybe motivated by a more rational, if no less daring, calculus? Is it driven by an aspiration to dominate the Gulf and its resources, achieve regional hegemony and use its status to export its Islamic revolution while challenging America's attempts to export democracy and the West's libertarian concept of social justice and human rights? Or is the quest for the bomb merely a tool to ensure the survival of a paranoid and isolated regime?

It is impossible, at this point, to provide a definitive answer to these questions, but it is clear that since the revelation of its clandestine nuclear programme Iran has followed a dual-track approach of accelerating its nuclear activities while pursuing a strategy of weaving itself ever more tightly into the fabric of the European economy. Its success in both of these endeavours is largely due to the fact that Iran proved itself exceptionally deft in the use of deception as a tool of statecraft and diplomacy, both in the realm of its nuclear programme and in its economic relationships.

Nor has Europe been immune to Iran's embrace. Europe has no wish to live under the shadow of an Iranian bomb, but the lure of short-term trade advantages appears to have trumped the longer-term threats posed by a nuclear Iran. European exports constitute 40 per cent of Iran's imports, and Europe is particularly involved in Iran's lucrative energy sector. Europe now appears to have invested too heavily in the Iranian economy to play a constructive role in attempts by the international community to dissuade Iran from pursuing nuclear weapons.

In his seminal book on Iran's nuclear programme, *Iran, le choix des armes*, French non-proliferation expert François Heisbourg confronted this contradiction, which is at the heart of Europe's relations with Iran. He concluded his assessment of Iran's nuclear dossier with an exhortation to European leaders. The policy of European nations, he wrote, 'must be inspired by their own fundamental values and vital interests alike: nuclear non-proliferation is at the heart of both'.

Heisbourg's plea underlies the entire structure of this book, whose goal is to offer a detailed argument in favour of robust European sanctions against Iran. In these pages, opinion-formers, decision-makers and the general public will find the necessary information to assess the nature of Iran's nuclear programme and the possible consequences of a nuclear Iran for both Europe's strategic interests and the stability of the region.

In spite of Iran's claims that its nuclear activities are

intended purely for civilian use, it is widely accepted that Tehran is determined to develop a nuclear weapons arsenal to match its extensive ballistic-missile programme. Preventing this development is a supreme European interest. But time is not on the side of those who fear the consequences of a nuclear Iran. Time is on Iran's side.

Although Iran does not seem to have fully mastered the nuclear cycle – and it has certainly not tested a nuclear device – such developments are only a matter of time. There is little to prevent Iran overcoming the technical hurdles and any remaining gaps in its scientific know-how.

With the publication of the National Intelligence Estimate's Key Findings on Iran's nuclear programme (NIE) in December 2007, the USA appeared to remove any credible military option from the table. A military attack launched from Israel might be possible (indeed, it might be inevitable), but that is less likely to provide the result that would come from military action by the USA. In spite of the country's awesome power, even a US strike could not be certain to reach all of the Iranian nuclear sites. And, besides, it is now estimated that no military action can be absolutely conclusive. Iran's nuclear plans may be degraded and delayed by external military action, but its march towards nuclear weapons capability can only, ultimately, be stopped by an Iranian decision that such a goal is not worth pursuing.

The NIE focuses mainly on two aspects of Iran's nuclear programme: first, the military component, which includes the development, construction and assembly of a deliverable nuclear device; and second, the political will that the Iranians must demonstrate to cross the technological threshold necessary to build nuclear weapons. According to the NIE,

> in fall 2003, Tehran halted its nuclear weapons program; …
> Tehran at a minimum is keeping open the option to develop
> nuclear weapons. … [T]he halt, and Tehran's announcement
> of its decision to suspend its declared uranium enrichment
> program and sign an Additional Protocol to its Nuclear Non-
> Proliferation Treaty Safeguards Agreement, was directed pri-
> marily in response to increasing international scrutiny and
> pressure resulting from exposure of Iran's previously unde-
> clared nuclear work.

Assuming the NIE was accurate, the 'pressure' to halt (or
suspend) work on Iran's nuclear weapons programme in 2003
might be explained by anxieties in Tehran that the USA would
extend its military operation against Iraq into Iran itself. After
witnessing America's easy military triumph over Saddam
Hussein's armies, the Iranian leadership may have worried
that they would be next if they were found to be secretly developing nuclear weapons. The Americans had, after all, toppled
Saddam ostensibly because of his weapons of mass destruction (WMD) programme, so why would they not seize on
Iranian WMD as a pretext to extend their operation into Iran?

But, still assuming that the NIE was accurate, an even
more pressing issue for Tehran may have been the presence
on their soil of highly suspicious inspectors from the International Atomic Energy Agency (IAEA), the UN's watchdog
on nuclear issues. The inspectors had reason for suspicion,
for they had just learned that they had been duped by the
Iranians for at least eighteen years. The inspectors had been
galvanised into robust and intrusive action when the National
Council of Resistance in Iran, an opposition group in exile,
revealed the existence of two clandestine nuclear sites – at

Natanz and Arak – during a briefing in Washington, DC, on 14 August 2002. The inspectors' mission was to authenticate the claims and determine whether Iran had breached the terms of its commitments as a signatory of the Nuclear Non-Proliferation Treaty (NPT).

Article 3 of the NPT stipulates that, in exchange for access to nuclear technology for peaceful civilian purposes, signatory states pledge not to pursue nuclear weapons. In other words, countries that sign the NPT undertake neither to develop nuclear weapons nor transfer nuclear technologies to non-NPT nations. They also commit themselves to open their nuclear sites and installations – whose purposes must be intended for peaceful civilian use – to inspection and monitoring by the IAEA. The benefits of signing the NPT are twofold: first, signatories can access assistance from other NPT states for the development of their own civilian nuclear energy programmes in compliance with the NPT stipulations; and second, so-called 'nuclear weapons states' that sign the NPT commit themselves to nuclear disarmament over time. As a signatory of the NPT, Iran was clearly entitled to pursue a nuclear programme. But it was emphatically not entitled to use that programme for military purposes. It was also obliged to be transparent. The revelation that it had been engaged in clandestine nuclear activities in Natanz and Arak for eighteen years had thrown its credibility in terms of its compliance into serious doubt.

If Iran had been secretly involved in developing a nuclear weapons programme, its discovery would have serious consequences. A declaration by the IAEA that Iran was in breach of its NPT obligations might lead to sanctions. The discovery of a smoking gun – actual evidence of a nuclear weapons programme – particularly with American forces deployed in both Iraq and Afghanistan, could have led to a war that Iran was ill prepared to fight. Under the circumstances, it seems reasonable to conclude that Iran would have decided, prudently and pragmatically, to suspend its weapons programme.

According to the NIE, Iran suspended only the military component of the entire programme. It noted that 'by "nuclear weapons program" we mean Iran's nuclear weapon design and weaponization work and covert uranium conversion-related and uranium enrichment-related work; we do not mean Iran's declared civil work related to uranium conversion and enrichment'.

These terms, however, are ambiguous. 'Civil work' alone is the most critical component of a nuclear military programme. Efforts to enrich uranium to weapons-grade level and to develop and improve the range and performance of ballistic missiles continue apace, with no attempt to dissimulate or deny the existence or scope of these twin components of a nuclear weapons programme. Besides, evidence shows that Iran has conducted work on designing a warhead, testing explosives and adapting ballistic missiles to accommodate a nuclear payload, as well as on uranium hemispheres, detonators and other components of a nuclear bomb.

Regardless of the reasons that may have pushed the Iranian regime to suspend the military aspects of its nuclear programme – if, that is, the NIE is correct – the intelligence assessment had two far-reaching diplomatic implications. The mood among many international leaders and commentators changed. There was, they happily concluded, no rush to pressure Iran. The gentle diplomatic dance could continue. The other consequence was to make the likelihood of a US military strike against Iran even more remote than it may have been before the NIE was published.

Beyond the headlines caused by the apparently benign NIE, some troubling details were revealed which should give cause for concern. For the first time, the NIE explicitly acknowledged that Iran was building a nuclear weapon. No government agency, and certainly no international organisation, had ever gone so far. It is, therefore, legitimate to ask how advanced the programme was when it was suspended, what suspension means and what has happened to the programme since 2003. The NIE also notes that Iran has the scientific capability to develop a nuclear weapon and that its choice to suspend its military programme is susceptible to being reversed. According to the NIE, 'Iran probably would be technically capable of producing enough HEU [highly enriched uranium] for a weapon sometime during the 2010–2015 time frame'. It adds that 'Iranian entities are continuing to develop a range of technical capabilities that could be applied to producing nuclear weapons, if a decision is made to do so'. It concludes therefore that

> convincing the Iranian leadership to forgo the eventual development of nuclear weapons will be difficult given the linkage many within the leadership probably see between nuclear weapons development and Iran's key national security and foreign policy objectives, and given Iran's considerable effort from at least the late 1980s to 2003 to develop such weapons. In our judgment, only an Iranian political decision to abandon a nuclear weapons objective would plausibly keep Iran from eventually producing nuclear weapons – and such a decision is inherently reversible.

Seen in this light, the NIE report is not as benign as the headlines suggest. But one cannot discount the impact of the Iraq War on decision-makers, opinion-formers and the public at large. After all, the invasion of Iraq was based on the premise that Saddam Hussein had a WMD programme which threatened regional stability and, by extension, Western security. In the event, that assessment was proved wrong: WMD were not found. This might explain the scepticism of some in the case of Iran's nuclear aspirations – a scepticism that the NIE reinforced. The main operational result of the NIE was to weaken the argument for a military strike on Iran's nuclear facilities – among those, at least, who were predisposed to scepticism.

Recently published reports highlight the possible fallout of another war in the Gulf. For Europe, the political consequences of the NIE are understandably important. It appeared to make the prospect of a nuclear Iran more remote, at least in the short term, and was particularly welcomed by those who oppose a military confrontation with Iran to prevent such a development. Most particularly, it was welcomed by Europeans who feared another 'military adventure' in the region. The NIE had another unexpected side effect: the diminishing threat of US military action against Iran coincided with a diminished appetite for a more rigorous sanctions regime to persuade Iran, via diplomatic means, to abide by its NPT commitments.

Iran still has not come clean on its nuclear programme and there is considerable cause to doubt Tehran's continued insistence on its purely peaceful nature. Iran is in no hurry to answer questions from the IAEA, let alone offer a convincing explanation – coupled with compelling evidence – of the fate of the clandestine military programme that was exposed by the NIE. Far from responding to requests for clarification from the IAEA, Iran has done everything possible to raise doubts and fears even among such traditionally cautious observers as the IAEA.

The fact that fresh American military intervention in the Gulf appears to be less likely in a post-NIE world does not reduce the risk that Iran will eventually master the nuclear cycle and arm itself with nuclear weapons. But such a development should not compel the West to reconcile itself to living with the strategic threat of an Iranian bomb. There are other options that could persuade Iran's leaders that the price of developing nuclear weapons is simply too high. One price-too-high is a direct threat to the survival of the Islamic Republic itself. It is conceivable that further deterioration of Iran's sclerotic economy could heighten popular disaffection, raise fundamental doubts about the Islamic Revolution and seriously destabilise the regime. Robust and rigorously enforced sanctions could hold the key.

In Europe, however, there is an increasing reluctance to intensify economic pressure on Iran. Trade relations with Iran are fruitful and expanding; a fact which has been given added significance by the credit crunch. Moreover, Europe is intrinsically averse to confrontation, preferring treaties, accords, agreements, memoranda of understanding, winks and nods. Its response to the Iranian nuclear challenge has focused on negotiations, with a plethora of carrots and a few small sticks, including sanctions on a level that would be ineffective and which Iran has treated with contempt.

But Europe is taking an enormous gamble by protecting its lucrative trade with Iran in the hope that the bellicose rhetoric emanating from Tehran is mere bluff. No evidence exists to support some European assertions that the mullahs will somehow emerge from their mystical, medieval mindset and behave rationally when their nuclear weapons start rolling off the production line. There is another factor that the Europeans should consider. They have largely welcomed America's lack of military will and they probably accept that, at the current level, sanctions will not work. But those are not the only options. If tough diplomacy fails to work and an American strike remains beyond the horizon, it is possible that Israel, which has been goaded by Iranian threats to 'wipe it off the map', will conclude that it has no alternative but to act independently and pre-emptively to prevent Iran from achieving the ability to carry out its threat.

Europe has no reason to be complacent when it comes to Iran. Even if the NIE is correct and efforts to build a nuclear device were interrupted in 2003, Iran did not abandon its ambition to master the nuclear cycle and acquire the technology and know-how to develop nuclear weapons. From all accounts, Iran's nuclear programme appears to be advancing inexorably towards the 'point of no return', the technological threshold beyond which nothing can stop it from acquiring nuclear weapons. Nor, strictly speaking, does it matter what Iran does once it is capable of constructing a bomb.

It could choose to go the way of Japan – that is, master the art without building the bomb and thereby remain a member of the NPT – or it could go the way of Israel (which has never signed the NPT) and adopt a policy of nuclear ambiguity. In such a case, Iran could simply allow the world to believe, with good reason, that it might have a bomb. The so-called 'bomb in the basement' is no less destabilising than an open declaration of nuclear-weapons status. After all, unless one aspires to initiate a nuclear holocaust, the role of the bomb is to act as a deterrent and to project power. The presumption that Iran possesses the bomb – even without a test to prove it – would be a powerful instrument of dissuasion.

If Iran were to acquire nuclear weapons, or even just the capability to build them, whether it uses them or not becomes largely irrelevant. The outcome is, at a minimum, that Iran will be able to radically destabilise and alter the regional and global balance of power. Its nuclear arsenal – or presumed arsenal – will threaten not only its Middle East and Gulf neighbours but also its Asian neighbours, particularly Pakistan, which is already a nuclear state and one, moreover, with nascent tendencies towards rival Sunni extremism. The effect will be dramatic for Europe, too.

Iran will no doubt use its enhanced regional power status to establish its hegemony over the Gulf – including a dominating role over the vital energy supply routes through which 40 per cent of the global supply of crude oil transits daily. It will also be able to coerce or threaten its neighbours and not a few European nations thanks to its ballistic missiles – which can currently reach southern Europe with a conventional payload. Regionally, a nuclear Iran will stir the already simmering tensions between Shi'a and Sunni powers; it will strengthen its proxies, notably Hezbollah and Hamas, by transferring – or threatening to transfer – weapons-grade material which could be used in 'dirty bombs'; and it could make the prospect of any peace deal with Israel (which it opposes) immeasurably more complex than it is at present. It could also thwart any hope of pacifying Lebanon, which would be at the expense of Iranian hegemony over Syria and Hezbollah. Iran would also compete with Saudi Arabia for supremacy as the Guardian of Islam and leader of the Islamic world, becoming the main sponsor of all Islamist movements in the region. Iran's nuclear capability would also trigger a regional arms race, raising the spectre of proliferation throughout the region. Already, a slew of states have put out feelers to suppliers of nuclear facilities.

The first victim would be the NPT regime and the international order that regulates the use of nuclear energy for peaceful purposes. From Egypt and Saudi Arabia to Morocco and Turkey, many regional players will seek to acquire nuclear arsenals to deter Iran. The risks for Europe are self-evident: what will be the future for NATO if Turkey becomes a nuclear power? Will European states respond by building their own deterrent nuclear force? And what will be the security implications for the Mediterranean if Egypt, Algeria and Morocco go nuclear?

Finally, it is difficult to see how Iran, with its revolutionary zeal protected by a nuclear arsenal, will play a constructive role in pacifying the regional tensions it is currently fomenting. The Iranian proxies would then be able to shelter under the destructive power and diplomatic prestige of Iran's nuclear umbrella. And their capabilities might actually be enhanced by the acquisition from Iran of radiological weapons and longer-range missile systems that will be able to strike deep inside Israel. This is not a hopeful scenario for Europeans who seek peace at home and aspire to stability in the Levant.

Iran's revolutionary ideology is not necessarily tinged with a yearning for the End of Days, though it would be foolish to dismiss the existence of such feelings among Iran's ruling elites. In spite of their rhetoric, Iran's leaders may be guided by a rational calculation – the desire to ensure the survival of the Islamic Revolution and to strengthen it, both internally and regionally, in order to achieve the regional hegemony that some in Iran believe is rightfully theirs. But the revolutionary nature of the regime means that, at a minimum, Iran aspires to redefine the regional order of power in its favour and remake it in its own image. Nuclear weapons would exponentially increase Iran's ability to achieve that goal, setting the Shi'a regime on a dangerous collision course with most of its Sunni neighbours. Given such premises, it does not even take a leadership driven by visions of religious utopia to slip into a war. Its revisionist ambitions are enough to set it on a collision course with the other regional powers.

Besides, Iran's ambitions go beyond the region. Tehran has repeatedly expressed its aim to become the global reference point for countries and movements that oppose the existing global order. The enhanced prestige and power Iran would gain from acquiring nuclear status would generate a stream of anti-Western governments and anti-global movements to Tehran. Offering them protection and material support, Iran would become the ideological counterweight of America, much as the Soviet Union was during the cold war. Finally, as the aspiring leader of the Islamic world, Iran would challenge Saudi Arabia and its ageing monarchy for the role of custodian of Islam's most sacred places. It would launch a race across the lands of Islam to regain supremacy over the Sunni rulers of Mecca and have Muslims the world over look to Tehran for guidance instead of to Riyadh. Western interests, including European interests, would suffer grievously from this development and would likely become the target of Iranian agitation, directly or through its new-found proxies, for years to come.

The international political constellation is hardly favourable to interdicting this gloomy forecast. Apart from the distant prospect of an independent Israeli military strike, the only obstacle standing between Iran and its nuclear ambitions is time – the time it will take to master the nuclear cycle. Sooner rather than later, Iran will achieve this breakthrough. But the industrialised world does not need to sit on its hands and await the fateful announcement from Tehran. It could hold the key to preventing this doomsday scenario.

That key is economic pressure – robust, rigorous, intrusive, extensive and sustained. Deep enough to threaten the very survival of the Islamic Revolution and make continued nuclear activity unfeasible. On the brink of the abyss, the Iranian regime will choose to follow its survival instincts and rethink its nuclear ambitions, regardless of the dreams that initially propelled it down the nuclear path. Success will require Europe to radically reassess its current fatalistic approach and, possibly, forgo short-term economic gain. Given its pivotal role in Iranian trade, Europe must dramatically increase its economic pressure on Iran.

The path of total sanctions will pose economic, political, strategic and, not least, psychological challenges for Europe. The internal process of achieving consensus for decisive economic action among the twenty-seven member states of the European Union will be difficult. Europe will collectively have to contend with the loss of lucrative Iranian markets for trade and possible Iranian reprisals. This could take the form of a loss of Iranian oil supplies and a consequent further steep rise in energy costs. Iranian reprisals could also take the form of attacks through its proxies. Europeans will also have to overcome their squeamishness at the loss, albeit temporarily, of the diplomatic option. The urgent imperative now is for hard-nosed confrontation. Short of a successful Israeli air strike that sets back the Iranian nuclear project for a decade, with all the consequent fallout, tough economic sanctions are the only means of stopping this destructive development. And it must be stopped.

There is the legitimate doubt – underscored by a series of unhappy precedents – that sanctions might not work. They may, indeed, produce unintended consequences: allowing the regime more time to pursue its nuclear programme, escalate its radical narrative, possibly throw IAEA inspectors out of Iran and even withdraw from the NPT. Critics of a more robust sanctions regime understandably cite the cases of Iraq, Serbia, Myanmar and Zimbabwe as example of why sanctions, far from achieving their political goals, have encouraged rogue regimes to accelerate their activities, inflicting much humanitarian suffering on civilian populations in the process. Even in cases where sanctions eventually worked – such as Rhodesia and South Africa – it took many years. And even then, success was at least as much a consequence of other international and internal political developments as it was of economic sanctions. This issue will be examined in greater depth elsewhere.

There is the innate European philosophy which informs its worldview. It is a view underpinned by an unshakeable faith in dialogue and multilateralism, in the supremacy of diplomacy as a means of suasion without the need for confrontational mechanisms, such as sanctions. Reluctance to pressure Iran is not only the result of cynical business calculations but also of a genuine belief that dialogue and engagement offer a better instrument to advance diplomatic goals in international relations. In short, there are many arguments against recourse to sanctions.

The problem is that these arguments end up paralysing any European initiative that is not merely an attempt to increase the incentives Europe offers to Iran in the vain hope that it will change its aberrant behaviour. Carrot after carrot, Europe will sooner or later find itself in the spectator's role while a new war in the Gulf erupts, the fourth in thirty years. Given that Europe is bound to bear much of the consequences of such conflict, whatever the outcome, and considering the scarce results so far achieved through dialogue and incentives, it is time for Europe's leaders to strengthen their resolve and play a leading role in averting the catastrophic consequences of a nuclear-capable Iran.

The nuclear stand-off between Iran and the West is perhaps the greatest foreign policy challenge for a united Europe in a generation. This book is intended to provide a users' manual for dealing with that challenge.

1

How We Got Here

Is Iran building a nuclear bomb? Is there hard evidence of such an intention? And is there evidence that such an intention is being translated into reality? Or are the claims and counter-claims about Iran simply a rerun of the case against Saddam Hussein's Iraq, when a flawed argument for war was based on faulty intelligence about weapons of mass destruction?

The nuclear stand-off between Iran and the international community is already into its seventh year. During that time, many sympathetic voices have been raised in Tehran's defence. Most advocates for Iran tend to advance three arguments. First, they contend, there is no evidence of Iran's intention to build nuclear weapons. The growing pressure on Iran, as in the case of Iraq, is focused on the presumption rather than the evidence of WMD in order to create a pretext for war. Second, they ask, so what if Iran is building nuclear weapons? No such fuss was made about Israel, India and Pakistan, all near neighbours which acquired nuclear arsenals. Why not Iran? Third, they argue, Iran has good reasons to build nuclear weapons. It is isolated, has suffered terribly from the Iran–Iraq War, is surrounded by enemies and has been the victim of a protracted American-led arms embargo. Moreover, they point out, Iran is not a belligerent power. It has never initiated war and, considering the regional context, it would seek nuclear weapons for defensive purposes only.

There is an inherent contradiction among these three points. Either Iran is building the bomb or it is not. India, Pakistan and Israel are not signatories of the Non-Proliferation Treaty (NPT), but Iran is a signatory. It therefore enjoys a privileged position and, at the same time, is bound by its treaty obligation not to pursue nuclear weapons. Such restrictions do not apply to non-NPT states like India, Pakistan and Israel. It is also hard to believe that, as an Islamic revolutionary power with regional hegemonic ambitions, Iran is seeking nuclear weapons for purely defensive purposes. On the contrary, it is entirely reasonable to assume that Iran is seeking the shelter of a nuclear umbrella in order to impose its will on the region – and to do so with impunity.

This applies to a range of issues, including Iran's intense and irrational hostility to the existence of Israel or to any political accommodation with the Jewish state. Given its active support for terrorist groups and insurgencies across the region, it is difficult to credit Iran's claim to be a peaceful nation, intent only on defending itself from external threats. Allowing Tehran to acquire nuclear weapons, whether by commission or omission, is the diplomatic equivalent of throwing a match into a tinderbox.

Regardless of these counter-arguments, objections to almost any intervention in Iran are understandable in the post-Iraq climate of cynicism and suspicion. It is, therefore, necessary to understand the history of Iran's nuclear programme and the parallels – or, more accurately, the absence of parallels – between the cases of Iran and Iraq.

*

Iran had a modest nuclear programme when, still ruled by the Shah, it signed the NPT in 1968 and ratified the treaty in 1970. By signing the NPT, Iran permanently renounced its pursuit of nuclear weapons and acquired the status of a 'Non-Nuclear Weapon State'. As such, it was permitted access to sophisticated nuclear know-how and technology from other NPT states in order to develop its own peaceful nuclear programme. Iran also assumed a further NPT obligation: it would make its civilian nuclear programme fully transparent and it would permit inspections by IAEA officials to confirm that it was indeed complying with its treaty obligations.

Iran's ratification of the NPT coincided with the extraordinary oil windfall of 1973, when an unprecedented injection of hard currency into the state's coffers enabled the Shah to embark on an ambitious modernisation programme. This included, among other elements, the military transformation of Iran into the leading regional power and a plan to construct twenty nuclear power plants. Armed with its new NPT status, Iran signed various agreements – with the United States in 1974, with Germany in 1976 and with France in 1977 – for an array of nuclear paraphernalia, including assistance in the construction of nuclear reactors, ostensibly for civilian power generation. The centrepiece was an agreement with the German company Siemens to construct two nuclear reactors near Iran's southern town of Bushehr, on the banks of the Gulf. Work at Bushehr started during the Shah's reign, while other nuclear-related deals were being struck abroad, including a deal with South Africa to supply, among other things, yellowcake, a form of uranium concentrate. Tehran insisted that it was pursuing peaceful nuclear goals, but Western intelligence agencies believe that this was not strictly true.

At the time Iran joined the NPT, nuclear power was a symbol of modernity among emerging nations, even oil-rich nations. The Shah is thought to have regarded his country's nuclear programme as a matter of national pride. But national pride may not have been his only interest. There is reason to suspect that, once his scientists had established access to sensitive nuclear technology abroad, the Shah decided to venture down the path to nuclear weapons. Western intelligence services believe that, even then, Iran's nuclear technicians were undertaking studies that had clear military applications. These studies were conducted at Tehran's Centre for Nuclear Research and they focused on a small, 5-megawatt thermonuclear reactor which was supplied to Iran by the United States for the purpose of civilian research. But under cover of their NPT status, Iran's nuclear scientists were, in fact, focusing their attention on other issues – plutonium extraction, laser enrichment and possibly the design of nuclear warheads.

All this ended after the Shah was overthrown in 1979. Almost immediately, the leaders of the Islamic Revolution ordered a halt to nuclear-related activity. Work on the two reactors in Bushehr was abandoned and the new Islamic Revolutionary Republic, following an ideologically motivated decision by its Supreme Leader, Ayatollah Ruhollah Khomeini, also closed down other nuclear activities and research facilities. Thousands of Western-trained nuclear scientists and engineers, who had been recruited to work in Iran's developing facilities, drifted away. In spite of the official shutdown, however, intelligence sources report that some work did, indeed, continue at Tehran's Centre for Nuclear Research after 1979.

Dramatic events soon led to a reverse in Iran's nuclear calculus. On 22 September 1980, barely seventeen months after the Islamic Revolution, Iraq launched an all-out attack against Iran over the Shaī al-'Arab waterway, which lies between the two countries. The eight-year war that followed resulted in hundreds of thousands of casualties, with some estimates putting the figure as high as one million. Iran found itself woefully unprepared for war. Its armed forces were in the midst of a brutal purge which had been instituted to expunge all traces of the Shah's regime. Iran was dangerously exposed and cruelly vulnerable to the Iraqi attack.

That was not its only problem. The military embargo imposed on the Islamic Republic by the United States and other Western powers prevented Iran from gaining access to new weapons and spare parts for the Western equipment with which the Shah had armed his country. Meanwhile, Iraq exploited its advantage and launched indiscriminate missile attacks against its Iranian enemy, at one point resorting to the use of chemically tipped warheads. Nor did Iraq confine its aggression to the battlefield. It targeted Iranian population centres, leading to mutual rocket attacks in what became known as the 'War of the Cities'. Both countries' nuclear programmes were targets. Iran tried, unsuccessfully, to bomb Iraq's nuclear reactor at Osirak in the autumn of 1980; Iraq responded by inflicting severe damage on Iran's nascent facilities at Bushehr in 1985. Both countries feared the other's nuclear programme, but Iran's special predicament heightened its anxieties.

Tehran's diplomatic isolation was accompanied by an arms embargo at precisely the time Iraq was receiving regular infusions of weapons from the Soviet Union, China and some Western states, such as France. This acute vulnerability is considered to have been pivotal in Iran's decision to revisit its nuclear programme. In Tehran, the revolutionary leaders, desperate to break out of their isolation, particularly their military isolation, could not allow a recurrence of the ordeal Iran endured during the eight-year-long war against Iraq. It became imperative for Iran to acquire not only a conventional military capability that was serious enough to deter its belligerent neighbour, but also a non-conventional option that could deter Iraq from using its weapons of mass destruction, including its stock of chemical weapons.

The Iranians had learned yet another lesson: they would never again allow themselves to be dependent on the international community for their defence. The priority now was to acquire a home-grown capability for producing both conventional and non-conventional weapons. Any lingering ideological objections to nuclear technology had evaporated.

The shocking circumstances of the Iran–Iraq War were no doubt a significant factor in changing Khomeini's mind on the nuclear issue. Less than five years after he had ordered a suspension of Iran's nuclear programme on religious grounds, he apparently reversed his ruling and, as early as 1984, the nuclear programme was revived, when a new nuclear research centre was inaugurated in Isfahan.

The context of Khomeini's reversal – Iran's isolation in the face of a brutal enemy which threatened the survival of its revolution – suggests that the decision to return to the nuclear drawing board may have been motivated by a defensive imperative. But there was another reason. Recalling the imperial ambitions of the Shah during his final years in power, the Islamic Revolutionary Republic now aspired to more than merely acquiring the tools to defend itself from Iraqi aggression; it was now intent on exporting its revolution and transforming Iran into a credible regional power.

By the end of the 1980s, with the country still bound by its NPT obligations, Iran's geo-strategic environment had undergone profound changes. It had acquired new commercial and strategic allies, such as Pakistan, China, the Soviet Union and North Korea. From such partners Iran could hope to obtain advanced weaponry and sensitive technology that would help it realise its ambition of regional dominance. Between 1987 and 1990, Iran signed agreements with Pakistan, the Soviet Union and China, which did indeed accelerate its nuclear plans. Not only would Iranian nuclear technicians and scientists be permitted to train abroad under these agreements, but Iran would also be able to purchase modern weapons and gain access – through its relations with North Korea – to advanced ballistic missile technology.

China supplied Iran with two small nuclear reactors as part of their 1990 agreements, while the Soviet Union, within the framework of an agreement also signed in 1990, undertook to rebuild the Bushehr nuclear power plant, which the German contractor declined to complete after the Iran–Iraq War. Pakistan, in all probability, offered critical assistance in the nuclear sector. According to IAEA reports, Pakistan nuclear scientist and revered 'Father of the Bomb' Abdul Qadeer Khan supplied Iran with vital nuclear technology and know-how, including the Chinese design for a uranium nuclear bomb. Khan had created a nuclear smuggling network that, unbeknown to Pakistani authorities, had sold nuclear material to countries such as Libya, Iran and North Korea. After confessing to his crimes in 2004, Khan was pardoned by Pakistan's president, Pervez Musharraf, under an arrangement that put the scientist under house arrest and imposed severe restrictions on contacts with the outside world.

During the 1990s, Iran devoted itself to acquiring the elements that would make its nuclear programme fully self-sufficient, indigenous and independent from foreign supplies. This objective was boosted by the discovery of vast fields of uranium deposits – reserves are estimated at up to five thousand tons of uranium oxide – near the town of Saghand, in the north-eastern province of Yazd. But progress was slow, hampered by intense opposition from the West, spearheaded by the United States, which sought to prevent Iran from procuring dual-use technology. At an early stage, Western intelligence agencies suspected the worst about Iran's nuclear ambitions.

Then, on 14 August 2002, the opposition-in-exile National Council of Resistance of Iran caused a sensation. At a briefing in Washington, DC, the organisation revealed the existence of two previously undeclared – and unknown – Iranian nuclear facilities, which were functioning in flagrant contravention of Iran's treaty obligations. The first was a uranium-enrichment plant in Natanz; the second, a centre for producing heavy water in Arak. The revelation was accompanied by a plethora of photographs and other evidence that left little doubt about the authenticity of the claim. The Natanz facility, for example, was shown to have two components – a relatively small pilot project and a larger plant intended for commercial production. When fully operational, the larger installation is destined to accommodate fifty thousand centrifuges for enriching uranium, ostensibly to power Iran's nuclear power plants. So far, however, Iran has no nuclear power plants and the Bushehr facility will be fuelled by Russian-supplied enriched uranium.

Iran's extensive nuclear programme consists of a complex web of installations and plants, some in universities, others in facilities that are linked to, or affiliated with, the military or defence industries. It is inside these installations that research and development are taking place. Among them are:

- the Arak heavy water plant;
- Tehran's Centre for Nuclear Research;
- Isfahan's Centre for Nuclear Technology;
- the Nuclear Research Centre for Agriculture and Medicine in Karaj, 160 kilometres north-west of Tehran;
- the Isfahan factory for uranium hexafluoride (UF6);
- the Beneficiation and Hydrometallurgical Research Centre (BHRC) in Isfahan;
- the multi-purpose laboratories of Jabr Ibn Hayan (JHL);
- the Department of Applied Sciences and Nuclear Physics at the Amir Kebir University in Tehran;
- Sharif University of Technology in Tehran;
- the University of Saghand;
- the Bonab Atomic Research Centre;
- the Rudan Nuclear Research Centre near the city of Fasa, south-east of Shiraz (reportedly a conversion plant for yellowcake);
- the nuclear fuel site of Ardekan, for uranium treatment;
- the uranium mines of Gchine, near the southern port of Bandar Abbas;
- the uranium mines of Talmessi, near Anarak;
- Darkhovin – a suspected clandestine nuclear site run by the Iranian Revolutionary Guard Corps (IRGC);
- Chalus – a clandestine nuclear installation built under the mountain near the coastal town of Chalus;
- Kholadouz – an IRGC-run military complex suspected of being a site for clandestine nuclear activities;

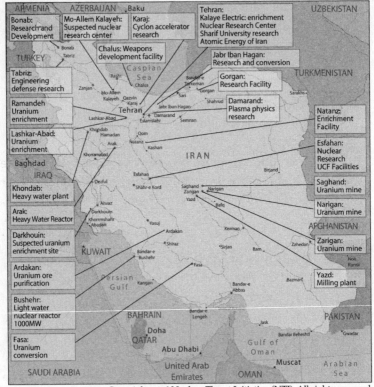

Iran's nuclear sites

- Lavizan – site of possible industrial military activities linked to Iran's non-conventional programmes; it was dismantled in 2004 after it was exposed in Western open sources;
- Mo'allem Kalayeh – a site suspected of underground clandestine nuclear activity and run by the IRGC;
- the pilot fuel enrichment plant at Natanz;

- Neka – near the Caspian Sea and suspected of being a site for nuclear research;
- Parchin – site linked to ballistic-missile and WMD programmes; it is thought to be a site for nuclear activities as well;
- Saghand – uranium mines;
- Yazd – university department for nuclear research.

A word of caution: some of these sites are noted in respectable sources, such as the Nuclear Threat Initiative (www.nti.org) or Global Security (www.globalsecurity.org), but have not necessarily been confirmed by Iran as part of its nuclear programme. Their existence and purpose, however, are usually flagged by opposition groups or diplomatic sources (or both) and are often confirmed by intelligence agencies. In other cases, NTI, Global Security and the third significant open source of information on Iran's programme, David Albright's Institute for Science and International Security (www.isis-online.org), support the claims, often basing their judgements on satellite imagery. Iran is unlikely to acknowledge such sites, given their nefarious nature.

Regardless of the qualifications, the list reveals an inherent flaw in the lofty non-proliferation goals of the NPT: success depends primarily on the integrity of its signatories. Iran has demonstrated that this is, perhaps, a fatal flaw. The IAEA inspectors can be, and apparently are, easily thwarted, misled, bamboozled or restricted, while entire networks of nuclear sites, small and big, are able to slip through the net and escape IAEA attention altogether. That has been the lesson of Arak and Natanz.

*

Given that some alleged nuclear installations in Iran are just that – alleged – why is the Iranian experience so different from that of Iraq? How can we trust intelligence on Iran's nuclear ambitions and progress, particularly as some of it comes from opposition groups with a vested interest in exacerbating Western suspicions of Iran? Should we not have learned the painful lesson of Iraq's alleged WMD? The answer is that the two situations are profoundly different. Many factors that exist in Iran simply did not exist in pre-war Iraq. There is, in fact, no comparison between the two.

It has now been conclusively established that for at least eighteen years – when the Centre for Nuclear Research and Enrichment was established in Isfahan in 1984 – Iran hid much of its nuclear activity and lied about it. That in itself provides cause for considerable suspicion, which explains the international community's insistence that Iran come clean and make a full disclosure of the history and nature of its nuclear facilities. Only then can it hope to restore confidence and be considered fully in compliance with the NPT. In the meantime, Iran is regarded as being in breach of its treaty obligations. This was stated explicitly and forcefully by the IAEA on 24 September 2005:

> ... Iran's many failures and breaches of its obligations to comply with its NPT Safeguards Agreement ... constitute non-compliance in the context of Article XII.C of the Agency's Statute ... [T]he history of concealment of Iran's nuclear activities referred to in the Director General's report, the nature of these activities, issues brought to light in the course of the Agency's verification of declarations made by Iran since September 2002 and the resulting absence of confidence

that Iran's nuclear programme is exclusively for peaceful purposes have given rise to questions that are within the competence of the Security Council, as the organ bearing the main responsibility for the maintenance of international peace and security.

As for what is suspected but not known for certain, the former UN chief weapons inspector, IAEA inspector and head of the Iraq Survey Group, David Kay, wrote in the *Washington Post* on 8 September 2008 that 'it's the only partially understood and suspected activities of Iran that are most alarming'.

In addition to the clandestine nature of Iran's nuclear activities, the discoveries that have been made by the IAEA inspectors in the course of their controls since 2003 give rise to further concern. Apologists for Iran argue that, in the absence of a 'smoking gun', why insist on accusing Iran of aspiring to nuclear weapons? Is this, they ask, not a rerun of the same old mistakes that were made in the case of Iraq? True, the IAEA has not actually accused Iran of developing nuclear weapons, but nor has it said in clear, explicit and unambiguous terms that it is not. As far as the IAEA is concerned, there are grounds for legitimate suspicion that a military component lies within Iran's declared activities. In his report to the board of governors, on 3 June 2008, the director-general of the IAEA, Dr Mohammad ElBaradei, stated that 'It should be noted that the Agency currently has no information – apart from the uranium metal document – on the actual design or manufacture by Iran of nuclear material components, of a nuclear weapon or of certain other key components, such as initiators, or on related nuclear physics studies.'

Iran is being asked to provide conclusive proof that its

nuclear activities are intended for purely peaceful purposes. This could be achieved swiftly through a policy of full transparency and disclosure on all its nuclear-related activities, past and present, coupled with free access to its nuclear sites and scientists for IAEA inspectors. Instead, Iran has chosen concealment over transparency. Its nuclear programme remains opaque and it continues to prevaricate and deny the international community the opportunity to conclusively verify the real nature of its programme. Iran is not, to be sure, refusing to cooperate with the IAEA, but it is engaging in an elaborate stratagem of delay, obfuscation and deception.

But the IAEA's failure to produce a 'smoking gun' does not mean that Iran is not developing nuclear weapons. Nor does it mean that the crisis over Iran is simply a repetition of the crisis that led to the invasion of Iraq. So why should we suspect that Iran is building nuclear weapons when it insists that its nuclear programme is intended for strictly civilian use? If Iran claims innocence in much the same way as Saddam Hussein did, and if the West cannot provide conclusive proof to the contrary, what makes the case against Iran different from the case against Iraq? Are we not repeating the same mistake, with potentially devastating consequences? Should we not learn the lessons of Iraq and avoid a war at all costs? There is no shortage of voices asking such questions.

David Kay, for one, wrote in the *Washington Post* in 2005 that 'now is the time to pause and recall what went wrong with the assessment of Iraq's WMD program and try to avoid repeating those mistakes in Iran'.

John Sawyer, director of the Pulitzer Center on Crisis Reporting in Washington, wrote in the *Los Angeles Times* on 29 October 2006 that 'as in the run-up to the Iraq war, there are assertions of a broad consensus of experts' views that Iran is intent on developing a nuclear weapons capability; and, just as in 2003, there are muted voices questioning how definitive the evidence is'.

Scott Ritter, another former IAEA inspector, has repeatedly denounced American policies towards Iraq. Lately, he has directed his fire against American policies towards Iran. In March 2007, he stated that 'we're doing it all over again. The policy in regard to Iran is regime change; [the claim of] a nuclear weapons programme is simply an excuse to rally support around the confrontation of Iran'. A year later, he drove the point home more forcefully. Writing in London's *Guardian* on 8 March 2008, he said that 'Iraq had been placed in the impossible situation of having to prove a negative, a doomed process which led to war. I am fearful that the EU-3 [Britain, France and Germany] is repeating this same process, demanding Iran refute something that doesn't exist except in the overactive imaginations of diplomats pre-programmed to accept at face value anything negative about Iran, regardless of its veracity'.

Also in the *Guardian*, John Pilger had already written on 13 April 2007 that

> Just as non-existent weapons of mass destruction or facile concerns for democracy had nothing to do with the invasion of Iraq, so non-existent nuclear weapons have nothing to do with an American onslaught on Iran. Unlike Israel and the United States, Iran has abided by the rules of the Nuclear Non-Proliferation Treaty. The International Atomic Energy Agency (IAEA) has never cited Iran for diverting its civilian programme to military use.

Rightly or wrongly, some commentators insinuate that current rhetoric against Iran is a reprise of the arguments that led to the 2003 invasion of Iraq. In fact, there are fundamental and substantial differences which demonstrate that the comparison is not only poorly made but also profoundly misleading. We must, of course, approach the issue prudently, but we should not be paralysed by the Iraq experience. The fact that the intelligence assessments were wrong on Iraq does not automatically make them wrong in the case of Iran. As the French non-proliferation expert Bruno Tertrais noted in his book *Iran, la prochaine guerre* (2007), 'The Iranian dossier is of a different order: it actually consists of a set of certainties that did not exist in the case of Iraq.'

He cites three reasons for this assertion:

- Iran's programme is conducted in many facilities that can be observed in satellite imagery, while in the case of Iraq there was a presumption of – but no evidence of the existence or location of – clandestine installations.
- Iran's programme relies significantly on supplies that came from the A. Q. Khan nuclear-proliferation network that was dismantled in 2003. Khan's network has supplied the IAEA with a wealth of detail on its nuclear transfers to Iran, and this has provided a clear picture of what Iran is pursuing through the technology it acquired from Khan.
- The most worrying details of Iran's nuclear programme have come from the periodic reports of the IAEA – 'the same IAEA', notes Tertrais, 'that asserted in early 2003, at the risk of enraging Washington, that Iraq did not appear to have resumed its nuclear programme

after 1991 and which sceptics therefore should take
seriously'.

Beyond Tertrais's three reasons, there is further cause for
concern. Not only is Iran suspected of engaging in clandestine
military activities but, as will be seen, it is dedicated to developing nuclear weapons. And Iran makes no secret about the
fact that it is building long-range ballistic missiles which are
integral to a comprehensive military nuclear programme. Any
nation that aspires to possess an independent, indigenous
nuclear capability must engage on three fronts: first, it must
master the nuclear cycle, which involves enriching uranium or
plutonium to weapons-grade levels. This is a complex process
which requires sophisticated equipment, technical skills and
many years of experience. Second, it must develop the appropriate means of delivery. A nuclear bomb can be dropped by a
strategic bomber, but a far more effective delivery method for
non-conventional weapons is a ballistic missile. This requires
a sophisticated and ramified missile programme. And third,
it must develop the necessary tools to weaponise the enriched
uranium or plutonium.

In the case of Iraq, we know that Saddam Hussein did have
a nuclear programme. After Israeli jets destroyed the Osirak
reactor at Al-Tuwaitha in 1981, Saddam Hussein rebuilt the
programme, dispersing various components throughout the
country. These were discovered and dismantled after the 1991
Gulf War. Rigorous import restrictions, sanctions and inspections, combined with the damage inflicted on Iraqi infrastructure during the war, made it difficult for the programme to
resume undetected.

In short, there is no evidence that the Iraqi programme

resumed after 1991, in spite of Saddam Hussein's evasiveness and the obstacles he put in the way of the IAEA inspectors. In the light of Iraq's murky past and its record of non-cooperation, the Federation of American Scientists felt justified to declare in a report published in November 1998 that 'even at the present level of highly intrusive monitoring and inspections, under some scenarios Iraq might be able to construct a nuclear explosive before it was detected. All Iraq lacks for a nuclear bomb is the fissile material'. The comparison with Iran, then, can be drawn only to the following limited extent:

- both regimes have in the past pursued ambitious and clandestine nuclear programmes aimed at building nuclear weapons;
- both regimes dispersed their nuclear installations widely – in some cases building underground facilities – to hide them from inspectors and make them less vulnerable to military attack;
- both regimes systematically lied about and concealed the nature of their nuclear activities to the international community;
- both regimes actively sought to delay and obstruct the IAEA's inspectors;
- both regimes made incendiary threats against Israel, referring to weapons of mass destruction as the means of making good on those threats.

From 1991 to 1998, the international community managed to uncover and dispose of most of Iraq's clandestine nuclear installations and other activities forbidden under UN Security Council Resolution (UNSCR) 687. When it came to other non-conventional weapons and ballistic missiles, which were denied to Iraq by UN resolutions after Operation Desert Storm, the international community could at least partially verify their destruction. But the suspension of inspections in 1998, before full Iraqi compliance with UNSCR 687 could be verified, meant that by the time inspectors resumed their task in the autumn of 2002 there had been a four-year hiatus in monitoring Iraq's WMD activities. And then Iraq did everything it could to delay and hamper the verification process, often appearing reluctant to cooperate or flatly obstructing the inspectors.

The difference between the cases of Iraq and Iran is obvious. In Iraq, the inspectors were attempting to locate clandestine sites that may have existed but whose existence was now hard to prove. In the case of Iran, it is not just a matter of locating possible clandestine installations, but also determining exactly what is under way at the existing, known sites.

ElBaradei seems to have clarified the issue. Speaking on the sidelines of the IAEA's annual general conference in Vienna in late September 2008, he effectively conceded that, under present circumstances, his organisation would never find concrete evidence of bomb-making activity in Iran. In spite of the IAEA's protracted investigations in Iran, he said, it lacked the means to discover covert nuclear activity. The crux of the problem, ElBaradei continued, was that Iran had failed to ratify a protocol permitting short-notice IAEA visits to ensure no secret bomb-making work was going on in areas that were not declared nuclear sites. 'Our legal authority is very limited. With Iran, we have discovered that unless we have the additional protocol in place, we will not really be able to discover undeclared activities,' he said. ElBaradei was more forthcoming, however, when he spoke to the German daily *Süddeutsche Zeitung*. In an interview published on 26 September 2008, he declared that Iran was on its way to mastering technology that would enable it to build atomic bombs. 'They have the cookbook,' he said, '[but] right now they don't yet have the ingredients – enough nuclear material to make a bomb overnight.'

More recently, the Wisconsin Project for Arms Control has published a timetable, mapping Iran's nuclear progress towards a bomb. According to the nuclear watchdog, 'Based on the amount of low-enriched uranium Iran has stockpiled, and the amount it is believed to be producing each month, the Wisconsin Project estimates that by inauguration day, Iran could have enough U-235 to fuel one bomb quickly. "Quickly," in this context, means two to three months – about the time it would take Iran to raise the level of U-235 in its uranium stockpile from 3.8 percent to approximately 90 percent.'

Of course, this leaves open the question of weaponisation. But if the estimate is accurate – and it is mostly based on information provided by IAEA reports penned by Mohammed ElBaradei and his team – then Iran's race against time might soon be over.

On the issue of ballistic missiles, Iraq claimed to have complied with the mandatory restrictions imposed by the UN Security Council. The task of inspections was to find missiles which, if they still existed at all, were concealed. Iran, on the other hand, makes no attempt to conceal its growing arsenal of missiles – in fact, it showcases them at military parades and publicises them whenever a new, longer-range missile is tested. Nor does Iran deny its intention to enrich uranium. The only element that Iran denies is that its programme has a military dimension. Only the most naive – or wilful – are prepared to believe it.

The vast bulk of the international community rejects Iran's claims on the basis of five empirically verifiable criteria:

- Iran pursued major elements of its nuclear programme in secret for at least eighteen years, in violation of its solemn NPT obligations.
- Iran procured much of its nuclear technology, including plans to build uranium metal hemispheres which can only be used for a nuclear device, from A. Q. Khan. The Khan network supplied Iran and other countries, such as Libya, with sensitive nuclear technology, including blueprints for a nuclear device. Iran never denied having received any of the above. On the contrary, it confirmed that it possessed the Khan documents.
- Iran insists that it intends to enrich uranium to feed several thermonuclear power plants. Apart from Bushehr, however, work has not started on any other plants. And the uranium needed to fuel the Bushehr plant will come from Russia. But the 60,000-square-metre centrifuge field at Natanz, constructed deep underground and protected by layers of reinforced concrete, is capable of producing highly enriched uranium for nuclear weapons.
- All research centres involved in Iran's nuclear programme have links to, or are an integral part of, the Iranian armed forces. This would be both inappropriate and unnecessary if the centres were designed for purely civilian purposes. The Iranian defence minister and leaders of the IRGC play key roles in all matters relating to the nuclear programme, while Iran's military industry manufactures the uranium-enriching centrifuges.

- The programme includes a heavy water research reactor, whose structure and dimensions suggest a military purpose – the enrichment of plutonium – given that Iran's power stations would ostensibly be fuelled by uranium.

Reviewing the history of Iran's nuclear and missile programmes, with its rich record of inconsistencies, prevarications, concealments and lies, it is hard to escape the conclusion that Iran's claim to be pursuing nuclear power for purely peaceful purposes is disingenuous.

Much of the evidence that is cited for indicting Iran comes from the IAEA and its reports, which focus on Iran's visible and declared activities rather than on its suspected unreported and clandestine installations. What concerns the IAEA is based on what is already known about Iran's nuclear programme, not on what is suspected, which explains why the IAEA had good reason for declaring Iran in breach of the NPT. It is this solid evidence which makes the best case for claiming that Iran is intent on building nuclear weapons.

Iran's voluminous nuclear file contains the evidence of Tehran's real intentions. Far from being a set of 'sexed-up dossiers', the IAEA's periodic reports over six years, alongside the actions and statements of the Iranian regime itself, demonstrate beyond doubt that Western suspicion about Iran's ambitions to clandestinely construct a nuclear-weapons capability are well grounded. At regular intervals since 2003, Mohammed ElBaradei has been reporting to the UN on what his organisation of nuclear inspectors, monitors and analysts has been able to learn from the Iranians and other sources. These reports have conveyed much sobering information, a tone of urgency, but no indication of any real progress in persuading the Iranians to be more transparent. On the contrary, what they reveal are the successful workings of an Iranian policy aimed at occluding the IAEA's mission through persistent denials, incomplete or misleading information, and just plain stalling.

The stalling is evident from ElBaradei's patient reminders of both the urgency of the matter and the speed by which the issue could be solved if Iran agreed to cooperate. On 18 June 2003, faced with mounting signs of a possible military nuclear programme, ElBaradei announced: 'We need to solve this issue as soon as we can.' Two months later, in late August, he worried: 'The information [we have procured] was in contrast to that previously provided by Iran. In addition … there remain a number of important outstanding issues, particularly with regard to Iran's enrichment programme, that require urgent resolution.'

A few days later, he permitted himself a note of impatience: 'Iran should not wait for us to ask questions and then respond; it should come forward with a complete and immediate declaration of all its nuclear activities. That would be the best way to resolve the issues within the next few weeks.'

The 'best way', indeed, but that is not how the Iranians saw it. By November 2003, without any further evidence of Iranian cooperation, ElBaradei reported that 'Iran's nuclear programme, as the agency currently understands it, consists of a practically complete front end of a nuclear-fuel cycle, including uranium mining and milling, conversion, enrichment, fuel fabrication, heavy-water production, a light-water reactor, a heavy-water research reactor and associated research-and-development facilities'.

These words should have been enough to confirm Iran's intentions, but they came just as America's failure to find WMD in Iraq had become a dominating issue on the diplomatic agenda. ElBaradei had played a significant role at the United Nations in attempting to stymie Washington's determination to topple Saddam Hussein. Now he appeared to be unwilling to join up the dots and say what seemed, according to his own reports, to be beyond doubt. Instead, he continued to caution that there was still no conclusive evidence.

Two years later, with still more facts surfacing, ElBaradei continued to display a seemingly infinite patience: 'In order to clarify some of the outstanding issues related to Iran's enrichment programme,' he declared, 'Iran's transparency is indispensable and overdue.' Once again the Iranians took a different view. On 27 January 2006, ElBaradei wrote of

> repeated requests for a meeting with Tehran to discuss information that had been made available to [the UN] about alleged studies, known as the Green Salt Project, concerning the conversion of uranium dioxide into UF_4 [the immediate precursor of fissile uranium] ... as well as tests related to high explosives and the design of a missile re-entry vehicle, all of which could involve nuclear material.

A month later, on 27 February 2006, the IAEA chief again reported failure: 'Iran has yet to address the other topics of high-explosives testing and the design of a missile re-entry vehicle.' And a few months after that, on 8 June 2006: 'Since the last report ... Iran has not expressed readiness to discuss these topics further.' The Iranians continued to ignore ElBaradei. On 31 August 2006, he wrote: 'Iran has not expressed any readiness to discuss these topics since the issuance of the ... report in February 2006.' More than a year later, after Iran had endured two rounds of UN sanctions for failing to comply with the IAEA, nothing had changed: 'Iran has not agreed to any of the required transparency measures, which are essential for the clarification of certain aspects of the scope and nature of its nuclear programme.'

The international community certainly did not demonstrate any particular zeal in the light of ElBaradei's sense of alarm. But ElBaradei had given Iran a welcome respite by complicating efforts at the UN to turn the screw on Tehran. In the summer of 2007, ElBaradei agreed on a timetable with Iran to address and clarify all outstanding issues, without any commitment from Tehran to halt its uranium-enrichment programme. This is what UN Resolutions 1696, 1737 and 1747 required. A looming UN deadline for Iranian compliance was neatly overridden by this new agreement.

Given all the circumstances, Iran might have been expected to finally cooperate, but in November 2007 ElBaradei wrote that 'Since early 2006, the Agency has not received the type of information that Iran had previously been providing ... As a result, the Agency's knowledge about Iran's current nuclear programme is diminishing.' Iran's response was not just evasive, but positively dismissive. On 22 February 2008, ElBaradei conveyed Iran's response to mounting signs of a clandestine military programme: 'Iran stated that the allegations were baseless and that the information which the agency had shown to Iran was fabricated.'

Ever patient, the IAEA chief gave Iran another chance to come clean. Tehran summarily turned him down. Iran had delivered its final word on the subject. And when the IAEA showed Iranian officials a warhead design, obtained from the hard drive of an Iranian computer and deemed 'quite likely to accommodate a nuclear device', Iran once more replied that 'the schematic layout shown by the agency was baseless and fabricated'.

Then, in May 2008, ElBaradei caught the attention of international media with a report in which he complained about Iran's failure to offer satisfactory answers, *especially in relation to the military dimension of its programme*: 'Substantive explanations are required from Iran to support its statements on the alleged studies and on other information with a possible military dimension.' In his 26 May 2008 report, which was presented to the IAEA board of governors on 3 June, ElBaradei noted that Iran had failed to explain the existence of a diagram for an underground testing facility; had failed to explain the testing of explosive detonators normally used for nuclear weapons; and had failed to explain the existence of documents, including a short video clip, relating to the modification of Iran's Shahab-3 missile to enable it to carry a nuclear warhead. Perhaps most disturbing in the report was an offhand passage about work being done by a scientist at the Institute for Applied Physics (IAP), an Iranian military research facility: 'The [IAEA] has also enquired about the reasons for inclusion in the *curriculum vitae* of an IAP employee of a Taylor-Sedov equation for the evolving radius of a nuclear-explosion ball with photos of the 1945 Trinity test.'

The Trinity test was a reference to the testing of a plutonium bomb in the New Mexico desert on 16 July 1945, the prototype for what was later dropped on the Japanese city of Nagasaki on 9 August 1945. Why would an IAP scientist have been working on this equation? One reason might be that his employers saw in it a possible application for Iran's own nuclear programme.

Indeed, IAEA inspections and reports have focused increasingly on the military aspects of the Iranian programme, based on a steady flow of intelligence the IAEA received from member states that it deemed serious and credible enough to warrant further inquiry. The intelligence, as it emerges from the IAEA reports, demonstrates that Iran is pursuing not only civilian nuclear power for peaceful purposes but also military components for its nuclear programme. All this was not necessarily suspended or abandoned in 2003, as suggested by America's National Intelligence Estimate (NIE), which was published in December 2007. In fact, the evidence indicates Iran is indeed pursuing a nuclear bomb.

At the very least, Iran continues to enrich uranium – the most important and technologically complicated challenge to overcome. It does so intensively and aims to install up to fifty thousand centrifuges to aid its enrichment activities. Iran currently has approximately four thousand centrifuges in operation, more than the quantity that experts consider necessary for the production of enough enriched uranium to build a nuclear weapon within a year. The most recent batch of centrifuges are said to be more advanced than their predecessors, and some of the early technical difficulties encountered in the enrichment process are now expected to have been resolved.

Iran's enrichment programme is not the only cause for concern. Iran has one of the most active and sophisticated missile-development programmes in the world. While Iranian missiles have appeared to be designed to carry a conventional military payload, recent models indicate that they have been reconfigured to carry a nuclear payload. In his IAEA reports, ElBaradei has expressed concern about Iranian efforts to build a nuclear warhead and a re-entry vehicle, as well as its attempts to conduct tests on high explosives and other activities that can only be explained in the context of a full-blown nuclear-weapons programme.

What, exactly, does the IAEA say about the possible existence of an active nuclear military programme in Iran? In the autumn of 2005, well after the date when the NIE says Iran suspended its programme, the agency received proof of Iranian experiments involving high explosives and other activities with clear military applications. ElBaradei accepted the evidence as precise and reliable enough to warrant both mention and action. In February 2006 he wrote that

> On 5 December 2005, the Secretariat repeated its request for a meeting to discuss information that had been made available to the Secretariat about alleged studies, known as the Green Salt Project, concerning the conversion of uranium dioxide into UF4 ... as well as tests related to high explosives and the design of a missile re-entry vehicle, all of which could involve nuclear material and which appear to have administrative interconnections.

As already noted, Iran declined to respond. Then, on 28 April 2006, ElBaradei revisited the matter, noting that Iran 'has yet to address the other topics of high explosives testing and the design of a missile re-entry vehicle'. On 8 June 2006, he reported that 'the Agency has continued to follow up on information concerning studies related ... to high explosives testing and to the design of a missile re-entry vehicle. Since the last report of the DG, Iran has not expressed readiness to discuss these topics further'. On 31 August 2006, he had little new to report: 'Iran has not expressed any readiness to discuss these topics [high-explosives testing and the design of a missile re-entry vehicle] since the issuance of the DG's report in February 2006.' And finally, on 23 May 2007 he commented that

> Iran has not agreed to any of the required transparency meas-
> ures, which are essential for the clarification of certain aspects
> of the scope and nature of its nuclear programme. These
> measures include discussion about information provided to
> the Agency concerning alleged studies related to the conver-
> sion of uranium dioxide into UF4, to high explosives testing
> and to the design of a missile re-entry vehicle.

The unmistakable message is that Iran is on the path to nuclear capability.

Meanwhile, the impact of the NIE was startling, not least because it apparently reflected the settled view of the United States intelligence community. It cast serious doubt on the nature and progress of Iran's nuclear programme, undermined diplomatic efforts to call Iran to account, and fuelled specula-tion that the impetus for more pressure might be running out of steam. The operative consequence of the NIE was to reduce the chance of a US military strike against Iran's nuclear sites, and it generated a debate, particularly in the USA, on the need, even the desirability, of engaging Iran in a dialogue.

While the NIE ignited a diplomatic firestorm in both

the United States and Europe, it also raised two important questions: how reliable was the intelligence and how politically motivated was the timing of its release and the manner of its phrasing? The former US Secretary of State Dr Henry Kissinger noted that 'the key judgements blur the line between estimates and conjecture'. And the former US Secretary of Defense and CIA director James Schlesinger wrote that 'clearly, the key judgements in the NIE were overstated. And that, in turn, may reflect the very late decision to declassify the key judgements, written in a kind of shorthand, and thus incautiously phrased'. The former US Special Envoy to the Middle East, Ambassador Dennis Ross, noted that, although the NIE was almost certainly the product of rigorous assessment and questioning, 'it may actually leave us less secure over time. How can such an improved product of spy-craft have such a negative effect? It can when it frames the issue mistakenly and is not combined with statecraft'. And the former US ambassador to the UN, John Bolton, took the NIE summary apart, calling it 'a flawed product'.

The expert community was similarly unforgiving. The Washington Institute's expert, Patrick Clawson, wrote that 'the NIE displays undue confidence that the US intelligence community knows not just what happened, but the reasons why'. He added that 'the report implies that the threat from Iran has diminished. But in fact, a careful and close reading of the NIE does not warrant this interpretation. In the end, the report will only make it harder to address a growing threat to world peace'. Iran Watch editor Valerie Lincy and Wisconsin Project for Arms Control director Gary Milhollin lamented that 'the report contains the same sorts of flaws that we have learned to expect from our intelligence agency offerings. It, like the report in 2002 that set up the invasion of Iraq, is both misleading and dangerous'. Former Iraq Survey Group leader David Kay went farther and said that the NIE 'looks like it was written by a really inadequately trained graduate student'. He later commented that 'the last US attempt to produce a National Intelligence Estimate on Iran ... led to a comedy remarkable even by Washington standards'.

Efforts to discredit the NIE were accompanied by attempts to draw a distinction between its headline, which seemed to let Iran off the hook, and its content, which was far more incriminating than any previous official public document on Iran's nuclear quest. Whatever the short-term effects of the NIE, the long-term effects are likely to be felt by the intelligence community itself. Still suffering from their flawed assessment of Iraq's WMD, Western intelligence agencies in general are likely to suffer further damage to their credibility as a result of the NIE on Iran.

Washington has castigated the hapless spooks for their casual use of language. The US National Intelligence Agency director, Admiral Michael McConnell, recently regretted the language used in the NIE. Under fire from Senator John D. Rockefeller IV (D-WV) and Senator Evan Bayh (D-IN) at a Senate hearing, the admiral admitted that, 'in retrospect', he 'would do some things differently'. Regrets are a sign of intellectual honesty, but they do not undo damage.

Perhaps the greatest damage the NIE inflicted was on the credibility of the Bush administration's claim that 'all options' – including war – 'are on the table'. 'Regardless of what one thinks about the National Intelligence Estimate's conclusion that Iran stopped its nuclear weapons program in 2003 – and there is much to question in the report – its practical effects are indisputable,' wrote Robert Kagan soon after its release. 'The Bush administration cannot take military action against Iran during its remaining time in office, or credibly threaten to do so, unless it is in response to an extremely provocative Iranian action.'

Iran is unlikely to oblige. An early sign that the NIE had emboldened Tehran came in late January 2008, when Iran's nuclear negotiator, Saeed Jalili, met a small group of diplomats and journalists in Brussels. He was quick to cite the US document as conclusive proof that Iran was not engaged in any illicit nuclear activity. Nothing could have served Iran's propaganda machine better than the apparently clean bill of health delivered by none other than American intelligence. Europe also provides ample evidence of how the NIE backfired. In the Czech Republic, for example, several national newspapers suggested that there was no longer any need to worry about missile defences. The NIE should have been warmly welcomed by those European leaders who were so ready to criticise Washington's insistence that 'all options are on the table' with Iran. In fact, the NIE had served to weaken their own argument for sanctions (alongside the bulging package of incentives they have offered Tehran).

And in post-NIE America, the call for a dialogue with Tehran was gaining traction. Mark Brzezinski and Ray Takeyh wrote that 'the intelligence estimate undercuts the Bush administration's attempt to craft (let alone broaden) an international coalition to impose sanctions against Tehran'. For Lee Hamilton, co-author of the Iraq Study Group report, the NIE represented 'a significant break with our intelligence community's previous assessments'. While acknowledging the risks of a direct dialogue with Tehran, he argued that 'we should be prepared to engage Iran diplomatically one-on-one, without preconditions'. Two former members of the Clinton administration, Flint and Hillary Leverett, hailed the NIE and declared that 'the idea of "engaging" Iran diplomatically is becoming less politically radioactive than it was early in the Bush years, when any officials who broached it were putting their careers in jeopardy'. Harvard scholar and former Barack Obama adviser Samantha Power further elaborated this premise in January 2008, arguing that

> [W]e need to broaden the range of policy tools we draw upon. That means refraining from redundant reminders that military force is still 'on the table,' which only strengthen the hand of hard-line Islamists and nationalists. It means broadening cultural contacts with the Iranian people, bypassing the regime through Voice of America and the Internet. And it means trying high-level political negotiations, something the Bush Administration has so far shunned.

The prospect of dialogue went hand in hand with the expectation that nothing could now happen until a new administration assumed office in January 2009. That, coupled with a widespread anxiety among European policymakers and businesses alike that the next administration would launch a dialogue with Tehran and in the process let US companies descend on Tehran, meant that little political progress could be made in 2008, short of an Iranian change of heart on its nuclear ambitions. Not a promising outlook given the dynamic nature of Iran's nuclear programme and Tehran's seemingly limitless ability to prevaricate.

Against this background, fresh intelligence began reaching

the IAEA. It contained concrete evidence that contradicted the NIE main findings. The sudden surge in supply of incriminatory material had a clear aim: that the NIE and the climate it had created should not give ElBaradei a pretext to close the Iran file on the grounds that Iran had no ongoing nuclear military programme. By proving the existence and progress of such a military programme, even after late 2003, the evidence made it impossible for the IAEA to give Iran a free pass.

Following the damaging fallout caused by the NIE, detailed intelligence on Iran's nuclear military programme started flowing into the IAEA. To its credit, the IAEA meticulously sifted through the material and took it seriously enough to abruptly change its tone. The February, May and September 2008 reports had nothing positive to say about Iran's compliance. Meanwhile, the UN Security Council approved yet another sanctions resolution against Iran – UNSCR 1803 – and a fifth resolution – UNSCR 1835 – that reaffirmed the international community's demands that Iran stop enrichment.

The reasons for the growing anxiety among Western governments were endorsed by the IAEA. The anxieties are not the product of warmongering among so-called foreign-policy hawks in Washington, as many will insinuate. That much is evident in ElBaradei's 22 February 2008 report:

On 8 November 2007, the Agency received a copy from Iran of the 15-page document describing the procedures for the reduction of UF6 to uranium metal and the machining of enriched uranium metal into hemispheres, *which are components of nuclear weapons*. Iran reiterated that this document had been received along with the P-1 centrifuge documentation in

1987 and that it had not been requested by Iran. The Agency is still waiting for a response from Pakistan on the circumstances of the delivery of this document in order to understand the full scope and content of the offer made by the network in 1987. (Emphasis added)

In other words, Iran admitted that it had received plans to build a nuclear bomb from Pakistan, which, in turn, eventually confirmed that the document received by Iran was identical to the blueprints for a nuclear device in Pakistan's possession. Whether Iran had asked for it or not is immaterial – for twenty years it held on to a blueprint for a bomb and failed to either return it or report on it to the IAEA. It later emerged that the A. Q. Khan illicit nuclear smuggling network that was selling nuclear technology and which had specifically provided blueprints for a nuclear bomb to both Iran and Lybia had a Swiss connection.

According to reports, Swiss authorities arrested members of the network and seized laptop computers, which contained plans to build nuclear devices far more advanced than those referred to in the IAEA's February 2008 report. According to nuclear proliferation expert David Albright,

But the designs in Switzerland included ones for smaller, more sophisticated nuclear weapons than the one found in Libya. These would have been ideal for two of Khan's other major customers, Iran and North Korea. They both faced struggles in building a nuclear warhead small enough to fit atop their ballistic missiles, and these designs were for a warhead that would fit. These designs would also simplify the task of building a nuclear weapon for anyone who obtained them.

The new design could well fit inside a warhead carried by a ballistic missile. It is perfectly conceivable that the network sold an electronic copy of this more advanced design to Iran. The arrested members of the network have not been willing to cooperate with Swiss authorities on the whereabouts of other electronic copies of the blueprints.

Apart from the nuclear-weapon design that Pakistan obtained from China and Khan sold to Iran – Iran did not deny having such a plan – the IAEA noticed several inconsistencies in Iran's nuclear activities which raise further questions about the nature of the programme. Among them, there is evidence of studies on high explosives and multiple detonators, which are typically used for nuclear weapons. And there is evidence of research and development relating to a nuclear warhead which is compatible with Iran's Shahab-3 missile, which was delivered to the country's armed forces in June 2003. Writing in February 2008, ElBaradei noted that

> the Agency made available documents for examination by Iran and provided additional technical information related to: the testing of high voltage detonator firing equipment; the development of an exploding bridge wire detonator (EBW); the simultaneous firing of multiple EBW detonators; and the identification of an explosive testing arrangement that involved the use of a 400 m shaft and a firing capability remote from the shaft by a distance of 10 km, *all of which the Agency believes would be relevant to nuclear weapon R&D.* (Emphasis added)

There was more:

During the meetings mentioned above, the Agency also described parameters and development work related to the Shahab 3 missile, in particular technical aspects of a re-entry vehicle, and made available to Iran for examination a computer image provided by other Member States showing a schematic layout of the contents of the inner cone of a re-entry vehicle. *This layout has been assessed by the Agency as quite likely to be able to accommodate a nuclear device.* (Emphasis added)

Clearly, coming after the NIE release, these meetings showed that the agency was still concerned by evidence in its hands. Confronting Iran with the evidence was yet another honest attempt to allow Tehran to exculpate itself and come clean. Instead, Iran demurred.

Two more items were added to this worrying picture in the May 2008 report: first, the agency mentioned 'the testing of at least one full-scale hemispherical, converging explosively driven shock system that could be applicable to an implosion-type nuclear device'. And second, it emerged that, as mentioned on page 42, a scientist employed at a military research facility, the Institute for Applied Physics of Tehran, conducted studies on the shock waves caused by a plutonium nuclear bomb explosion. Iran has so far declined to answer these questions and has denied the IAEA inspectors any access to the relevant individuals.

Six years after Iran's clandestine nuclear programme was revealed to the world, there remains a long list of question marks about its history and its real goals. Iran, so far, refuses to answer these questions, though it is obliged to do so under the NPT regime. It is important therefore to list the outstanding issues and the reasons why Iran's nuclear programme, when viewed in the light of the dozens of reports authored by Mohammed ElBaradei, cannot be dismissed as a rerun of Iraq.

- Iran has concealed its nuclear programme from the world and the IAEA for eighteen years – in clear violation of the NPT to which it is a signatory.
- Iran seeks to enrich uranium, although it has no nuclear power plants that require the nuclear fuel it is trying to produce (the Bushehr plant, which is being constructed with Russian assistance, will be fuelled by Russian-supplied low enriched uranium).
- Iran's facility at Arak is bound to produce plutonium, which can be explained only by a desire to make weapons-grade fissile material (its declared goal is to use enriched uranium to generate its nuclear power plants).
- Iran has the blueprint to build a nuclear weapon.
- Iran is said to be building an underground shaft which includes a 400-metre-deep tunnel and several control points to test explosives with military applications.
- Iran has conducted studies on high explosives and multiple detonators, which are suited for nuclear weapons.
- Iran has tried to build uranium metal hemispheres and has conducted tests on 'a full-scale hemispherical, converging explosively driven shock system'.
- Iran has conducted studies – documented by a video that the IAEA deemed credible – to install a non-conventional warhead on its ballistic missile, the Shahab-3.

- Iranian scientists have conducted studies on the progression of the shock wave caused by the Trinity test – the prototype of a plutonium bomb later dropped on the Japanese city of Nagasaki.
- All the above activities – but especially those with clear military applications – have administrative interlinks.

As David Kay wrote,

Signs of [suspected] activities include detection by International Atomic Energy Agency inspectors of samples of highly enriched, weapons-grade uranium; more extensive plutonium separation than Iran has admitted; weapons design work; construction of a heavy-water reactor and its associated heavy-water production facility; design work on missile re-entry vehicles that seem to be for a nuclear weapon; and reports of yet-undiscovered programs and facilities. If all of these activities are real, it would mean that Iran is moving faster and is closer to obtaining a nuclear-weapons capability than the hard facts suggest. Obtaining that last 20 percent of the elements needed to make a nuclear weapon would take perhaps one to two years, instead of the four to seven years needed if they were not.

It is true that Iran vigorously denies all the accusations. Nor has the international community so far offered conclusive evidence about its nuclear-weapons programme. But given the clandestine nature of the programme, given the risks and opportunities involved, it is hard to imagine that inspectors will ever stumble on to a site that displays a sign saying 'Welcome to Iran's Clandestine Nuclear Weapons Factory!' Those who take Iran's arguments at face value will probably settle for nothing less as evidence of what Iran is up to. But policymakers, who have privileged access to intelligence files, cannot take such a risk. It will be too late if we do nothing until we receive confirmation of what Iran is doing through an announcement that it is withdrawing from the NPT – or worse, through an announcement of an underground nuclear test. Pundits can take the risk of getting it wrong. Political leaders must err on the side of caution. And it is certainly prudent to assume that Iran is well down the path to acquiring nuclear weapons.

The evidence that already exists offers incontrovertible proof that Iran has not been transparent about its activities. It has behaved with duplicity in its dealings with the IAEA, which has been seeking to reach a definitive conclusion about its nuclear programme, and it has been running rings around the European Union emissaries who were sent to persuade Iran to cease its enrichment activities. Meanwhile, Iranian scientists, who have been made inaccessible to the IAEA, draw ever closer to their goal of completing the nuclear cycle, which will deliver nuclear weapons into the hands of the leaders of the Islamic Revolutionary Republic.

The minimum threshold involves enriching uranium to at least 5 per cent. And that is the hardest part of the process. Uranium enriched to 5 per cent is sufficient for a nuclear power station, but it is not yet sufficient to fuel a nuclear device, which requires enrichment to 90 per cent. Here, the time frame becomes telescoped, for it takes just half the time to enrich uranium from 5 per cent to 90 per cent as it does from 0 to 5 per cent. Iran has declared that it is enriching to 4.7 per cent; IAEA inspectors claim Iran has managed to reach the level of 4 per cent. With Iran installing more and higher-quality centrifuges, it is reasonable to suggest that the process will be accelerated.

As David Kay wrote in the *Washington Post* on 8 September 2008, 'Given what we know and what we can best-guess, it looks as if Iran is 80 per cent of the way to a functioning nuclear weapon.' There is still time, but not much.

It is known that the Iranians are digging tunnels under the Zagros mountains and near Isfahan, but it is not known exactly what purpose the tunnels are intended to serve. One suggestion is that they will store weapons-grade nuclear material at depths that cannot be reached by American bunker-busting bombs. Three elements must guide Western foreign policy in the months ahead.

First, if the NIE is accurate, Iran was, at least until 2003, building a nuclear weapon – and it is likely that this work continued afterwards. Far from supplying the necessary information on what happened to the military component of its programme, Iran has done everything in its power to obstruct the inspection and monitoring activities of the IAEA. Meanwhile, ElBaradei can do nothing but acknowledge that our knowledge of Iran's nuclear programme is 'diminishing'. Inspections are not helping the IAEA to fulfil its task of verifying whether Iran is complying with its NPT obligations, but they are facilitating Iran's efforts to buy time. Second, Iran has systematically lied about the nature of its nuclear-weapons programme, and there are good reasons for assuming that it is continuing to lie. Third, the West's technological supplies, commercial relations and political dialogue with Tehran have failed to persuade the regime to change course by even one iota. On the contrary, Iran exploits these contacts to raise false hopes that it will be more amenable to reason, while continuing to pursue its nuclear goals.

Those who still support dialogue and engagement with Tehran should ponder the NIE and what it truly means for dialogue. If it is true that Tehran *was* building a nuclear weapon in the autumn of 2003, that means that it was doing so under the presidency of Mohammad Khatami, the man hailed as a moderate and a reformer. At the time, Khatami was energetically promoting a 'dialogue of civilisations' with the West, while simultaneously supervising a clandestine programme to build nuclear weapons in his own backyard.

If these are the reformists, the moderates, what can we hope for from the regime of Mahmoud Ahmadinejad? To the Iranians, it seems, the concept of a dialogue with the West is a tactic designed to channel the West's frustration and concern, while buying time for work to continue in the underground facilities at Natanz and a dozen other nuclear sites around Iran. Investing any hope in a dialogue with the current regime is surely an exercise in futility.

When the IAEA inspections started, the file on Iran's nuclear-weapons programme could have been closed 'in a matter of weeks', to quote ElBaradei's statement in June 2003. But Iran chose the path of prevarication rather than cooperation with the IAEA. And so the weeks turned into months and years. Five years – and counting. Meanwhile, the nuclear countdown continues, and unless effective action is taken, we will, sooner rather than later, wake up to the fateful news from Tehran that it has acquired nuclear weapons. The world will have undergone a transformation, and nothing will then be able to put the genie back in the bottle.

2

In the shadow of Iran's bomb

'The first US shot on Iran would set the United States' vital interests in the world on fire.'
  – *Ali Shirazi, personal representative of Iran's Supreme Leader, Ayatollah Ali Khamenei, to Iran's Revolutionary Guards*

'If we have to choose between Iranian nuclear deterrence and intimidation, or accept military action as a solution, we'll accept military action.'
  – *Mustafa Alani, an analyst at the Gulf Research Centre in the United Arab Emirates*

So what if Iran wants nuclear weapons? In its quest for a nuclear capability, Iran is in breach of its NPT obligations. Its non-compliance is beyond dispute and the IAEA has referred it to the UN Security Council because it continues to breach its treaty obligations. This has been confirmed by five UN Security Council resolutions.

But international law aside, can Iran's objectives be viewed as unacceptable on ethical and political grounds as well? Three other countries with nuclear arsenals – India, Pakistan and Israel – inhabit Iran's neighbourhood. If they have the bomb, why not Iran? What ethical reasons can be adduced for denying nuclear weapons to Iran while its neighbours – and potential adversaries – possess such weapons? And why should the West insist on using the NPT regime to deny Iran membership of the small and exclusive 'nuclear club'? Is this not a recipe for encouraging systematic violations, since the only countries to have nuclear weapons today are either the five permanent members of the UN Security Council or those nations that were smart enough and fast enough to develop nuclear capabilities on their own – and then relied on their strategic relationship with the West to avoid retribution?

One answer could be that Iran poses a threat to regional peace while India, Pakistan and Israel do not. But if one looks at recent conventional wars, it is commonly assumed that Iran has never displayed any aggressive vocation. From 1979 to 2008, Iran fought only one war – with Iraq – and in that case Iran was the victim, not the aggressor. Given that Iran is historically viewed as a predatory enemy by Arab states, particularly Arab Gulf states; given the rivalry between Iran and Iraq, in spite of the overriding adherence to Shi'a Islam by a majority in both states; given the historic hostility between Shi'a and Sunni streams of Islam; given Iran's vulnerability as a result of decades of Western embargoes, both commercial and military; given America's military presence in the region … is it any wonder that Iran would seek the sanctuary of nuclear weapons? That would, surely, be the only credible means of deterrence in such a hostile and volatile environment.

Rhetoric aside, what evidence exists to suggest that Iran's leadership is so irrational that it is prepared to risk the existence of its country – and certainly the future of its revolution – by launching a nuclear attack on Israel? Iran is not a paranoid one-man dictatorship like Saddam Hussein's Iraq or Kim Jong Il's North Korea. Iran's power structure is more diffuse and there is a modicum of pluralism even within its admittedly authoritarian regime. Despite its restrictions, it is a relatively sophisticated, complex and open society, and at least some important elements in Iran aspire to an open dialogue with the rest of the world. Finally, its vibrant civil society sets it apart from Saddam's Iraq and the Dear Leader's North Korea. It is not quite a democracy, but it is at least partially open to criticism, the exchange of views and limited public dissent.

Such a state must know that a nuclear attack against Israel would trigger a devastating response from Israel itself. And it must know that it might even invite retaliation from other countries – if one is to believe the statements of solidarity and support for Israel's existence from a range of Western leaders. If Iran were to attack Israel and trigger a response in kind, the consequences for the entire region would be catastrophic. There are enough studies from the cold war era to underscore this point. There are no winners in a nuclear winter.

That does not mean that a nuclear Iran is no threat at all. But if nuclear deterrence, based on the doctrine of mutually assured destruction (MAD), secured the peace in western Europe for more than forty years during the cold war, is there any reason to assume that this will not also be true for a nuclear Middle East? A similar balance of terror could take root between Israel and Iran. Similarly, Western nuclear powers could take serious steps to extend their nuclear umbrella over the region. As it is, there are already nuclear weapons near by. Israel aside, NATO has a stock of tactical nuclear weapons at its Incirlik missile bases in Turkey. Deterrence, of course, is a fragile business that might require adjustments to the postures of the USA, NATO and the European Union. But while it is not ideal, it is preferable to the alternative: a pre-emptive military strike against Iran.

So far, so plausible. But is this argument not, in fact, simply a rationalisation of the West's capitulation to Iranian resolve and a way of reconciling itself to Iran's apparently unstoppable quest for nuclear weapons? The bellicose rhetoric emanating from Tehran has persuaded many in Europe and the USA that Iran may indeed constitute an existential threat to Israel – though fewer people believe it to be a threat to Europe, existential or otherwise. But even those voices are quick to qualify their concern by pointing out that Israel itself has a nuclear arsenal and can take care of itself. Anyway, the distance between the two states would render an Iranian military strike perilously difficult. Pragmatic Iran, they say, would never be so foolhardy.

Can we be so sure? Can we afford to be so complacent? Can we, 60 years after the destruction of Europe's Jews, gamble on Israel's existence? Even if we accept the best-case scenario and assume that Iran will not attack Israel, its nuclear capability will dangerously destabilise the rest of the region and inevitably lead to an arms race and further proliferation. Can we afford the risk of such a development?

The problem with all of these arguments is that they miss one absolutely central point. They are based on the assumption that Iranian leaders think and behave as Western leaders might. The West projects its own mindset – its rational, deductive reasoning process, its pragmatic logic, its liberal democratic values, its humanitarian aspirations – on to a state whose own values are locked in a seventh-century world of divine transcendental supernaturalism, whose strategic objective is the attainment of an obscurantist mystical destiny. In that critical respect, Iran is very different from India, Pakistan and Israel.

The most risible of all the propositions that seek to minimise the impact of an Iranian nuclear capability is that Iran has never threatened anyone. It did. It does. And it will continue to do so in its subtle and not-so-subtle ways. To Iran's credit, the Iran–Iraq War – the only occasion when Iran fought a conventional war under the Islamic Republic's regime – was initiated by Iraq, not Iran. Even so, Iran has been involved in aggression ever since the Peacock Throne was replaced by Khomeini's revolution.

First, within months of the revolution, the US embassy in Tehran was seized and about seventy US diplomats were taken hostage for more than a year. Since then, Iran has made extensive use of suicide bombers, exporting their lethal menace to areas where its enemies could be slaughtered in great numbers. In 1983, its wholly owned Hezbollah proxy struck first the US embassy in Beirut (60 dead), and then the barracks of the US Marine peacekeepers in Beirut (241 dead) and the barracks of the French peacekeeping paratroopers (53 dead). Iran is suspected of being responsible for the bombing of US airmen in the Khobar Towers at the King Abdul Aziz Air Base in the Saudi city of Dhahran in 1996 (19 dead). And Iran is also widely regarded as the real culprit in the downing of Pan Am flight 103 over the Scottish town of Lockerbie in 1988 (270 dead).

It was certainly responsible for the 1992 bombing of the Israeli embassy in Buenos Aires (29 dead) and of the Jewish communal organisation AMIA in 1994 (85 dead, mostly Argentine citizens). Following the AMIA attack, Argentina's authorities issued an international arrest warrant for several Iranian officials, including the then president, Akhbar Hashemi Rafsanjani, the then foreign minister, Ali Akhbar Velayati, and the then Iranian ambassador to Buenos Aires, Hadi Soleimanpour. Interpol turned down these three requests (Argentina's warrants against the trio are still outstanding). But Interpol upheld warrants against Ahmad Vahidi, who in 2007 was deputy minister of defence; Mohsen Rezai, a former commander of the IRGC; Ali Fallahian, who at the time of the warrant was a National Security Adviser to Iran's Supreme Leader, Ayatollah Sayyed Ali Khamenei; Mohsen Rabbani, who was the cultural attaché at the Iranian embassy; and Ahmad Reza Asghari, another official at the Iranian embassy at the time of the attack. A further warrant, also relating to the AMIA bombing, was issued against 'Imad Mughniyeh. He was said to have been the mastermind of Hezbollah's terrorist activities until his assassination in Damascus in February 2008. Argentina is said to have been targeted because it had suspended a shipment of nuclear material to Iran.

In addition to its campaign of mass murder across the world, Iran also fanned the flames of conflict across the Middle East and Europe, dispatching assassins to kill its opponents in exile, often in friendly countries. It has not launched a war in the traditional sense of the term – not yet, at least. But it is hardly a hapless victim.

Why do states that intrinsically oppose the burgeoning ambitions of Iran oppose tough measures to halt its march to nuclear weapons? As for individual pundits, intellectuals and politicians vigorously arguing Iran's case in the Western public sphere, there is no doubt that some would welcome the rise of a new regional power that is capable of containing and counterbalancing American influence in the Middle East. They loathe the values of the West and remain nostalgic for the return of an ideological challenge to Western hegemony far beyond the region. They believe that Iran is well placed to champion the 'oppressed of the earth'. And Iran, for its part, is ready and willing to take up the mantle.

Still some states in the developing world support Iran's 'right' to nuclear weapons in order to prevent the creation of a precedent that might foil their own future nuclear ambitions. There is little to discuss with those who wish to see Iran succeed out of an ideological commitment to the Iranian cause, those who wish to spike the West's aspirations or those who secretly harbour nuclear ambitions of their own. Elements that do not fall into these categories must regard Iran's nuclear quest with undiluted apprehension.

States that fear that a precedent will be created if Iran is denied the right to a nuclear programme do have a case in principle. They are concerned about the demands, contained in a slew of UN Security Council resolutions, that Iran suspend its enrichment programme. According to Article 4 of the NPT, Iran is entitled to enrich uranium. Denying such a right seems to suggest that any nation could be barred from enjoying the benefits of the NPT unless they are in a state of grace with America and its allies. This is particularly so when Iran's programme is set alongside the cases of India, Israel and Pakistan, countries that built their nuclear arsenals in violation of, or disregard for, the NPT. They got away with it. Those who oppose action against Iran would argue that if Iran cannot enrich uranium for political reasons or because it is believed to be proliferating, what guarantees are there that other countries will not find that their rights under the NPT are being denied in the future? Surely, they might argue, the right to enrich must not be granted or denied on the basis of subservience to the West? Who, then, they ask, can blame Iran for its defiance?

They would also argue that Iran, surrounded by enemies, isolated and subject to an embargo, seeks only to have its rightful place in the sun recognised by other regional powers. Instead, it suffers a political double standard that rewards its enemies, while denying Iran its fair entitlement under international law.

It would be a convincing argument, were it not for several important omissions: Iran, unlike Israel, Pakistan or India, has signed the NPT and has permanently and unconditionally relinquished any claim to nuclear weapons. The ban on enrichment is not the result of a double standard; rather, it stems from justified concern that Iran is enriching uranium specifically to build nuclear weapons rather than to generate electricity. It is also not an absolute ban: if Iran restored full international confidence in the peaceful nature of its activities, cooperated with the IAEA in its efforts to establish the history and inconsistencies of Iran's nuclear programme and became fully compliant with its NPT obligations, there would be no reason to continue denying the country its right to enrich. It is up to Iran to prove it is compliant with the commitments it solemnly undertook to uphold, and Iran has so far failed to live up to this standard.

According to the obligations set by the NPT, Iran must

declare all its nuclear activities swiftly. It must also accept the kind of inspections and controls that the IAEA deems necessary. It must commit itself not to proliferate and it must undertake to limit its nuclear activities to peaceful goals. It is precisely because Iran signed up to these obligations that it has benefited from access to nuclear technology and know-how, as well as research and commercial reactors. The benefits of the NPT are offset against the commitments that signatories undertake – and which Iran has violated. India, Israel and Pakistan, on the other hand, are not signatories to the NPT, they are not bound by it and therefore have neither enjoyed its benefits nor violated its terms.

This may seem unsatisfactory, even heartless, because it is technical and legalistic. But the reality is that international treaties leave no room for sentiment. Violations of the NPT undermine the entire NPT regime. And the NPT is one of the key building blocks that support and sustain the international order. It is the crucial, if imperfect, instrument for containing the spread of nuclear weapons.

Undermining the credibility of the treaty in order to make the case for Iran carries significant risks. If successful, Iran's defiance of the NPT and of the collective will of the UN Security Council could – and would – be copied throughout the region and beyond. Successful defiance would tell the world that international treaties can be violated with impunity and that violations are rewarded. If Iran acquires nuclear weapons in spite of its treaty obligations and in spite of Security Council resolutions calling it to order, the fragile balance of international affairs will have been seriously eroded. Not least, it will tempt others, particularly non-democratic regimes, to reassess the risks and opportunities when they are confronted by treaty obligations. A high price should be attached to non-compliance.

There is also the danger that Iran might be tempted – as have others – to transfer its nuclear technology and know-how to other states, such as Venezuela, which would further undermine the NPT and contribute to proliferation. Worse, Iran could arm its proxies with 'dirty bombs' – briefcase bombs – that are highly portable and can be deployed and detonated anywhere on earth. While authorities will suspect that Iran is complicit, these devices will not leave a definitive, telltale 'fingerprint'. This is yet another nightmare scenario that the NPT seeks to avoid. Undermining the treaty out of contempt for the exclusive nature of the 'nuclear club' is not just infantile, when it comes from pundits, but downright folly. It would make the world infinitely more dangerous.

The NPT is important not only because it prevents proliferation but also because it reverses the process by encouraging states to significantly decommission their nuclear arsenals with the goal of complete disarmament. In the case of Russia and the United States, it has involved the destruction of thousands of nuclear warheads. In addition, France and the United Kingdom have announced their intention to reduce their nuclear stockpiles. In a world threatened by weapons of mass destruction, the proliferation risk deserves to be treated very seriously. The survival of the NPT should be a top political priority for both governments and anti-nuclear activists. Violations should be dealt with by making the rules of compliance more strict, not less.

The more effective the non-proliferation regime, the fewer are the risks of nuclear catastrophe, regardless of which states are denied the opportunity to join the 'nuclear club'. And herein is the contradiction: many of those who cite the cases of India, Pakistan and Israel as shocking evidence of Western hypocrisy and double standards against Iran also tend to be in favour of what they describe as 'a Middle East free of nuclear weapons'. This principle, if it is a genuine political goal and not merely a rhetorical feint to attack Israel, should include a nuclear-free Iran. It is not clear how well the goal of a nuclear-free Middle East is served by attempts to excuse, or even actively defend, Iran's nuclear programme on the grounds that India, Pakistan and Israel already have their own.

The bottom line is that criticism of these three countries' nuclear programmes expresses a *political* opposition to their nuclear status. It has nothing to do with the NPT. Iran signed the NPT and violated its terms. One can either like the idea of a world where Iran is a nuclear power or dislike it. But one cannot ignore the differences that exist between Iran and the other three nuclear powers beyond the question of the NPT. In the case of India and Pakistan, it is clear that their nuclear arsenals are not regarded as existential threats outside the binary context of the Pakistan–India rivalry.

After four wars in the past 61 years, India and Pakistan have acquired nuclear weapons as a strategic instrument of deterrence in their continuing stand-off. It is a dangerous instrument, but, in their hands, it poses a fundamentally different challenge from that of a future nuclear Iran. In the India–Pakistan case, one can say that the doctrine of mutually assured destruction, with all its unknowns and its shortcomings, is working. Clearly, Pakistan is shaken by spasms of terrorist violence, and the Islamist stirrings of some of its provinces may bode ill for its future and the reliability of those in power. But so far, Pakistan's nuclear arsenal has not served any of the aggressive goals that a nuclear arsenal would undoubtedly serve in Iranian hands. In the case of India and Pakistan, nuclear weapons remain instruments of mutual deterrence.

This did not prevent Pakistan from being a source of proliferation. One cannot underestimate the damage to the goals of non-proliferation caused by A. Q. Khan, the Pakistani nuclear scientist and 'Father of the Bomb', who sold nuclear technology and know-how through his illicit network to Iran, Libya and North Korea (among others). But this only reinforces the argument against Iran. Every time a new country crosses the nuclear threshold, there is a danger of further proliferation. It underscores the need to rigorously enforce the NPT to limit proliferation and thus forestall any chance of a future nuclear conflict.

Pakistan's nuclear posture was not established to extend Pakistan's influence beyond the Indian Ocean and in the Persian Gulf; it was not developed to offer succour to insurgents in Central Asia and western China; it was not conceived to foment subversion in Latin America; it was not devised to project a messianic vision beyond the region. It was designed to deter nuclear-armed India, ten times its own size. Nor was the Pakistani bomb intended to remake the world in a radical Sunni image. Its sole intention was to achieve strategic parity in the subcontinent. And what applies to Pakistan also applies to India, which does not aspire to turn the world into the playground of a fanatical Hindu revolution but seeks to balance and deter the power of China and Pakistan.

The case of Israel differs slightly from that of India and Pakistan. Israel reportedly built its nuclear facilities in the 1950s – well before the NPT was drafted – and probably achieved nuclear capability some time towards the end of the 1960s. It chose not to join the NPT and it never admitted to conducting a nuclear test – though it possibly did so in the late 1970s. Its precise status is intentionally unconfirmed and its opaque nuclear power is based on a doctrine of ambiguity. Israel's deterrence rests on this ambiguity. Its adversaries suspect it has nuclear weapons, and, without showing its hand, Israel does nothing to allay these concerns. No doubt, its adversaries are not overjoyed by Israel's perceived nuclear capability, but a nuclear Israel – like nuclear India and nuclear Pakistan – is not regarded by its neighbours as an existential threat or, indeed, a challenge to the region's political status quo.

Despite the virulent anti-Israel rhetoric that routinely appears in much of the Arab media, Middle East states have never perceived Israel as a power intent on imposing its ideology on its neighbours. Israelis may be seen as usurpers by most people in the region, but nobody in the Gulf or North Africa has ever considered that Israel would use its nuclear might as a tool of aggression in order to have its way in the region or compel its neighbours to adopt its worldview. Israel has shown no signs of seeking to transform the Gulf into a Zionist entity.

It is instructive that none of the moderate Arab regimes have sought to acquire nuclear weapons in response to Israel, but they are scrambling to do so now that Iran is building its own nuclear capability. Arab leaders sleep soundly under the shadow of Israel's nuclear umbrella; it is Iran's nuclear quest which gives them nightmares. They know – they have always known – that Israel's military prowess serves its survival and does not seek to impose a political diktat on its neighbours. The same cannot be said of Iran, with its hegemonic ambitions and its desire to refashion the region.

In order to understand the unique nature of the threat posed by a nuclear Iran it is worth mentioning another example of proliferation, where the international community's insistence on diplomacy at all costs led to capitulation. North Korea not only clandestinely developed a nuclear capability (and tested a bomb) but also has an advanced ballistic-missile programme whose technology has been sold to Syria and Iran. In addition, it is believed to have supplied Syria with nuclear know-how and assistance.

Pyongyang should be on the receiving end of treatment similar to that visited upon Iran. But a different approach was adopted in the case of North Korea. The international community did not threaten military action; instead, it offered a range of incentives to Kim Jong Il's regime, in spite of the fact that his regime treats its subjects more brutally and repressively than Iran's, to say nothing of its lamentable behaviour on the international stage and its less than satisfactory implementation of its commitments. Why did the international community negotiate with and reward a worse offender than Iran? If we are prepared to live with North Korea's nukes, why can we not tolerate Iran's?

The reason for this differential treatment is no doubt that South Korea demanded that negotiators reach a diplomatic solution with Pyongyang, effectively slapping a veto on confrontational tactics. This has effectively let a dangerous, brutish, irresponsible and threatening regime withdraw from the NPT, develop a nuclear capability, make a mockery of international law, threaten its neighbours – and still exact a prize for bad behaviour from the international community.

The diplomatic approach has failed to secure the region and instead has laid it open to the blackmail of an erratic dictator, even though North Korea has never aspired to export its weird worldview beyond its own borders. North Korea does not wish to transform South-East Asia into a permanent gulag governed by its grotesque dictator, and it does not wish to spread the message of its revolution to the four corners of the earth. Its successful nuclear quest has made the area a much more dangerous place. It has also made a mockery of international diplomacy – the same approach the West has tirelessly pursued to persuade Iran to change its course. Clearly, from Iran's vantage point, North Korea is an example to learn from and emulate. If Iran succeeds in reaching the technological threshold where it can test a nuclear device, it could follow in Kim Jong Il's footsteps and exact a heavy price from its foes.

It should be obvious, then, that this precedent strengthens the case for a blunter approach with Iran, not the opposite. From the perspective of the international community, North Korea is a textbook case on what should not be done. The international community fumbled when it came to North Korea, in spite of the fact that North Korea is a repeat offender when it comes to proliferation, in both the missile and the nuclear fields, and in spite of its aggressive posture vis-à-vis its neighbours. By seeking an accommodation, the international community acquiesced in the face of a nuclear-capable North Korea that has flouted agreements and destabilised the region.

First and foremost, an argument that gives a pass to Iran because one was given to North Korea effectively acknowledges the death of the NPT. The NPT is not the perfect tool for keeping the world safe, but undermining it is not going to make the world any safer. Second, if negotiations were exploited to advance the nuclear programme and agreements were flouted only to seek a better deal later, there is something to be said also about the wisdom of endless negotiations and the unshakeable belief in accommodation. Iran has been extraordinarily adept at dragging out negotiations and at constantly pushing back the international community's red lines. And third, given the consequences for its neighbours of a nuclear North Korea, the world should not delude itself that a nuclear Iran is something the Middle East, and indeed the international community, can easily accommodate.

This is especially true because Iran is a revolutionary power. It is not pursuing nuclear capability in order to up the ante and improve its bargaining position. It does not simply aspire to obtain weapons that will deter enemies and guarantee its survival. Iran is seeking instruments of ideological coercion and intimidation. As Iran affairs expert Ray Takeyh observes in his book *Hidden Iran*: 'The nuclear program is a national investment beyond money. Having the bomb would serve as more of a political tool than a tangible threat.' This is a somewhat artificial distinction: a tangible threat *is* a political tool. But what Takeyh probably means is that Iran is less likely to drop nuclear weapons on the heads of its enemies and more likely to use them as a way of expanding and consolidating its influence.

If this is so, Iran is seeking to use its future nuclear arsenal to advance its foreign policy. This, according to Takeyh, is driven by two main factors. The first derives directly from the revolutionary ideology of Iran and is reflected in the idea of state, which is described by Iran's Supreme Leader, Ayatollah Ali Khamenei, as 'the realisation of God's will on earth'. The Supreme Leader is regarded as the *Velayat-el-Fakih*, 'God's shadow on earth', and as such, his word on what constitutes the realisation of divine will on earth is final. Opposing Khamenei's will on the nuclear issue – and he has repeatedly said that Iran's nuclear programme is the realisation of God's designs – is equivalent to opposing God.

What, then, are the goals that God supposedly bestowed on Iran which nuclear weapons would serve? God's design is surely not so Irano-centric as to limit itself to deterring Iran's enemies and guaranteeing the integrity of its borders. More likely, God wants Iran to become the beacon of Islam and to reassert Shi'a predominance over the Sunni world. Khomeini himself explained that 'we shall export our revolution to the whole world. Until the cry, "There is no God but God" resounds over the whole world, there will be struggle.' Nuclear weapons greatly enhance the ability of a country like Iran, blessed with oil riches, to export its dream – by persuasion, if possible; by force, if necessary.

According to Takeyh, the second factor driving Iranian foreign policy stems from Iran's history as 'a defensive, paranoid, narcissistic state which imagines itself to be the "biggest dog in the yard"'. Persian nationalism, combined with this sense of paranoia, creates an explosive cocktail: Iran obsessively sees itself as the target of plots and conspiracies. Its sense of vulnerability is in stark contrast with the greatness to which Iran aspires – a greatness that Islamic revolutionary zeal has exponentially enhanced beyond Iran and the region. In these circumstances, the combined weight of destiny, paranoia and zeal makes the bomb a profoundly dangerous instrument in the hands of those who are determined to promote imperialist aspirations.

Kenneth Pollack, another Iran affairs expert and former director of Persian Gulf Affairs at the US National Security

Council, shares the view that Iran's historic hostility towards outside pressure leads inevitably to an 'anti-status quo foreign policy'. The combination of the divine and the subversive is the recipe that makes Iran a country constantly searching for a new regional status quo. The new world that Iran seeks to create will be dominated by Tehran. It will be characterised by fierce competition with the USA for hegemony over the Gulf and by efforts to cement alliances to confront Iran's ideological antagonists: America and Israel.

It is not so much a choice, then, between a millenarian and apocalyptic Iran that wants to destroy its enemies with the ultimate weapon or a fearful and isolated Iran that seeks the bomb as the ultimate deterrent to guarantee its survival. One must worry not only about the possible catastrophic consequences of a nuclear attack on Iran's foes. Rather, policymakers should be concerned about the indirect use Iran, in its current political configuration, would make of a nuclear arsenal. Iran would use its acquired nuclear capability as a force-multiplier in order to project its power across the region and beyond in unprecedented ways in pursuit of its imperial and revolutionary ambitions.

There is no diplomatic instrument that can dissuade an irrational leader who is driven by delusions of divine inspiration and the desire to hasten the End of Days. If the vision of Iran's President Ahmadinejad prevails, then it might be difficult to dissuade Iran from using nuclear weapons after it has acquired them. If sanctions fail, the choice will be between pre-emption to deny Iran access to the final parts of the technological puzzle or acquiescence in Iran's rise as a nuclear power. Many would – and do – argue that we should just accept the inevitability of a nuclear Iran. They assume that a nuclear Iran would act rationally, and therefore it could be deterred. But a nuclear Iran would constitute a grave danger even if its leadership were driven by a rational calculus, its aspirations were not millenarian and apocalyptic and its politics were more prudent than its rhetoric suggests.

It is wrong to assume that nuclear deterrence is successful only if the party to be deterred behaves rationally. The Soviet Union was not a revolutionary power by the time it acquired nuclear weapons, but it is hard to argue that Josef Stalin, its leader at the time, was rational. The same can be said of Mao's China when it acquired nuclear capability. Rational, perhaps, but not in a Western sense. Yet both the Soviet Union and China could be deterred. In this sense, there is virtually no power that is immune to deterrence because deterrence ultimately appeals to a state's most primitive, basic survival instinct. Deterrence is intended to instil fear. It relies on ambiguity and uncertainty: the enemy can never be certain of the consequences of crossing a red line, but it knows for sure that the consequences will be catastrophic.

An important US Army study on nuclear deterrence released after the cold war tackled the potential challenges posed by rising nuclear powers from non-Western cultures. Defining deterrence, it stated clearly that 'Deterrence [is] a process that goes beyond the rational'. The reason for this is that 'the very framework of a concept that depends on instilling fear and uncertainty in the minds of opponents was never, nor can it be, strictly rational. Nor has it ever strictly required rational adversaries in order to function'. But given the expected cultural gap that is likely to characterise a possible future nuclear stand-off, the study suggested that nuclear deterrence must now engage in 'value targeting'. First, we must understand our enemies' value systems; second, we must be able to make this understanding manifest to them; and third, we must convey beyond doubt our willingness to strike ruthlessly and mercilessly where it hurts most according to the value system in question:

> The concept of 'value-based targeting' is not new. But just as for deterrence itself, it is similarly fraught with difficulty if one tries to be too rational in considering how best to determine what a particular adversary values. Determining what a nation's leadership values is complex, since, to a considerable extent, it is rooted in a nation's culture. One is almost certain to err [if] 'mirror-imaging' is used as a surrogate for understanding an adversary's values.

At the same time, it is imperative that our adversaries understand our own value system so that they do not misinterpret our actions. It is important, too, that communications are compatible with their frame of reference. This is not always easy. Our opponents are unlikely to share our frame of reference and it is not safe to assume that our inclination to be reasonable, moderate and pragmatic, our willingness to negotiate, conciliate and compromise, will be interpreted as a sign of strength. The contrary is true. Clearly, in its dealings with Iran, Europe has not conveyed a message that, according to Iran's cultural frame of reference, instils fear and encourages prudence and accommodation. The approach of Europe's negotiators might make perfectly rational sense in a European context. To the Iranians, however, it has projected weakness.

Americans in a position of authority have consistently

emphasised that 'all options are on the table'. Implicit in this statement, of course, is the idea that the USA is keeping open the military option. This periodic reiteration of the fact that America might ultimately resort to force has had a frosty reception in Europe, where many leaders fear an American attack on Iran even more than Iran's success in its nuclear goals. There are frequent statements that condemn a possible military strike in such terms as 'disastrous' or 'inadmissible'. In an interview with the Israeli daily *Ma'ariv*, for example, Italy's former foreign minister, Massimo D'Alema, described a military attack as 'a disastrous possibility'. His successor, Franco Frattini, used precisely the same term and made the same assessment during a recent visit to Israel. Many other European leaders have used similar language, expressing firm opposition not only to an attack but even to the threat of an attack. As former British Foreign Secretary Jack Straw declared in April 2006, 'the reason why we're opposed to military action is because it's an infinitely worse option [than diplomacy] and there's no justification for it'. This sentiment was echoed by the then leader of Germany's Social Democratic Party, Matthias Platzeck, who said that 'military options must be taken off the table' in Europe's engagement with Iran. What kind of message did European negotiators convey to their Iranian interlocutors? Whatever the outcome of its efforts to wean Iran off nuclear weapons, Europe will remain 'reasonable', open to continuing the dialogue and ready to negotiate? So far, they are sticking to their guns. According to the American study on deterrence in a post-cold-war world,

Because of the value that comes from the ambiguity of what the US may do to an adversary if the acts we seek to deter are carried out, it hurts to portray ourselves as too fully rational and cool-headed. The fact that some elements may appear to be potentially 'out of control' can be beneficial to creating and reinforcing fears and doubts in the minds of an adversary's decision-makers. This essential sense of fear is the working force of deterrence. That the US may become irrational and vindictive if its vital interests are attacked should be part of the national persona we project to all adversaries.

Deterrence is less preferable than prevention in the case of Iran. It requires a language, a posture and a behaviour that are the antithesis of what Europe has done, said and hinted at so far. What should remain at the centre of European foreign policy is the possibility of strong diplomatic language, but there must also be other strings to its bow. These should include a precise and credible formulation of the price Iran will pay if it crosses certain clearly defined red lines. And that price must be enormous.

The implications of a revolutionary power acquiring a force-multiplier, such as a nuclear weapon, are simply intolerable from Europe's perspective. And this does not refer to a revolutionary power that actually uses its arsenal to attack its enemies, but simply to the possibility that such weapons will be used, indirectly, to support Iran's revolutionary ambitions. Europe needs to know the consequences of a nuclear capability in the hands of Iran and it needs to convey to Iran, in no uncertain terms, the consequences that will confront the Islamic Republic if it is continues along its present path.

The *Washington Post* columnist David Ignatius has published a fascinating essay with the German Marshall Fund on the subject of Iran as a revolutionary power. Ignatius, who draws heavily on the writings of Henry Kissinger, the former US Secretary of State, outlines the theme of confronting an adversary who is driven by a revolutionary ideology. Kissinger, Ignatius reminds the reader, defined a revolutionary regime as 'a power which considers the international order or the manner of legitimizing it oppressive'. In such circumstances, 'relations between it and other powers will be revolutionary' – that is, geared towards undermining the foundations of the existing international order and replacing them with new foundations which the revolutionary power considers more just.

Drawing a parallel between revolutionary France and the Islamic Republic, Ignatius explains that while their ideologies are substantially different they share an important objective: the will to change the existing political order. The challenge confronting the international community is to understand that this is the primary goal of a revolutionary power and that its search for resources is geared towards increasing its chances of success in challenging the status quo. As Kissinger wrote, referring to status quo powers dealing with a revolutionary state,

> Lulled by a period of stability which had seemed permanent, they find it nearly impossible to take at face value the assertion of the revolutionary power that it means to smash the existing framework. The defenders of the status quo therefore tend to begin by treating the revolutionary power as if its protestations were merely fanciful; as if it really accepted the existing legitimacy but overstated its case for bargaining purposes; as if it were motivated by specific grievances to be assuaged by limited concessions.

The mistake of failing to recognise the threat that revolution poses to the status quo is being repeated with regard to Iran. European leaders are deluding themselves that Iran's actions are driven by legitimate grievances. No doubt, historians, intellectuals and commentators line up to remind diplomats and politicians that they should not worry unduly about Iranian ambitions; that they may not repeat the arrogance of Europe's colonial past and presume that they know what is best. Rather, Europe must accommodate the Iranians. At what price?

In the history of Europe, there have been three significant revolutionary powers – France in 1789, the Soviet Union and Nazi Germany. These three experiences are as different from one another as Iran is from each of them. Similarly, outside Europe in the twentieth century, there were other revolutionary powers, such as Mao's China, Nasser's Egypt or Castro's Cuba. Clearly, these were diverse movements, reflecting their ideology, size, geography and their ability to impact on the fate of the world. In spite of the differences, however, and bearing in mind the limits of the analogies and precedents in history, one can identify common elements which can also apply to Iran:

- A revolution aspires to radical change because it sees society as so incorrigibly corrupt that it must be destroyed and rebuilt from scratch in order to be reformed.
- Its desire to produce ideology-driven radical change will not stop at the international frontiers but will aspire to bring utopian change to other societies – perhaps to the entire world. Its aspirations to export

its revolution will be directly proportional to the universality of the ideas it nurtures.

- Its desire to export its ideology will lead, sooner or later, to a collision with neighbouring countries, other regional powers and, eventually, part, if not all, of the international community. This clash will be conducted in the name of changing the iniquitous status quo.
- As ideology is at the heart of the conflict, a revolutionary power cannot be dissuaded through economic incentives; its progress can be delayed and it can be denied the means to pursue revolution beyond certain boundaries, but revolutionary fervour cannot be quelled by economic mechanisms. Ideological struggles do not lend themselves to appeasement or compromise.

Driven by the passion for the universal principles it proclaimed in 1789, France embarked on a drive to export these principles to the rest of Europe after it had implemented them at home. The result was two decades of wars and conflicts, which came to an end only after the final defeat of Napoleon Bonaparte. The Soviet Union, whose revolutionary ambition was accompanied by great scientific and technological advances, sought to export its communist revolution and supported anti-Western regimes and movements throughout the world long after it had lost its revolutionary passion.

In the case of the Soviet Union, there was no need for a mortal military defeat because the communist system ultimately imploded spontaneously. But the price paid to avoid a world war with the Soviet Union was an acceptance of the partition logic of Yalta in 1945. This concession left central and eastern Europe under Soviet domination until 1989 and it did not avoid several 'minor' conflicts, often fought by proxies, as part of the cold war. Nor did Yalta offer foolproof guarantees against a nuclear war. After all, the two superpowers came close to direct confrontation several times – the 1962 Cuban missile crisis and the 1973 October War between Israel, Egypt and Syria are just two examples. Even as the Soviet Union acquired nuclear weapons at the end of its genuinely revolutionary phase, this did not prevent Moscow from using proxies across the world to promote wars, foment revolts and, in one case, the missile crisis, which brought the world to the brink of nuclear war.

Nazi Germany's revolutionary vision clearly had little in common with the universal elements of the French Revolution or even the communists, but that did not prevent Adolf Hitler from dragging Europe, the cradle of Nazi ideology, into total war and genocide. It took some years to materialise, during which Germany rebuilt its military power and conditioned German society to its revolutionary vision. But it was just a question of time before Nazi Germany would turn aggressively on the rest of Europe to pursue its goal of reshaping the continent according to its racist doctrine. The result of appeasement in this case was catastrophic.

Mao's China devoted much of its revolutionary zeal to defeating its nationalist foes and the last remnants of empire and capitalism, ensuring in the process that millions of its victims were Chinese. But being revolutionary, China also ensured that, amid Mao's Cultural Revolution, it could export its Asian version of agrarian 'reform' throughout the region, fanning conflicts in the Korean peninsula and elsewhere.

Castro's Cuba and Nasser's Egypt also did their best, given their more limited resources, to agitate, foment and instigate revolution. In spite of the poverty of their societies and economies, they did not hesitate to undertake ambitious military campaigns abroad and waste their limited wealth to help other revolutions – as Nasser did in Yemen and Castro did in Angola and Ethiopia. They offered financial and military assistance to revolutionaries far and wide as long as the beneficiaries were perceived to be willing to change the world according to the vision of their patrons.

Sooner or later, a revolutionary power aims to export its revolution, both as an instrument of radical change and as a tool to establish its hegemonic role. If that is so, then the revolutionary power will in due course find itself at war with its neighbours or other regional and global powers that see themselves as guarantors or beneficiaries of the status quo. In the case of Iran, the objective is to export Khomeini's revolutionary vision. Such acts will in time set Iran on a collision course and drag the Islamic Revolutionary Republic into theatres of conflict, near and far, wherever Iran sees fertile territory for interpolating its vision.

It is only a matter of time, as French philosopher Michel Foucault noted in a prescient analysis of the Islamic Revolution. Between 1978 and 1979, Foucault wrote a series of articles expressing enthusiastic support for the revolution. In an article entitled 'A powder keg named Islam', which was published in Italy's daily *Corriere della Sera*, on 13 February 1979, a few days after Khomeini's return to Iran from his Paris exile, Foucault wrote,

> Maybe the historical significance will be found, not in its conformity to a recognized 'revolutionary' model, but instead in its potential to overturn the existing political situation in

the Middle East and thus the global strategic equilibrium. Its singularity, which has up to now constituted its force, consequently threatens to give it the power to expand. Thus, it is true that as an 'Islamic' movement, it can set the entire region afire, overturn the most unstable regimes, and disturb the most solid ones. Islam – which is not simply a religion, but an entire way of life, an adherence to a history and a civilisation – has a good chance of becoming a gigantic powder keg, at the level of hundreds of million of men. Since yesterday, any Muslim state can be revolutionised from the inside, based on its time-honoured traditions.

A nuclear arsenal offers a cover, a protective umbrella, a shield of immunity and impunity for Iran's pursuit of future objectives which Foucault predicted with great foresight 30 years ago. Those goals, alongside others that Iran has explicitly announced, are what must concern Europe before Iran bursts on to the global stage as an irresistible nuclear power.

How would the world change if it woke up to the news that it was now under the shadow of Iran's nuclear arsenal? This does not require Iran to test a nuclear device or even withdraw from the NPT. All Iran needs to do is to prove that it has successfully completed the nuclear fuel cycle and that it has the ability to enrich uranium to weapons grade (about 90 per cent). As noted by IAEA chief ElBaradei in an interview with the Arabic TV station *al-Arabiya*, once the Iranians master the fuel cycle and enrich sufficient uranium, it would take up to year to construct a nuclear weapon. Iran would then be in a position to project its power across the region without the need for a test and by pretending it remains in compliance with the NPT.

This does not mean that Iran will choose the Japanese model (having the ability to enrich uranium without creating nuclear weapons) or the Israeli model (an ambiguous 'bomb in the basement'). Iran might ultimately choose to have a functioning arsenal rather than merely the potential to create one. It might also choose to make use of its weapons to make good its threats against Israel, in spite of the attendant risks.

Israel's reprisals would no doubt bring about the annihilation of Iran and its regime. And only a regime driven by an apocalyptic view of international relations could possibly seek this outcome. But Iran's rhetoric does nothing to assuage the fears of those who believe that this is the goal of its leaders.

No matter how remote, this scenario deserves being spelled out in some detail. We need to confront the worst possible scenario, even assuming that, more realistically, Iran will use its nuclear capability merely to boost its regional influence and hegemonic ambitions, which include exporting its revolution. But even a mildly less nightmarish scenario leaves no room for complacency.

In recent times, a stream of virulent rhetoric emanating from key figures in Iran's clerical and political establishment has fed fears that Iran intends to use its nuclear weapons as a means to pursue a precise goal: the destruction of Israel. So far, this has been contained in rhetoric, but it is accompanied by other tangible, hostile acts against Israel, as well as Israeli and Jewish targets, throughout the world.

First, Iran funds, equips and, via its Revolutionary Guards in south Lebanon, trains and organises the radical Shi'a Hezbollah (Party of God). Hezbollah is a wholly owned subsidiary of the Islamic Revolutionary Republic and serves as Iran's proxy against Israel and other enemies, both real and imagined. Hezbollah gives Iran, for the first time in 60 years, a direct role in the Arab–Israeli conflict.

Hezbollah operates beyond the borders of Lebanon. Some of its leaders were involved in training Shi'a militias in Iraq, while it maintains sleeper cells in Europe and North America, and it operates with relative impunity in Latin America. Iran also has a direct role in the Arab–Israeli conflict through its patron–client relationships with radical Palestinian groups, including Palestinian Islamic Jihad (PIJ) and Hamas. PIJ reports directly to Tehran, while Hamas, although a predominantly Sunni movement, has slid inexorably into Iran's orbit and now benefits from Iranian shipments of cash, arms and Revolutionary Guards, who have been introduced into the Gaza Strip.

All these conflict areas would be profoundly influenced by the advent of a nuclear element. As the French philosopher André Glucksmann says, Iran could now infringe the two great taboos of the twentieth century – Auschwitz and Hiroshima – by acquiring a nuclear capability that would enable it to re-enact both and destroy Israel.

Iran's rhetoric does nothing to dispel fears that this may be precisely what the Islamic Republic aspires to achieve. Iran's president, Mahmoud Ahmadinejad, has repeatedly called for Israel to be 'wiped off the map'. Nor is his a lone, rogue voice within the regime, as some in the West have claimed. Other senior members of the political elite in Tehran have joined the genocidal rhetoric, including his immediate predecessors, the pragmatic-conservative Hashemi Rafsanjani and the modernising-reformist Mohammad Khatami.

Iran's Supreme Leader, Ayatollah Ali Khamenei, himself

has repeatedly expressed his desire to see Israel disappear. In December 2000, he said that 'Iran's stance has always been clear on this ugly phenomenon [Israel]. We have repeatedly said that this cancerous tumour of a state should be removed from the region'. In February 2001, Khamenei made it clear that he regarded the elimination of Israel as being not only a desirable outcome, but also a clear political objective of the Islamic Republic. 'It is', he said, 'the mission of the Islamic Republic of Iran to erase Israel from the map of the region.' In the spring of 2001, Khamenei defined 'the Zionist regime' as 'the symbol of bloodthirstiness [and] barbarianism', and its leaders as 'wild beasts'. In a speech on 24 April 2001, he proceeded to trivialise and negate the Holocaust, saying that 'there are documents showing close collaboration of the Zionists with Nazi Germany, and exaggerated numbers relating to the Jewish Holocaust were fabricated to solicit the sympathy of world public opinion, lay the ground for the occupation of Palestine, and to justify the atrocities of the Zionists'.

As recently as 1 October 2008, Khamenei reasserted Iran's support for the Palestinians and the Hamas government. In an Eid el-Fitr message, Iran's official Fars News Agency quoted him as saying that Israel was being 'weakened day by day' and that 'they are moving towards ... destruction and defeat. The world of Islam will see that day and hope the existing generation of the Palestinian people will watch the day Palestine is at the disposal of the Palestinian people'. Ominously, too, he noted that 'Iranians are taking major steps towards progress. Their achievements belong to all Muslims'.

If one takes into account Iran's power structure, the utterances of the Supreme Leader are even more significant than those of President Ahmadinejad, whose influence is limited by constitutional impediments. The president is still subordinate to the Supreme Leader. In spite of differences in style among the leading figures of Iran, there is little difference in the substance of their sentiments about Israel.

Mohammad Khatami is regarded by many in the West as Iran's leading reformist, 'a leader with whom we can do business'. During his presidency, he devoted himself wholeheartedly to promoting a 'dialogue of civilisations'. But his comments on Israel suggest that there is little room for dialogue on this issue. In 2000, as president, Khatami defined Israel as an 'illegal state'. When the then Palestinian leader, Yasser Arafat, visited Tehran, Khatami told him that the peace process was destined to fail and that 'all of Palestine must be liberated'. On 25 April 2001, Khatami declared that Israel was 'a parasite in the heart of the Muslim world'. It was during Khatami's presidency, too, that the International Anti-Zionist Movement was established with the explicit mandate of sabotaging the Arab–Israeli peace process. Its first head was Mohsen Rezai, the former commander of the IRGC, who is on Interpol's wanted list as a suspect in the 1994 AMIA bombing in Buenos Aires. In a communiqué issued shortly after his appointment, Rezai called on the Islamic world to 'mobilise to destroy Israel and create problems for those governments who defend it'. Iran, he declared, 'will continue its campaign against Zionism until Israel is completely eradicated'.

Before Khatami, there was Rafsanjani, whom many in the West still regard as a pragmatic figure and a possible future interlocutor. In a sermon he delivered in December 2001, Rafsanjani said, 'If a day comes when the world of Islam is duly equipped with the arms Israel has in its possession, the strategy of colonialism would face a stalemate because application of an atomic bomb would not leave anything in Israel, but the same thing would just produce damages in the Muslim world.'

The current president, Mahmoud Ahmadinejad, in a speech to a conference entitled 'A World without Zionism' on 26 October 2005, declared:

> There continues a historic war between the World of Arrogance and the Islamic world, the roots of which go back hundreds of years. In this historic war the battlegrounds have shifted many times. On some occasions, the Muslims had the upper hand and advanced. Regrettably, in the past three hundred years, the Islamic world has been on the retreat in the face of the World Arrogance. One hundred years ago the last trench of Islam fell, when the oppressors went towards the creation of the Zionist regime. It is using it as a fort to spread its aims in the heart of the Islamic world ... The skirmishes in the occupied land are part of a war of destiny. The outcome of hundreds of years of war will be defined in Palestinian land ... Some wonder whether there would come a day when one would see a world without the United States and Zionism ... This slogan and goal is one which is attainable and could definitely be realised. There is no doubt that the new wave in Palestine will soon wipe off this disgraceful blot [Israel] from the face of the Islamic world.

Ahmadinejad then went on to address himself to the late Ayatollah Khomeini, father of the Islamic Revolution and founder of the Islamic Republic:

O dear Imam [Khomeini]! You said the Zionist Regime is a usurper, an illegitimate regime and a cancerous tumour that should be wiped off the map. I should say that your illuminating remark and cause is going to come true today. The Zionist Regime has lost its existence philosophy ... the Zionist regime faces a complete dead end and under God's grace your wish will soon be realised and the corrupt element will be wiped off the map.

More recently, Ahmadinejad defined Israel – in terms that would have made the old Nazi propagandists proud – as a 'filthy germ' and a 'savage beast'. His foreign minister, Manouchehr Mottaki, in the face of shocked and dismayed Western reactions, made it clear the day after Ahmadinejad's speech that the president had said nothing new. He was right. Ahmadinejad's speech was consistent with the message of the Islamic Revolution since 1979. On the same day, the point was reinforced by the spokesman of the IRGC, Seyyed Massoud Jazayeri:

If this cancer [Israel] is not removed from the Islamic world, Muslims will sustain immense harm ... This wound was opened more than half a century ago and has still not been healed because some leaders and regimes in the Islamic world which have not been democratically elected by their own people continue to rule, with the help of Western imperialism. A world without Zionism, and the obliteration of Israel from the face of the earth, is not only the objective of Iran, but of the whole Muslim world.

A few weeks after Iran received an Italian parliamentary

delegation, which the Iranian rulers had promised not to embarrass by threatening anyone in the region, in February 2008, the then Speaker of the Majlis (parliament), Adel Gholam Hadad, said that 'the countdown for Israel's destruction' had begun. A former commander of the IRGC, Rahim Safavi, echoed his sentiment in remarks following the assassination in Damascus of Hezbollah terrorist mastermind 'Imad Mughniyeh, a few days earlier. He expressed the hope that 'with such anger, the definite death of Israel will arrive sooner'. And the former deputy foreign minister, Mohammad Larijani, brother of the current Majlis Speaker (and former chief Iranian nuclear negotiator) Ali Larijani, told a gathering in Berlin in June 2008 that 'the Zionist project has caused only violence and atrocities' and should be 'eliminated'.

This language is routinely accompanied by crass anti-Semitism and an obsessive campaign of Holocaust denial. Not surprisingly, this cocktail of vitriol, combined with Iran's march towards nuclear capability, is a matter of profound existential concern for Israeli leaders. They know that, sooner or later, Iran's nuclear bomb will be aimed at their population centres.

This apocalyptic scenario can take two forms. The first is a direct Iranian missile attack against Israel, which would probably be accompanied, or followed, by a joint offensive from Hezbollah in the north and Hamas in the south. Israel has an advanced anti-missile system, the Arrow, and it may be able to stop some of the incoming warheads. But the Arrow system is not 100 per cent impenetrable. If a missile managed to elude Israel's defences – and all it takes is one missile – and struck one of Tel Aviv's suburbs, it would affect an area that is home to 3 million people and which constitutes the heart of Israel's economy. A nuclear strike would kill tens of thousands of people, while wounding and contaminating thousands more. It would cause terrible damage to the infrastructure and paralyse the country.

Damage assessment would, of course, depend on the size, power and precision of the strike. According to Professor Anthony Cordesman, a specialist at the Washington-based Center for Strategic and International Studies and the author of a study on the possible consequences of a nuclear war in the Middle East, Iran could realistically establish an arsenal of several dozen nuclear weapons in the next few years. Their power would consist of up to 100 kilotons (a kiloton is the energy released by an explosion of 1,000 tons of TNT). If a 20-kiloton device struck Tel Aviv's metropolitan area, Cordesman estimates a minimum of 37,000 and a maximum of 132,000 casualties *within the first 48 hours after impact.* All metals would be vaporised in a 600-metre radius from ground zero and would melt within a radius of 1 kilometre. All plastics would melt or ignite within a 2-kilometre radius. Third-degree burns can be expected in a 3.5-kilometre radius.

The lethal ellipse of radiation generated by the explosion would spread fairly quickly in the hours following the impact, reaching up to 100 kilometres, if it did not encounter significant geographic obstacles along the north–south coastline, for example. In the event of an attack on the Tel Aviv area, one could expect that the mountain range east of its airport would somewhat contain and slow down the radioactive cloud, but it would move quickly northwards or southwards, depending on the winds. A north-easterly wind could push the radioactive cloud along the coast towards Israel's two southern port cities of Ashkelon and Ashdod and beyond, to Gaza, affecting at least another two hundred thousand Israeli citizens and over a million Palestinians in the Gaza Strip.

Tens of thousands of people would be likely to die in the weeks following an attack. Exposure to radiation would make their rescue unlikely: Israel lacks nuclear shelters for its civilian population and an attack would leave much of its critical civilian infrastructure, including hospitals, unable to cope.

Clearly, if Iran decides to attack Israel it would not do so with a single, nuclear-armed missile because this is likely to be stopped by the Arrow or, perhaps, a US anti-missile device before Israel launches a devastating, potentially nuclear, retaliatory strike against Tehran. One can, therefore, expect Iran to launch multiple warheads along the Tel Aviv–Haifa coastal axis. Multiplying the effect of a single impact, as described above, one can expect a minimum of two hundred thousand deaths and a maximum of one million deaths within the first three weeks after impact.

The second possibility is that Iran might transfer a nuclear device to one of its proxies, such as Hezbollah, to be deployed against Israel. There would be no need to install it on a missile and it could be delivered by a suicide commando mission. It could come by sea, on a speedboat, which could penetrate Israel's maritime defences, or even via a microlight aerial vehicle (one of which has already been used to successfully penetrate Israeli airspace).

If it were detonated in Haifa Bay or a few hundred metres from Tel Aviv's beaches, the outcome would not be significantly different. Iran could, however implausibly, deny any responsibility, but such a disclaimer is unlikely to prevent a non-conventional Israeli retaliatory strike against Iran. In addition to sophisticated aircraft and highly accurate missile systems, Israel is reported to have a small fleet of submarines with second-strike nuclear capability.

Meanwhile, it is possible that the spectre of a stricken Israel might awaken the enthusiasm in Arab countries, which would fall on their wounded prey in an attempt to reverse history and deliver a swift *coup de grâce*, while seizing the Palestinian territories, which are likely to be contaminated, in order to deny Iran its claim to victory.

The aftermath of such a trauma might mean that Israel would not be in a position to engage in a conventional war of defence and containment. Faced with such a scenario, it would likely respond to such an attack with nuclear weapons. Its reaction would, therefore, include an immediate, explicit and detailed warning to all Arab countries that Israel's response would wipe out all their major urban centres and other strategic sites in case of an attack on Israel. This nightmare-within-a-nightmare would quickly drag the entire region into a conflict that would turn the Levant and the Gulf into nuclear wasteland.

In the best-case scenario, Arab governments would exercise restraint and let Israel respond to Iran without getting dragged into the conflict. Such calculated, pragmatic processes are not, however, characteristic of the region, and this would not be the first time that the better judgement of some Arab rulers succumbed to pressure from the street and the agitation of populist leaders.

But even an Israeli attack that was limited to Iran alone would have far-reaching implications for the region. First, Israel would most likely hit all known Iranian nuclear sites. It could probably achieve that by conventional means (it could also choose to launch a pre-emptive strike on Iran's nuclear sites). But faced with a landscape of nuclear devastation, enormous human losses and with its own survival in the balance, Israel would most likely launch a barrage of missiles against dozens of targets inside Iran. It would make it clear to the world that no one could launch such an attack on Israel with impunity.

Israel might, therefore, choose to hit urban centres in Iran, such as the capital, Tehran, Isfahan, Kormanshah, Mashad, Qom, Shiraz, Tabriz and Yazd; nuclear sites such as Natanz and Arak, as well as the nuclear reactor in Bushehr; the port of Assaluyeh with its important refineries; and Bandar Abbas and Qaeshm Island, in the Gulf, with their important naval bases, military sites and petrochemical facilities. Bushehr's destruction, if it were to occur after the activation of its reactor, which is expected to be commissioned in early 2009, could potentially result in the formation of a giant radioactive cloud. And given the terrain around Bushehr, it could quickly contaminate the southern shore of the Gulf, killing thousands in Kuwait, Saudi Arabia, Bahrain, Qatar and the Emirates, while terminally damaging their economies. Once the Gulf is covered by a giant radioactive cloud, oil prices will spiral out of control, triggering an unprecedented global economic crisis.

In its choice of targets, Israel might prioritise important Persian centres and spare the periphery and its minorities. But its response to an Iranian nuclear strike would most likely involve Israel's nuclear arsenal, which is estimated to contain several hundred thermonuclear warheads, whose power varies from 20 to 100 kilotons, possibly 1 megaton. These weapons would inflict vastly more devastating consequences on Iran than an Iranian attack on Israel, in both relative and absolute terms. According to Cordesman, Iran's losses could be up to 28 million within the first three weeks of the attack. The entire civilian and military infrastructure would be devastated and Iran's chances of long-term recovery would be close to zero. It would be the end of the Persian civilisation.

Iran's annihilation would likely trigger a firestorm across the region. Regimes might be destabilised and pressured to join Iran's suicidal mission by their angry publics. In addition, an Israeli–Iranian military exchange would make any American presence in the region highly vulnerable. US troops and bases would become prime targets of the seething anger, along with other Western symbols in the region.

The spectre of nuclear war clearly shows the importance of preventive and pre-emptive measures. But it is doubtful that a military attack against Iran *before* the country crosses the nuclear threshold will be enough to stop Iran's nuclear programme (although it could deter and delay the inevitable). Even so, the price would be high.

The apocalyptic scenario is less likely in the short term. But it cannot be discounted, if only because history is often written by irrational actors and because, in the power struggle in Tehran between the conservative clergy and the messianic president, Ahmadinejad might gain the upper hand. But it is much more plausible to assume that, rhetoric aside, Iran is not seeking to build nuclear weapons for the purpose of committing national collective suicide, even in the cause of exterminating Israel. Iran's radical revolutionary goals, coupled with its hegemonic ambitions, are the combustible formula for future conflict in the area. Whether it will be nuclear or conventional is a matter of debate.

The Soviet Union and the United States never reached the

nuclear brink, but they did confront one another in conventional wars, mostly through proxy armies. Fear of mutually assured destruction (MAD) alone did not necessarily prevent a nuclear holocaust. MAD worked, more or less, in a binary context where there were only two nuclear powers. Whether MAD can work when there are multiple nuclear powers confronting each other is a different question. This is crucial in the context of Iran because one of the expected consequences of Iranian nuclear capability is a regional nuclear arms race. Even if the MAD doctrine could work between Israel and Iran – and that is a big 'if' – it is far from certain that it could work when one adds Saudi Arabia, Syria, the United Arab Emirates, Egypt, Turkey, Algeria and others to the equation.

There is an additional reason why MAD cannot be applied to the Middle East. Not only did the two superpowers have diplomatic relations, but even at the height of the cold war, channels of communication existed between Moscow and Washington. These channels, including the 'hotline' which was installed following the Cuban missile crisis, enabled the leaders of the superpowers to talk to each other and, where possible, defuse crises. They could discuss disputes, provide reassurances, send signals, and correct misunderstandings and misinterpretations of events on the ground. No such mechanism of consultation exists between Iran and its potential nuclear foes, notably Israel. The risk of a mistaken reading of one's adversary, their intentions and behaviour, could increase the margin of error and trigger a conflict even when there is no intention to initiate one.

In that case, the region might find itself plunged into nuclear conflict even without an apocalyptic, trigger-happy leadership that regards nuclear weapons as instruments for hastening the End of Days. All it would take is a combination of Iran's hegemonic ambitions, a nuclear arsenal enabling the Islamic Republic to export its revolution, and a total lack of comprehension and communication between adversaries to converge in a crisis, such as a renewed conflict in Lebanon. That could provoke a terrible storm.

Even without pressing the button, Iran's acquisition of nuclear weapons would have far-reaching implications for the region, if not as a doomsday weapon then as a force-multiplier, to project Iran's influence and establish its hegemony throughout the region.

The prospect of a nuclear Iran is no less problematic than the prospect of a pre-emptive attack on Iran's nuclear sites. Those who would be among the most affected by this radical change in the balance of power are Iran's small and vulnerable neighbours in the Gulf. A diplomat from one Gulf state recently conceded that if Iran were to succeed in acquiring nuclear weapons, 'the Iranians would lead us like sheep'. Another Gulf diplomat lamented the ineffectiveness of sanctions and forcefully suggested that 'a siege' might be better. Obviously, these off-the-cuff remarks, made in private, would never be repeated in public. Nevertheless, the remarks reflect a full understanding of what the success of Iran's nuclear programme would entail.

What exactly would it entail? The first and most obvious effect of Iran's acquisition of nuclear weapons will be on the price of oil. The recent dramatic rise in the price of crude was caused, in part, by the insatiable need for fossil fuels on the part of the rapidly expanding economies of China, India and Brazil. Similarly, global economic turmoil brought the prices down because of an anticipation of economic slowdown. Another compelling reason is the political instability in oil-producing countries like Nigeria and Iraq. Talk of war in the region also has an important effect, and with global markets anticipating some sort of confrontation in the Gulf, prices have inevitably been affected. This has less to do with supply and more to do with fear of the sudden disruption of supply. Four episodes in recent months favoured a sudden oil-price rise based on pure political speculation and without relation to changes in the supply and demand of crude:

- In January 2008, an incident near the Strait of Hormuz involving three US warships and five Iranian speedboats caused oil prices to rise from $90 to $100 a barrel.
- Bellicose statements aimed at Iran by Israel's former chief of staff and then minister of transport, Iranian-born Shaul Mofaz (he said he believed an Israeli strike on Iran was inevitable), caused prices to rise from $122.3 to $138.5 a barrel within 48 hours at the beginning of June 2008.
- In late June 2008, an Israel Air Force exercise conducted hundreds of kilometres away from Israel over the Mediterranean and involving hundreds of aircraft gave the impression that an Israeli attack on Iran was indeed imminent. This contributed to a further price increase to $145 a barrel.
- During the first week of July 2008, an Iranian military exercise in the Strait of Hormuz, which allegedly included the launch of new ballistic missiles that would bring Israel in range, caused prices to rise from $136 to $138 a barrel.

Clearly, oil prices are highly sensitive to events, although high oil prices caused by spasms of crisis and instability are not necessarily sustained in the long term. In the case of Iran, the obvious fear is that Tehran would respond to an attack by immediately sealing the narrow, highly strategic Strait of Hormuz, choke-point of global oil supplies. This would disrupt supplies from other states in the Gulf, a region that produces about 40 per cent of world consumption. Iran might also attack gas facilities and oilfields, desalination plants and US military bases along the Gulf's southern coast.

But this scenario need not materialise only as a consequence of an Iranian reprisal against a pre-emptive Israeli or American attack. Under the protection of a nuclear umbrella, for example, Iran could blackmail its neighbours by issuing credible threats aimed at forcing them to reduce production quotas, thereby raising world prices. Iran could also link levels of supply to political change. It could, say, demand a reduction in the US presence in countries like Qatar, Bahrain, Saudi Arabia and the United Arab Emirates, insisting that Iran alone would 'protect' the waterways.

While the focus of concern is usually the Gulf – the immediate repercussions of a nuclear Iran almost certainly would be felt there – Iran's nuclear arsenal would extend its shadow into the oil- and gas-rich Caspian basin, too. As the Georgia crisis of August 2008 clearly indicated, the Caspian basin is another strategically vital area for European interests. Iran could exploit its nuclear status to blackmail neighbouring countries to the north, too, with the aim of controlling energy prices and, by extension, the policies of European countries that are most dependent on those supplies. It is wrong to assume that in this area Iran's bullying tactics may be countenanced by Russia. After all, the Kremlin is on the same page as Iran when it comes to energy prices.

So, anxiety about the negative impacts on energy prices of a pre-emptive military strike against Iran must also take account of the possibility that Iran might be able to manipulate prices in a far more direct and protracted manner when it actually acquires nuclear capability. The price of oil is destined to remain affected as long as regional instability persists. A nuclear Iran would compound that instability for decades in a far more damaging way than it can through the occasional harassment of US warships by fast-moving dinghies.

Nor will Iranian interference stop at threats and provocations over oil prices. There is further potential for Iran to project its aggressive power in the drive to expand its influence. For one, its Gulf neighbours, already at a significant disadvantage, would be unable to resist Iranian interference. With significant Shi'a communities across the Gulf, Iran might be tempted to use the model of Russia's intervention in Georgia 'on behalf of its ethnic kin' to act in a similar way 'on behalf of the Shi'a populations' in Bahrain, Kuwait, Saudi Arabia and elsewhere in the Gulf.

Hossein Shariatmadari, the editor of the conservative Iranian newspaper *Kayhan*, and reported to be a confidant of Supreme Leader Khamenei, wrote an editorial on 9 July 2007 calling for the Shi'a majority of Bahrainis to be 'reunited' with their Iranian motherland. Shariatmadari's editorial also raised questions about the legitimacy of Bahrain's independence, which the small principality gained in 1970. Such provocative demands could be made with greater effect if backed by even a tacit nuclear threat. Hegemony does not require bombs to rain down on neighbours. Simply possessing the option is enough to scare others into submission. And while submission might be the political posture of states in the area, individuals might choose to seek safer shores for their businesses and their endeavours. An exodus of elites would not be a surprising side effect of Tehran's nuclear rise.

Bahrain is not the only Gulf country to fear Iranian interference. It could destabilise any country in the area, support subversion inside their territories and use the threat of Armageddon to coerce their governments. Even Saudi Arabia, which, unlike the Gulf emirates, is not a tiny city-state but a powerful and populous nation, is bound to suffer, perhaps even more than its smaller Gulf neighbours.

Ever since the Islamic Revolution, Tehran has been competing with Saudi Arabia for dominance within the Islamic world. Indeed, Khomeini defined the revolution as an attempt to redress the 'wrongs' of Islamic history. This was generally interpreted to mean the restoration of Shi'ism and the successors of Imam Husayn as the rightful heir to the Prophet after the Sunnis defeated and martyred him in Kerbala in the seventh century. The Saudis, for their part, regard Shi'ism as apostasy.

And then there is the millennia-old rivalry between Persia and Arabia, which still exists. A nuclear-armed Iran would finally be in a position to humiliate the Saudi monarchy and destabilise it from within, perhaps even bring it down. This could be achieved by financing and supporting terror inside the kingdom by targeting sensitive and strategic oil sites inside Saudi Arabia, which are largely inhabited by Shi'a. It could encourage daring actions, such as a repetition of the Shi'a occupation of the Sacred Mosque in Mecca in November 1979 (which was then led by an indigenous Sunni messianic group). And it could promote a Shi'ite insurgency, as it is already doing in Yemen. It could use the 400,000 Iranian residents in the Emirates to wreak havoc among the flourishing but fragile economies of the Gulf. It could intimidate its rulers and force them to expel Americans on their soil. It could even force the indigenous rulers themselves to go.

Nor would it end there. Iran could demand safe and unfettered passage for its navy through the Suez Canal in order to supply its proxies, Hezbollah and Hamas, in the Mediterranean. It could use all the means at its disposal to impose virtually unfettered influence over the reluctant but weak Gulf States in order to squeeze Western presence out of the area and establish Iranian control of the waterways – and of the oil price.

Iran's potential for blackmail would stretch beyond its immediate neighbourhood. A nuclear Iran would certainly continue to support terrorist organisations across the region and beyond. Today, Hezbollah in Lebanon and Hamas in Gaza operate under the aegis of Iran. They are trained, funded, ideologically guided and politically supported by Tehran, which also supports Shi'a militias in Iraq and Shi'a guerrillas in Yemen, as well as elements of the Taleban in Afghanistan.

With Iran already an actor in all these theatres of conflict, its behaviour could degenerate still further. Today, it is trying to gain a foothold in those areas by destabilising them. Tomorrow, supported by a nuclear fist, Iran will become indispensable to solving all of those conflicts (most of which it instigated and nourished in the first place). The solutions that Iran would be prepared to accept would not be to the liking of the West. But at that point, the West, expelled from the region, will have lost its voice.

Finally, one cannot rule out the possibility that Iran might transfer weapons of mass destruction to its clients. There are already unconfirmed reports that Iran has passed chemical and biological warheads to Hezbollah. Iran is certainly equipping them with missiles that are capable of carrying non-conventional warheads. Iran might soon be able to hand a briefcase nuclear device to a terrorist commando. As the French security and non-proliferation expert Bruno Tertrais says, 'If you like the way Hamas and Hezbollah are behaving now, you are going to love it when Iran goes nuclear!' Briefcases might be harder to trace. And Iran has a history of operating in the shadows, through proxies and alter egos who do its bidding while the leadership in Tehran pleads innocence and laments threatening conspiracies against a peace-loving nation.

All these are strategies Iran could adopt and goals that Iran could achieve once it has nuclear capability. But Iran aspires to much more than just removing America from the Gulf or empowering Shi'a communities in the region. Iran's true wish is to export the revolution, as France did after 1789. The French armies did not invade and conquer Europe only to raise the revolutionary flag over the palaces of Europe's ruling dynasties. They aspired to export the universal values of July 1789 beyond their borders, changing the social structures and balances of power in European societies. Iran wants nothing less.

Regional hegemony would not stop at a confrontation with America. Alongside Iran's embassies and military bases would sprout myriad 'revolutionary cultural centres', a massive physical presence of Iranian emissaries and institutions. Iranian money would pour into projects (it already does in places like Lebanon and Syria) and Iranian missionaries would spread Iran's version of Shi'ism throughout the region. Soon, the project would cross the waters, a symbol of Iran's rising power and prestige in the Levant and the Gulf. Iran would claim patronage over Shi'a communities throughout Europe and would offer its protection to Muslim communities outside the Middle East. As it transforms South Lebanon into an Islamic revolutionary republic in its own image, Iran would aspire to do the same elsewhere. And it might just succeed if its quest is backed by the might of a nuclear arsenal.

The prestige of a nuclear arsenal and its emergent military power would exponentially enhance Iran's reach, influence and power. Tehran makes no secret of its aspiration to become the reference point for all anti-Western and anti-global movements. Today's Iran dreams of transforming itself into a Soviet Union redux, racing to the aid of anti-Western revolutionaries. Tomorrow's nuclear Iran will be able to fulfil that dream. It will be in a position to act as the sponsor for myriad radical, possibly violent, groups. Tehran will then be a small step from being a potent sponsor of subversion throughout the world.

This scenario is not as far fetched as it might appear. Iran has friends in Europe. After all, the links between Europe's far left and radical Islam are well established. Their mutual loathing of Western values trumps differences they might have on issues like misogyny and homosexuality. At the opposite end of the political spectrum, expressions of sympathy and support for Iran are evident among the far right. Italy's Roberto Fiore, a member of the European Parliament and leader of the neo-Nazi Forza Nuova, was among the few Italian politicians who met President Ahmadinejad in Rome in June 2008. In an interview published in the Italian *Corriere della Sera* on 5 June 2008, he proudly boasted of having shaken Ahmadinejad's hand.

Awash in oil revenue, a nuclear Iran could be tempted to open its purse to both extremes in Europe. Their ideological distance does not prevent them from sharing a profound hatred of liberal-democratic societies, free-market economies, America, Israel and, in some cases, Jews. Twenty years after the fall of the Berlin Wall left them orphans of their ideological sponsor, political extremists of all shapes and sizes might once again find a feisty, well-armed patron state that is ready to project its might and open its coffers to sponsor their ideological battles.

This strategy would not stop at Europe and anti-global political forces. It would reach out and embrace an international coalition of states that share its ideological antagonism towards the West. If elements of the hard left in Europe become attractive candidates for the role of 'useful idiots', Iran would seek even more assiduously to cement its alliances with countries such as Ecuador, Bolivia and Venezuela in Latin America, Nicaragua in Central America, Cuba in the Caribbean, Zimbabwe and Sudan in Africa, and North Korea in Asia. Not to mention a slew of failed and failing states throughout the Third World.

Iran would become their paladin. It would invest in their economies, fill the bank accounts of compliant leaders, train and supply their armies, give them political support in international forums, and it would open the door to resources and technology. In exchange, Iran would rely on those countries as a base for its financial activities, for its agents, for the logistical needs of its operations, and as a launching pad for the spread of its religious and revolutionary zeal beyond the Lands of Islam.

But most of all, Iran would rely on the steadfastness of these allies in its confrontation with the United States outside the Middle East. After all, in October 1962 the Soviet Union did not hesitate to 'lend' nuclear-tipped missiles to the Cuban dictator, Fidel Castro, who happily proceeded to deploy them. Iran might do the same with its current best friend and ally, Venezuela's Hugo Chávez. It could contemplate the transfer of nuclear technology to some of its ideological allies, thus potentially triggering a nuclear arms race in Latin America as well – on the US doorstep.

No one watching this disconcerting spectacle could sit back and do nothing. The most likely consequence of a nuclear Iran is that most other powers in the region would seek nuclear weapons, too. A report published by the London-based International Institute for Strategic Studies in May 2008 suggested that at least thirteen Middle East states would pursue nuclear programmes in response to Iran's acquisition of nuclear weapons.

Egypt, which has had no diplomatic relations with Iran since 1979, would be unlikely to allow Iran to snatch away its role as regional leader. Cairo would watch with profound concern the rise of a hegemonic power which aims to change the regional status quo. It might, therefore, consider speeding up its nuclear activities, which so far have been modest. The same can be said of Turkey, Algeria and Morocco, all medium-sized countries with ambitious plans to modernise and diversify their energy supplies in coming years.

In the Gulf, Saudi Arabia leads the way. Rumours are rife that the kingdom has already acquired nuclear weapons through its close ties with Pakistan, while senior Western intelligence sources have expressed a mixture of surprise and alarm that the Saudis chose to buy expensive, Chinese-made Silkworm missiles, whose main selling point is their ability to carry nuclear warheads.

And then there is the Levant, where Syrian and Jordanian energy needs go hand in hand with their need to modernise. Syria clearly would not feel threatened by the nuclear programme of its closest regional ally. It is said that the alleged nuclear installation that Israeli jets destroyed in eastern Syria in September 2007 was a joint Syrian–Iranian programme that was operated with the help of North Korean scientists. If Iran acquires nuclear capability, Syria would no doubt enjoy its protection, and it could also act as the launch pad for the deployment of Iran's nuclear missiles in the Mediterranean. As such it would not only threaten Israel, but all of Europe.

Jordan, on the other hand, has much to fear. It was Jordan's King Abdullah II who warned in 2004 against a rising 'Shi'a Crescent' in the region. He was referring to a single, continuous stretch of extremist, Iran-backed Shi'a power running from Iran through Iraq and Alawite-controlled Syria into Lebanon.

In short, the regional landscape that emerges from Iran's acquisition of nuclear weapons (or at least the capability to build them) is one where most regimes will no longer rely on America for their security. After all, every imperial power in the history of the region eventually retreated. Why should America be the exception? What is certain is that a nuclear Iran would cause unbridled proliferation throughout the region. And a nuclear Middle East – particularly one in which the burgeoning nuclear powers are innately hostile, without channels of communication and, perhaps also by then, in the hands of more radical political forces – would be disastrous for regional stability.

That is not all. If, as expected, Turkey seeks to join the nuclear club in order to balance Iranian power, what will be the consequences for NATO and for Europe? Will a new doctrine of nuclear deterrence have to be defined? Will NATO feel compelled to offer a nuclear umbrella to its allies in the eastern Mediterranean and beyond? Will the world then be dragged into a horrifying nuclear stand-off? Will Paris and London be risked for Manama and Amman? And if Turkey goes nuclear in response to Iran, how will some European countries, such as Greece, Cyprus and Germany, respond to this development? And, finally, what will happen to the NPT and its goals of preventing proliferation and encouraging long-term disarmament? If a nuclear arms race is unleashed in response to Iran, that is likely to be the end of the NPT and, with it, the end of the current overarching structure of international security, of which the NPT is a fundamental, if imperfect, building block.

All these are possible long-term consequences of a nuclear Iran. Worst of all, none of them suggests that by allowing Iran to have what it wants, war could be avoided through deterrence. After all, the Cold War spared Europe another global conflict. The balance of terror between the superpowers also greatly reduced and, ultimately, avoided a nuclear war. But the price was a number of local conflicts which the two superpowers fanned and used to alter the balance of power between them elsewhere across the globe. All these consequences must, then, be taken into account, as must the possibility that war will just happen at a later and more dangerous stage – after rather than before Iran acquires nuclear weapons. Such a scenario, not an uneasy modus vivendi with a nuclear Iran, must provide the instrument for assessing the impact of a pre-emptive military strike on Iran's nuclear installations.

There is little doubt that a military strike launched against Iran's nuclear installations, especially if initiated by the USA, would not present overwhelming difficulties from a strictly operational point of view. Israel, too, could accomplish the mission, but this would likely be a more limited action targeting only Iran's main nuclear installations. It would also involve considerable political and operational risks for Israel. This would be the case even with the tacit support of a US administration. For the time being, however, even this appears to be lacking.

An Israeli attack, even without American complicity or simply approval, would most surely expose American troops and bases to Iranian reprisals. An Israeli attack is thus fraught with political hazards before its military leaders overcome the logistical challenges. At any rate, a US-led operation would have a much higher chance of success. The US has far greater firepower, precision, proximity and air and naval supremacy, all factors that increase the chance of success.

A pre-emptive strike against Iran would not include a full-scale land invasion under any circumstances. There is a consensus among analysts that a war against Iran that involved the use of ground troops and an occupation force would not only involve unbearable costs but also would hinder rather than facilitate the attainment of US goals. There is, instead, a consensus on the type of attack that would succeed and which is more likely to be used if Washington were to launch an attack on Iran.

It would comprise three elements. First, there would be

a systematic bombing of all nuclear sites known to Western intelligence services (not necessarily just those listed in the previous chapter). This strike would rely on Tomahawk missiles and bombings by air forces deployed from bases and aircraft carriers in region, as well as Diego Garcia, and B-2 bombers from both the Diego Garcia bases and the base in Missouri.

Second, US forces would seek to neutralise Iran's military capability by targeting its military bases, prioritising air and naval bases, which Iran could use to block the Strait of Hormuz and launch reprisal attacks. This would also extend to bases of the IRGC, command-and-control centres, telecommunications facilities and, possibly, part of the critical civilian infrastructure, such as bridges, railways, highways and refineries.

Third, less certain and more controversial, would be an all-out attack aimed at decapitating Iran's leadership and destroying its regime.

Finally, attacks would be preceded and accompanied by special-forces operations that would help designate and identify targets, and initiate sabotage behind enemy lines.

Iran will put up quite a fight. It has a respectable air force, including approximately five hundred aircraft. Among them is a fleet of MiG-29s, which were bought from Russia and are considered to be the best fighter aircraft available in the world today. Iran also has sophisticated anti-aircraft defence systems, including the Russian-made Pantsir S-1 SAM. But conventional Iranian military responses should not pose an insurmountable problem for the US Army and Navy, which are capable of deploying up to two thousand advanced aircraft that can operate out of reach of the Iranians.

The Americans gained some experience against Iran in 1988

– the only direct military clash between the two countries – when the US Navy inflicted a humiliating defeat on Iran's navy during the operation codenamed Mantis. In that engagement, two Iranian vessels were destroyed (one was sunk) and the Iranians also lost six IRGC speedboats, while two platforms that the Guards used in the Gulf to launch their operations were destroyed. On the Iranian side, 77 military personnel were killed and 300 were wounded. The USA lost two soldiers. There is no doubt that in any future clash the USA would prevail. The question is not whether such an operation would succeed, but how Iran would respond.

Iran has submarines and Chinese missiles, which are quite capable of inflicting damage on ships, as the Israelis learned during their 2006 war with Hezbollah, when one of their vessels off the coast of Lebanon was hit by an Iranian-supplied, Hezbollah-fired Chinese C-802 missile.

Then there is the experience Iran accumulated during the Iran–Iraq War, especially during the phase of the Tankers' War. Iran could launch missiles against US targets throughout the Gulf, including Iraq. It could mine the Strait of Hormuz and would most likely try to seal it off to commercial traffic. It would use its IRGC flotilla of speedboats, which are based along the Gulf, including on the islands Iran has seized from the Emirates – Abu Musa, and the Greater and Lesser Tunbs.

Iran would also unleash a wave of terror attacks against the West, particularly against American and Israeli targets, across the Middle East, starting from the Gulf, and moving on to Europe and beyond. Iran would probably also consider using the militias and terror groups that it supports in the region to open new fronts against the USA and its allies in the hope of inflaming anti-American and anti-Israel sentiment.

Any attack must therefore take this scenario into account and integrate countermeasures in the planning stage. An attack that is limited to Iran's nuclear installations will immediately ignite a conflict and invite widespread reprisals. The more extended the list of additional non-nuclear targets, the harder it will be for Iran to respond with full force.

It can be assumed, for example, that Iran's fleet of highly armed speedboats is likely to swarm through the waters of the Gulf in an attempt to block the Strait. An early landing of special forces at Abu Musa and other islands to destroy this fleet of high-speed miniature vessels might make it harder for Iran to disrupt the strategic oil routes. The more a US operation is able to anticipate Iranian reprisals and implement pre-emptive countermeasures, the less 'disastrous' the consequences of Iran's response will be.

No plan can guarantee that Iran's response will be strictly conventional. An American strike would expose US forces in the region to attacks, both conventional and non-conventional. All diplomatic missions in the Gulf, all expatriate residential areas, all places of entertainment and worship, all foreign companies – along with the civilian and military infrastructure that supports and protects them – will be potential targets.

Iran might activate sleeper cells in Europe and North America to organise 'spectacular' responses against civilian targets. And from the early hours of the attack, Iran can be expected to open a second front in south Lebanon, ordering Hezbollah to launch a missile barrage against Israel. After all, Hezbollah's military build-up in south Lebanon *is* the first line of defence for Bushehr. And given Iran's increasingly organic link to Hamas, one could even imagine Hamas entering the fray and dragging Israel into a two-front war against two guerrilla movements.

Equipped with Iranian weapons, Hamas and Hezbollah would wreak havoc on Israel's densely populated heartland and issue calls for jihad across the region, severely compromising US efforts. With Iran's Mediterranean proxies engaged against the Little Satan, the Arab friends of the Great Satan would find it hard to continue siding openly with America. They would face widespread protests and, possibly, popular disturbances within their own countries. If this were to happen, Iran could succeed in transforming a pre-emptive attack against its nuclear programme into a wider regional conflict. The ramifications would be dramatic.

One cannot underestimate the possibility that Iran will exploit an attack on its nuclear programme to trigger a regional war. That is why it has been a great mistake to allow Iran's proxies to become increasingly powerful in Lebanon and the Gaza Strip; that is also why it was right to take on the pro-Iranian militias in Iraq. It is doubtful whether the much-romanticised 'Arab street' will force their governments to join a war against Israel and the USA. After all, moderate Arab regimes stood on the sidelines, sometimes quietly cheering, when Israel took on Hezbollah in July 2006. They did not go out of their way to condemn Israel's strike against a suspected Syrian nuclear installation in September 2007. And not a few of them were pleased to see Hezbollah's terror mastermind, 'Imad Mughniyeh, blown into a thousand pieces on the streets of Damascus.

The distance between the incendiary rhetoric of the 'street' and the mood of the palace is significant in itself. It pales in comparison with the distance between the lip-service that

Arab regimes pay to 'public opinion' in the name of pan-Arab solidarity, and the concrete actions and policy choices made in the corridors of Arab power. Their national interest, with the exception of Iran's arch-ally, Syria, is diametrically opposed to Iran's. Even as conflict erupts along the Lebanon–Israel and the Gaza–Israel borders, most Arab countries will do their utmost to stay out of the conflict. They may also strive not to become political burdens on their American ally and even on Israel.

The real test will be the effectiveness of the American or Israeli actions. Arab leaders' embarrassment at what America and/or Israel might be doing in the region will be directly proportional to the length and nature of the operations, as well as the extent of 'collateral damage' – namely the civilian casualties that are the inevitable consequence of striking strategic targets in densely populated areas.

In the final analysis, the success of a military operation makes its risks and its costs tolerable. Failure is not an option. Such an outcome would trigger a wave of condemnation and a reassessment of strategic relations by countries in the region. As Mustafa Alani, of the Emirates-based Gulf Research Centre, recently told the London-based *Guardian*: 'If we have to choose between Iranian nuclear deterrence and intimidation, or accept military action as a solution, we'll accept military action … We in the Gulf can live with Iranian retaliation for a week or a month. That's manageable compared to the possibility that Iran will be a nuclear power.'

An attack on Iran would also have important political consequences which must be taken into account. According to Ken Pollack, there are two clocks ticking in Tehran. The first is faster – and it is the nuclear programme. The second is slower – and it is called regime change. No doubt, Iranians are not uniformly and enthusiastically loyal to their regime, even if those parts of Iran's civil society which aspire to a democratic Iran are too weak to assert themselves. For Pollack, the political challenge the West now faces is how to accelerate the latter clock (regime change) while slowing down the former (the nuclear programme).

The conventional wisdom is that an attack on Iran might not stop the nuclear programme but would rally all Iranians around the regime, thus hindering any prospect of an Iranian 'velvet revolution'. Iranians are presumed to be profoundly nationalistic, regardless of their sympathies for the regime, and an attack would trump their misgivings about their rulers with an upsurge of national pride. In other words, an attack would, paradoxically, strengthen domestic support for the regime.

Further evidence of this is the widespread popularity of Iran's nuclear programme. Even if the clerics vanished in a puff of smoke, Iranians would still want to pursue the programme. After all, the Shah wanted it, and his ambitions to turn Iran into a regional superpower were not so different from those of the Islamic Republic. Why would a democratic Iran be different? A more democratic regime would be more responsible and benign in its endeavours, both towards its citizens and towards its neighbours. Why, then, antagonise them if a free Iran with a nuclear programme would not pose the same threat to Western interests as do the Islamic revolutionaries?

This dilemma is not a simple one. Iranians are certainly a very proud people whose nationalism can reach jingoistic, even xenophobic, proportions. Love of motherland and a constant (and paranoid) fear of external interference and foreign plots are deeply engrained in the national psyche, regardless of the nature of the regime. It was patriotism which saved the Islamic Republic after Saddam Hussein launched his surprise attack in 1980. Even those who were alienated by the revolution rallied around the regime. It could happen again.

Policymakers must therefore carefully weigh this possibility. And in so doing, they must be aware of the counterpoints that may mitigate its impact:

- A considerable part of Iran's population is non-Persian and belongs to ethnic, religious or linguistic minorities that mostly live in the border areas of the country. Even though the precedent of the Iran–Iraq War suggests that they will not necessarily join their ethnic kin against Iran, they may not necessarily stand by the regime in case of an external attack.

- The impact of humiliating defeats on dictatorships cannot be discounted. The nationalist argument could well have been made for Argentina before the Falklands war in 1982, for Slobodan Milosevic's Serbia before the Kosovo campaign of 1999, or even for Saddam Hussein before Operation Desert Storm in 1991. In all three cases, military defeat and the regime's humiliation triggered either the downfall of the leaders – the military junta in Buenos Aires and Milosevic in Belgrade – or popular uprisings such as the Shi'a and Kurdish rebellions in Iraq (if external support for those two rebellions had been forthcoming, Saddam might have been toppled in 1991).

- Public opinion is irrelevant to the equation. Even if

100 per cent of Iran's population opposed the nuclear
programme and supported democracy, its impact on
the regime's policies is currently zero. Worrying about
a possible change of public opinion inside Iran as a
consequence of an attack is either a pretext or a gross
misreading of the situation. What matters is whether a
military operation is successful, not the percentage of
Iranians who will applaud as bombs fall on their heads.

The possible domestic consequences that pose anxieties
are of a different order. An attack may cause the collapse of
the clerical regime, with the IRGC seizing power from their
theocratic masters. The question then would be about the
damage inflicted on the nuclear programme and the ability of
a weakened military junta to resume work on it, particularly if
sanctions are able to prevent Iran from replenishing its stocks
of raw materials and components.

The Iraqi precedent – Operation Desert Storm – achieved
just such an outcome. It did not bring democracy to the belea-
guered Iraqis. It did not cause the downfall of a particularly
brutal tyrant. If anything, it made him more brutish, more
paranoid and more oppressive. But it degraded his ability to
produce weapons of mass destruction, and the subsequent
sanctions and inspections ensured that Saddam would never
reconstitute his non-conventional programmes, at least to the
pre-war levels he had achieved.

No doubt, an attack on Iran would retard the chance of
Iran's civil society regaining its lost liberties, and would force
the regime to reassess its national priorities. But those who
support regime change as a way out of the current nuclear
stand-off are doomed to disappointment. Revolutionary

regimes do not sit on their hands as their revolutionary goals are eroded by either domestic or external pressure. Indeed, in his discussion of revolutionary powers, the *Washington Post*'s David Ignatius continued his parallel between revolutionary France and revolutionary Iran by saying, '[I]f Iran holds to its revolutionary goals of challenging the other powers of the region and, indeed, the legitimacy of the established order, then diplomatic concessions will be very dangerous. An accommodation that is forged on Iranian terms would be harmful to the United States and its allies, from Egypt and Israel all the way to Pakistan.'

The problem is that the only way to persuade a revolutionary power to renounce its goals beyond its borders is through a decisive military defeat. In Napoleon's case, these defeats were delivered first in Russia and then at Waterloo. Those events opened the way for the end of France's revolutionary zeal.

The same happened with Nazi Germany in 1945 and Nasser's Egypt after its humiliating defeat in the 1967 Six Day War with Israel. Unlike Napoleon and Hitler, Nasser survived in power, but the 1967 defeat was the end of Arab nationalism and Nasser's aspirations to export it from the Gulf to the Atlas mountains. The Soviet Union, whose survival depended in no small measure on its nuclear shield, had a different ending. Nevertheless, one could argue that the Soviet Union did collapse – under a combination of military adventures (Afghanistan), political incompetence, economic exhaustion and ideological decay. In all events, its collapse derived from the failure of communism and its irreversible decline as a force for radical change in the world. The same can be said of Iran.

Iran would find it difficult to recover from a decisive defeat on the battlefield. It would certainly inhibit Iran's hegemonic ambitions and would cut the revolution down to size. It could even cause the collapse of the regime and lead, eventually, to a government that would view the regional status quo more benignly. Iran's success in its nuclear quest, by contrast, would defy any effort to contain the country, would strengthen the revolution, embolden the regime and give it a new lease of life. It would also extend its licence to quash internal dissent and restore the original revolutionary orthodoxy. Needless to say, it would also leave the region exposed to Iran's subversion and at the mercy of its ambitions.

All options – attack or containment, regime change or accommodation – raise enormous and difficult questions, legitimate doubts and understandable anxiety. The consequence of each course, in the worst-case scenario, is the sum of all the West's fears. If an attack bears too many risks and deterrence does not reduce them – in fact, it may magnify them without shielding the region from a future conflict – is there a third way between conventional war now and nuclear war later which can avoid both scenarios?

3

Human rights and the illusion of 'Iranian Democracy'

Majid Kavoosifar was executed in a Tehran square on 2 August 2007. Swinging from a crane next to him was his cousin, Hossein. The two youths had been found guilty of murdering a conservative judge. Hassan Moghadas, dubbed the 'Hanging Judge' by opposition groups, had presided over trials of regime opponents and had sentenced many to death. After the murder, the Kavoosifar cousins fled to the United Arab Emirates, where they were arrested and returned to Iran to meet their judicial death before a large crowd, which included state and local officials. Some of the mob photographed and filmed the event on their mobile phones; others shouted words of encouragement to the executioner. Soon, videos of the event were flashed around the world, mainly via the YouTube web-sharing site, while pictures of the lifeless bodies dangling from the cranes were published by Iranian news agencies.

To Western viewers, the grisly images were particularly shocking, both for their brutality and for the public nature of the event. Not so to Iranians, who had become inured to the sight of lifeless bodies swinging from cranes. In the early days of the Islamic Republic, thousands were executed in this way throughout the country. Then, the crane was an expedient way to execute more people more quickly. Almost thirty years later, the death sentence is still carried out from the business end of cranes, often of Western manufacture.

Any embarrassment these images might cause leaves the Iranian regime unmoved. Such events have become routine, standard fare in the Islamic Revolutionary Republic. It is hard to believe that the Western companies that supplied the cranes, and whose logos feature prominently in images of executions, remain so sanguine. In spite of international protests at what appears to be a barbaric punishment, hundreds of Iranians, including minors, continue to end their lives at the end of a crane. Their crimes range from murder and rape to drug-trafficking, armed robbery, espionage and sexual crimes, including homosexuality.

Executions are mostly carried out by hanging, though stoning is still known to occur. The only change in this gruesome business is that the regime recently opted to conduct executions in private, inside prisons and away from the public eye – unless otherwise specified. These days, when executions are conducted in public, photography and filming are forbidden. The restrictions were instituted by the judiciary in January 2008, but they were motivated more out of discomfort at Iran's vilification in the international media than out of a sense of shame at what was being perpetrated or a sense of empathy for the victims and their families.

Iran is a paradox. On the one hand, there are the IRGC, a revolutionary fervour that infuses the regime, blood-curdling genocidal rhetoric, support for terrorism, public executions and nuclear ambitions. On the other, there is a vibrant civil society, political and cultural manifestations of dissent, a limited measure of pluralism, carefully measured differences of opinion in the political and media sectors – and, of course, there are elections.

To the untutored eye, Iranian elections may appear to be genuinely open to competition among political parties, individuals and organisations, sometimes with apparently significant differences in opinion. So what, some may ask, if Iran retains the death penalty? Europe abandoned the death penalty decades ago, but several states in the USA continue the practice. The death penalty does not inherently contradict the democratic nature of a country. If that were the case, France would not have been a democracy until the mid-1980s, when capital punishment was abolished under the presidency of François Mitterrand.

The difference is that, in democracies, the death penalty is applied to criminals guilty of particularly abhorrent crimes, and then only after the most testing judicial process which could itself take years. In the United States, the accused is entitled to the presumption of innocence, habeas corpus, trial by jury, stringent criteria for the admission of evidence, the right to legal counsel, the transparency of the system, layers of appeal, the possibility of appeal to the Federal Supreme Court, and so on. Criticism voiced in the West about America's use of the death penalty has to do with the nature of the punishment, not the procedures through which punishment is handed down.

Nothing of the sort can be said of Iran. Victims are often executed even before their lawyers and families are informed of their fate. In Iran, the death penalty is part of a deeply oppressive, arbitrary and unjust judicial system that is devoid of respect for due process or the protection of the most basic rights of the suspect. That does not, however, make Iran a totalitarian dictatorship in the image of Saddam Hussein's Iraq or Kim Jong Il's North Korea.

It is understandable that those who promote dialogue with Iran emphasise the democratic nature of Iran's political institutions, the pluralism that exists within the admittedly narrow boundaries imposed by the Islamic Republic, the relatively free atmosphere – at least compared to other countries in the region – and the fact that Iran's civil society is much less anti-Western and bellicose than its leaders. Those who fear a military attack on Iran's nuclear installations and doubt the efficacy of sanctions often emphasise the need to encourage moderate elements to exploit the regime's internal divisions, the nuances between factions and leaders, the society's openness to the West. All these factors add to the impression that Iran is susceptible to reason and argument about a range of issues, not least its nuclear programme.

There is a problem with this superficial reading. Despite positive signals from Iranian society and its obvious differences to its neighbours in terms of governance, Iran remains one of the most repressive regimes on earth. The impact of civil society on the regime is nil. Before Iran can be described as a democracy and before its leaders and their policies can be treated as if they were responsible, transparent and democratic, it would be prudent to look more closely at Iran's political system. Here, the true nature of Iran is revealed – a country run by a small clique of fanatics, among whom differences – played up in the West – are a matter of style. When it comes to substance, the differences are mostly irrelevant and meaningless. A country that treats its citizens brutally and threatens its neighbours cannot be trusted with nuclear weapons.

Western diplomats nurture the hope that Iran's presidential elections, scheduled for the late spring of 2009, will put an end to the bizarre and ghoulish rule of Mahmoud Ahmadinejad. His departure, they believe, could open the door to a new, more constructive dialogue, which would include the nuclear issue – the more so if he is replaced by an amenable challenger, such as one of his two predecessors, Mohammad Khatami or Akhbar Hashemi Rafsanjani. But Iran's nuclear programme was not Ahmadinejad's brainchild, and it will outlive him.

The programme was, in fact, resumed during Rafsanjani's tenure as president. And if the NIE is accurate, the suspension of the military component of the programme would have happened in the sixth year of the Khatami presidency. That means that during the first five years of his term, Khatami had few scruples about presiding over a military nuclear programme. As for his much-touted reformist credentials, it is hard to see how Khatami brings any succour to those who aspire to a democratic Iran. The brutal repression of student protests on 9 July 1999 and 9 July 2003 occurred on his watch. The only meaningful change he oversaw while in office was a significant opening of the media to dissent. It was an opening that his successor quickly closed.

It is true that tensions between Iran and the international community have deteriorated since Ahmadinejad's electoral triumph. These tensions derive, in part, from the more militant and offensive political discourse that Ahmadinejad has fostered on a host of issues, including the nuclear issue.

Western diplomats have felt more comfortable, more able to entertain a dialogue, with other, less confrontational figures in Tehran – Khatami, Rafsanjani, even the former chief nuclear negotiator and current Speaker of the Majlis, Ali Larijani. These men are more polished, sophisticated and worldly. They are consummate diplomats. They are also more aware than the current president of the need to maintain civil, even cordial, relations with the West. It was under Khatami, after all, that Iran decided to suspend uranium enrichment as a constructive measure. It was under Ahmadinejad that Iran broke the IAEA seals at Natanz, thus igniting the current crisis.

The problem, though, is not so much with differences – real or imagined – between past, present and future presidents, or even between parliamentary factions in the Majlis. The problem is that, according to Freedom House, the US-based democracy advocacy organisation, Iran is 'not an electoral democracy'. Real power is not in the hands of elected leaders. There have been important changes since Ahmadinejad assumed office: he is the first president who is not a cleric and his credentials stem from a mixture of grassroots populism and revolutionary fervour. Accordingly, power has shifted towards the presidency, a sign that Ahmadinejad's attempt to return Iran to its early revolutionary days enjoys the blessing of the main power brokers in Iran.

Ultimately, though, power rests in the hands of the IRGC and the clergy. Above all, it rests with the Supreme Leader. The elected representatives of the people are subordinate to these complex structures, which include the revolutionary and religious courts, as well as the security apparatus, all of which, in turn, are subordinate to the Supreme Leader.

Ayatollah Ali Khamenei, as Supreme Leader, sits atop this

pyramid. He has ruled over Iran since the death in 1989 of his predecessor, Ayatollah Khomeini, the founder of the Islamic Republic. According to a doctrinal pronouncement by Khomeini, the Supreme Leader of the Revolutionary Republic is the 'representative of God on earth'. No less. As such, the Supreme Leader is the guardian of God's will and God's authority by virtue of his role as the ultimate 'jurisprudent'.

On seizing power in 1979, Khomeini introduced the doctrine of *Velayat-el-Fakih* to the country's new power structure. This stipulates that, in the absence of the Hidden Imam, whose return to earth to reclaim his legitimate throne over all Muslims is eagerly anticipated by all Shi'a, the Supreme Leader rules in his stead. The Supreme Leader is thus not just a political figure; nor is he just a religious figure. He is the shadow of God, the absolute ruler of Islam. Iran's Supreme Leader is, therefore, not the representative of the people in the conventional democratic sense of the term, but a leader whose authority is divine and whose words cannot be challenged without challenging God Himself.

The Supreme Leader is selected by an Assembly of Experts made up of 86 members of the clergy who are elected by universal suffrage for eight years. Candidates are selected from a list drafted by the government. The Supreme Leader is the commander-in-chief of the armed forces and he appoints the most senior officials in the judiciary and in state-owned radio and television. He also appoints the commander of the IRGC and he has de facto veto power over the appointment of the interior, intelligence and defence ministers.

Then there is the Council of Guardians, which has twelve members. Six are appointed by the Supreme Leader and the remaining six by the highest judicial authorities, who are themselves appointees of the Supreme Leader. Members of the Council of Guardians are elected for six-year terms and their appointments are rubber-stamped by the Majlis.

The Majlis is a unilateral chamber of 290 members, including five representatives from the religious minorities that the Islamic Republic tolerates: Christians, Zoroastrians and Jews. The Council of Guardians is in charge of vetting candidates for parliamentary and presidential elections and of verifying that laws passed by the Majlis are compatible with Islamic law. This means that the Council, guarantor of the regime's Islamic orthodoxy, has effective veto power over all legislation. Disputes may be referred to the unelected and clerical Council of Expediency, an institution with the power to adjudicate over discrepancies between man-made and God-made rules in the name of national security and Iran's supreme national interest.

Iran's constitutional structure does not actually pretend to be democratic in the conventional sense. True, Iranians go to the polls, but at the most recent election, held between March and April 2008, the Council of Guardians disqualified no less than three-quarters of the candidates who applied to run for office. Aware of the contagious power of democracy, the Iranian authorities have taken care to reserve a limited and tightly controlled space for dissent. Even after candidates have been vetted, their power is restricted, particularly when it comes to matters of foreign policy and national security, including the nation's nuclear issues. As for the president, his power depends largely on the approval and protection of the Supreme Leader. As if to prove who is really in power, Ayatollah Khamenei has recently declared that the responsible party in the advancement of the nuclear issue is the Supreme National Security Council headed by the honourable president. What is said by the president and authorities is shared by all authorities of the country and heads of the three branches of the state and representatives of the Supreme Leader in the Supreme National Security Council, which follows this issue in a committed manner ...

Clearly, the Supreme Leader has the last word.

All of this must be placed in Iran's political context, which few understand well. It is evident that Iran has a complex and sophisticated power structure. Power is indeed diffuse within several centres of influence, which sometimes compete among themselves, though even in the context of authoritarian regimes this is hardly unique to Iran and therefore hardly a profound insight.

The diffusion of power means that those in power are not impervious to external influence and pressure. Some groups may conclude that they have more to lose than gain from a confrontation with the West and use their influence in an attempt to find an accommodation. It is also true that there are internal battles, power struggles, nuances of opinion, dissent and disagreement. Sometimes these clashes become public, providing an opening for the intrusion of outside influences if pressure is cleverly imposed. Inside the system, the influence of leaders rises and falls. And there are popularity contests. All this attests to the fact that Iran is not a monolithic Stalinist dictatorship where power is concentrated in the hands of a leader, a family or a small military clique, as in Saddam's Iraq, North Korea or Myanmar. But that does not make it democratic.

The overarching structure does not remotely resemble a Westminster-style democracy. Iranians are ultimately ruled by their clergy and the IRGC, not by genuinely elected representatives. In order to truly understand the system, however, it is necessary to appreciate the dominance of the clergy – with all its doctrinal differences – in the hierarchical structure and governance of the Revolutionary Republic. Scratch the thin patina of 'democracy' and an inflexible theocratic reality is exposed.

First, there is Iran's record on human rights and its systematic violations of the most basic democratic rights. In spite of the limited degree of pluralism that makes Iran different from the sort of authoritarian and dictatorial regimes the region has experienced in the past, there is a coherent power structure that is under the control of the Supreme Leader, as well as the institutions charged with safeguarding the Islamic Revolution and its objectives. In these structures one must include revolutionary and religious courts and the ubiquitous IRGC, with their suffocating presence in society, in the economy and national security. The Guards enjoy a virtual monopoly over vital and strategic sectors of the economy, where they prevent economic transparency and competition. Their economic power feeds into, and is supported by, their military might. It is a structure that exists in parallel with Iran's regular armed forces and, as with the SS in Nazi Germany, it is animated by an uncompromising loyalty to Khomeini's revolutionary ideals.

These power centres – the clergy, the Guards, the courts and the unelected institutions in charge of maintaining Islamic and revolutionary orthodoxy – are responsible for decision-making. They are the ultimate arbiters of politics, not the elected institutions or a vibrant civil society. The fact that these institutions exist at all is meaningless when it comes to classifying Iran: ultimately, it is an illiberal, repressive, revolutionary regime.

International developments have obscured the meaning of the word 'democracy' in recent years. In the Middle East, insistence on free elections before other basic elements of democracy had been put in place has enabled illiberal and undemocratic forces to win popular elections – sometimes by massive majorities – and claim power. The victory of Hamas in the elections for the Palestinian Legislative Council in January 2006 highlighted the problematic nature of the 'democracy = elections' equation. Democracy is not simply the ability to elect representatives in free elections. To be genuine, a choice must occur in an environment that is free of intimidation and free from the fear of reprisals for dissenters. Moreover, voting must be genuinely secret and it must be based on information that enables voters to make an informed decision based on the platforms and programmes of candidates and parties. And other elements must be in place – guarantees of transparency, which make the electoral competition truly free, safeguards that ensure the democratic nature of politics between elections, and the protection of minorities and dissenting views.

These measures are the legal and substantive cornerstones of democracy. Without the protection of fundamental freedoms and political rights, democracy can neither exist nor survive. Those who claim that Iran is a democracy must contend with the absence of freedom of religion, opinion, expression and the press, along with the systematic denial of fundamental rights, such as rights to a fair trial, association, trade unions and professional associations, socio-economic rights, and the rights of women, especially the right to equality before the law. The electoral process is a smokescreen that shields a brutal, repressive and authoritarian regime.

According to Freedom House, Iran is not a free country. On its ranking scale, Iran is rated alongside such beacons of liberty as Algeria, Angola, Azerbaijan, Bhutan, Brunei, Egypt, the United Arab Emirates, Iraq, Kazakhstan, Oman, Pakistan, Qatar, Russia, Tajikistan and Thailand. Not many countries fare worse than Iran in the field of political rights – the exceptions are Saudi Arabia, China, Cuba, Eritrea, Equatorial Guinea, Laos, Libya, Myanmar, North Korea, Syria, Somalia, Sudan, Tunisia, Turkmenistan, Uzbekistan, Vietnam and Zimbabwe. In the field of civil rights, Iran is in the same category as Saudi Arabia, China, Eritrea, Equatorial Guinea, Iraq, Laos, Syria and Zimbabwe. It is surpassed only by countries like Cuba, Libya, Myanmar, North Korea, Somalia and Sudan.

Beyond the constitutional structure of the Islamic Republic, Freedom House identifies other areas that highlight Iran's democratic deficit. First, there is widespread corruption, which is aggravated by the many monopolies (in cement, sugar and pistachios, among other commodities) that the IRGC and the clerical establishment control. This is exacerbated by the role of religious foundations and their tax-exempt economic empires. Not only do these monopolies prevent fiscal transparency, encourage corruption and distort the market, but they also guarantee enormous income for the clerical establishment, which uses its privileges to maintain its predominant role in Iran's power structure.

*

For a brief period during the late nineties, Iranians enjoyed a faint hint of freedom – freedom of the press and freedom of expression, two critical freedoms that are used in assessing the democratic status of a nation. Then, just as suddenly, the glimmer of light was extinguished. The ability of civil society to express criticism and gain access to information was abruptly curtailed in a fresh spasm of repression.

During the Ahmadinejad presidency alone, almost six hundred publications have been closed down. Journalists were informed that they were not permitted to 'insult Islam' or to 'undermine the foundations of the Islamic Republic' – two 'offences' that were open to such broad definition as to constitute outright intimidation and an attempt to impose self-censorship. Journalists were also forbidden to report particular events, as dictated by the authorities and implemented by ad hoc and arbitrary censorship machinery.

Not even foreign reporters could escape the regime's long and oppressive reach. A Canadian photographer of Iranian origins, Zahra Kazemi, was arrested in 2003, allegedly because she had photographed the notorious Evin prison in Tehran, where political prisoners are held and sometimes executed. Kazemi suffered torture and random acts of violence in jail. She eventually died. No one has been prosecuted or punished for her murder. More recently, foreign citizens visiting Iran on behalf of Western NGOs – and an academic visiting her ailing mother – were arrested and arbitrarily detained.

According to Freedom House, President Ahmadinejad believes that the media's role is to 'recount and support government actions, not comment on them'. Clearly, those who criticise government decisions and cross arbitrary red lines risk becoming enemies of the state or, worse, 'foreign agents'. The consequences can be severe. Journalists are often persecuted, arrested and sentenced to varying degrees of punishment, including the death penalty, as demonstrated by the recent case of Kurdish journalists Adnan Hassanpour and Abdolvahed Botimar. They were accused of endangering national security and of being 'God's enemies'. Among the evidence cited was a string of interviews that Hassanpour had given to Voice of America. Both had worked for a magazine that Ahmadinejad banned soon after taking office, in August 2005. They were both hanged in late July 2007.

A similar fate befell a Baluchi journalist, Yaghoob Mirnehad, who was sentenced to death in February 2008 and executed in early August in the city of Zahedan. He had allegedly been a member of a terrorist organisation, Jandullah, which is active in Baluchistan, and guilty of involvement in unspecified activities against the 'security of the state'. Mirnehad had been writing for a Tehran-based newspaper and was running a charity to improve the education of children. His criticism of local officials, reports say, is what got him into trouble. The New York-based International Campaign for Human Rights in Iran called his execution 'state-sanctioned murder'. Many journalists have been imprisoned for publishing 'false information'. As reported in Amnesty International's 2008 report on Iran, cases of abuse and sentencing for undefined crimes are numerous. Ali Farahbakhsh, for example, was imprisoned for eleven months on charges of espionage. His crime: attending a press conference in Thailand.

Punitive, restrictive and intimidating measures against journalists have gone hand in hand with the censorship of literary works and other cultural events. Iran's Ministry of Culture must approve the publication of any book in Iran.

It also determines whether foreign books may be distributed in either the original or translated version inside Iran. Any work that is perceived to criticise the regime or the values of the revolution is banned.

Restrictions on freedom of expression do not stop at the punishment of those whose ideas are considered to be dangerous by the regime. The Iranian authorities also target the means through which the average citizen tries to bypass the censorship regime and gain access to information from abroad. The government has, for example, targeted both the Internet and satellite dishes.

The Internet is severely restricted and routinely ravaged by targeting of local bloggers. Satellite dishes were tolerated in the past; more recently, they have been randomly selected for confiscation. Under Ahmadinejad, raids against dishes have increased – and so have the penalties for illegal possession. The regime has also acted energetically to block radio and television broadcasts that are beamed to Iran from abroad. This has applied particularly to the BBC, Israel's Farsi service and Radio Farda, a Persian-language radio station based in Prague and Washington. A regime that suppresses information, fears dissent and persecutes dissenters – real or imagined – cannot be counted among the family of democracies.

As with other repressive, Islamic-inspired regimes, Iran views women as lesser beings. The percentage of female graduates in Iran is higher than that of male graduates. Women make up half of Iran's university population. But in spite of their high level of literacy and educational achievement, women are barred from a range of professions. They cannot, for example, be judges and their status in society is intrinsically subordinate to that of men. Women cannot divorce their husbands, but they can be repudiated by their husbands. Women's testimony does not hold the same weight in a court of law. By some bizarre measurement, a woman's word is regarded as being worth half that of a man.

In addition, women must adhere to a strict code of state-imposed 'modesty', which is intended to protect them, but is really aimed at upholding the peculiar brand of misogyny practised in the Islamic Revolutionary Republic. The appearance of women in public is thus monitored by a special branch of the police, which has been set up to ensure the protection and defence of public morality. Women who show too much – arms, hair, ankles – are frequently the object of abuse. They can be arrested and are subject to a range of punishments. Other typically feminine aspects of life are also strictly regulated by the modesty police, including the use of make-up, lipstick and nail polish.

The Islamic Revolutionary Republic sometimes seems to be obsessed with sexual matters. In response to a question about gay rights, President Ahmadinejad made the astonishing claim that the 'phenomenon' of homosexuality did not exist in Iran. The claim, which followed his address at Columbia University in 2007, was met with contempt and derision that extended far beyond the New York campus. The reality, of course, is that homosexuality does exist in Iran and the fact of its existence can be found in another 'phenomenon' – the judicial executions of homosexuals. In fact, Ahmadinejad's claim reflects a certain truth – that the Islamic Republic does not see homosexuality as a condition of existence. In revolutionary Iran, human beings are, by their nature, heterosexual.

There are no homosexuals, only homosexual *acts*, which are considered to be contrary to the will of God.

A recent case highlighted the plight of homosexuals in Iran. Mehdi Kazemi is an Iranian student who travelled to the United Kingdom for university studies. Kazemi is homosexual. While he was in the United Kingdom, his former partner was arrested and tortured in Iran. During the course of his interrogation, he revealed the names of past partners, including Kazemi, who understandably feared that, like his former partner, he would end his life at the end of a crane if he returned home. Following a three-year legal battle, Kazemi persuaded the Home Office to consider his application for asylum in 2008.

Many were less fortunate. Executions, alongside 'lesser' punishments, such as lashings, are routinely inflicted on those who are accused of having engaged in homosexual acts. The struggle for sexual freedom has not even begun in Iran.

Iran's capital offers a range of choices for the faithful. There are, of course, many Shi'a mosques. Jews and Christians have their places of worship, as do Zoroastrians. But beyond the state religion and these three 'tolerated' religious minorities, there are no facilities for other minority religions. Baha'is do not enjoy that privilege, nor do Sunni Muslims (who constitute more than 80 per cent of the world's Islamic population).

That does not mean Christians, Jews and Zoroastrians are accorded equality within Iranian society. They are second-class citizens and may not vote in general elections. Five members of the Majlis represent the three faiths, but they are elected separately, within their communities. They are subjected to a number of formal and informal limitations and are periodically accused of plotting against the regime when the government needs to find an external cause to explain its own domestic shortcomings.

If 'tolerated' minority faith groups enjoy a limited space for religious practice and political representation in Iran, they are hemmed in by a welter of restrictions. They are denied access to senior government posts and any role in the military. Education rights and access to universities are restricted. Some professions are closed to minorities. They may not buy certain types of properties in specified areas, and their communal activities are monitored and often censored by the regime. These restrictions include school curricula, prayers and social events. Grocery stores that are not owned by Muslims must indicate clearly that the owners are non-Muslims.

Sunni Muslims and members of the Baha'i faith are even more restricted. They cannot practise their religion or have their own places of worship. The Baha'i religion follows the teachings of Baha'ullah, a Persian preacher who was born in 1817 and died in an Ottoman jail in Acre, now part of Israel, in 1892. For the Baha'is, Baha'ullah is the last prophet after Moses, Jesus and Muhammad. They believe he completed their message. Iran's clerical regime views Baha'ullah as a heretic and his followers are considered the exponents of a deviant and subversive version of Shi'ism, Iran's state religion.

Baha'is are, therefore, first and foremost enemies of God because they are considered to be heretical. And as Iran's Supreme Leader is considered to be God's representative on earth, they are also considered to be enemies of Iran. In other words, their political offence derives from their theological divergence, and the charge of heresy triggers a punishment that also has political implications. Not surprisingly, then,

Baha'is are actively persecuted. All their activities are closely monitored and are regularly disrupted.

Baha'is must register with the police as members of a forbidden faith. Their young are barred from attending university and all their adherents are the object of regular abuse, persecution and punishment. Hundreds of Baha'is have been sentenced to death and executed by the Islamic Revolution. During one recent wave of arrests, 54 Baha'i leaders were sentenced to prison terms on 29 January 2008, for having promoted anti-regime propaganda. Sentences varied. Three received three years each and 51 were sentenced to one year, which could be suspended on condition they agreed to attend classes run by the Organisation for Islamic Propaganda, a state institution in charge of indoctrinating the population – a form of re-education that aims to coerce Baha'is into converting to Shi'a Islam. While Iran 'tolerates' some non-Shi'a religious communities, this does not extend to allowing Muslims to convert to these 'tolerated' religions. Such acts are regarded as apostasy and are punishable by death.

Iran's religious minorities are not alone in suffering from the regime's intrusive attention. Iran is home to a mosaic of ethnic and linguistic minorities that constitute a significant percentage of the overall population. Outside the Persian centre, the country is inhabited by non-Persian ethnic groups. The main minorities are Arabs (Ahwazis), Azeris, Baluchis and Kurds. In theory, they enjoy the same rights as the Persian majority, including the right to use their own language in their schools and the right to promote their own culture. In practice, however, these rights are often denied and suppressed, while leaders of such minorities are the object of arbitrary and frequent abuse and arrest.

In the case of the Ahwazi Arabs, the situation has deteriorated drastically since 2005. Demonstrations by Ahwazis, which sometimes degenerated into riots, followed the appearance of a document, whose authenticity Iranian authorities deny, which purports to describe a government plan to ethnically cleanse the oil-rich province of Khuzestan of its indigenous Ahwazi Arab inhabitants. A wave of arrests followed the unrest and seventeen Ahwazis were sentenced to death.

The Azeris also suffered repressive measures after riots broke out in support of their demands to have their language used in schools in areas where Azeris form a majority. The same fate befell Baluchis and Kurds, who, in the past, were also the target of random acts of brutality and mass killings. In their areas, tensions are worse owing to the active presence of terror groups and separatist organisations, especially in Baluchistan, which have targeted the regime.

Individuals suffer on account of their views, their faith or their ethnicity in Iran. They are also targeted by the regime if they seek to organise themselves in order to promote the interests of the group or individual members of the group. This applies also to non-governmental organisations that are involved in civil rights campaigns. Authorities intentionally delay the registration process that is required for formal recognition. And without formal recognition, they are technically illegal. As such, they are exposed to arbitrary arrest and punishment.

The same applies to independent unions, a thorn in the side of the regime and among its most vulnerable victims. In spite of Iran's huge potential wealth, its economy is weak and in a state of decline. Inflation is estimated to be more than 25 per cent and unemployment is running at more than 20 per cent.

With an ever-expanding workforce owing to the relatively youthful population (70 per cent of Iranians are under the age of 30), this is bound to become an increasingly major problem for the regime.

Every year thousands of workers, many of whom are skilled, join the labour market. This makes it imperative for Iran to constantly create jobs. But in order to do this, Iran needs a robust and steadily growing economy. In fact, Iran's labour market is stagnant and its relative success in maintaining competitiveness is due to the exploitation of workers, who are treated, in effect, as slave labour. This is exacerbated, first, by the absence of much-needed foreign investment to modernise Iran's antiquated industry, and, second, by a deeply corrupt public administration. The net result of this stagnation is that Iranian workers often do not get paid. And when they do, inflation significantly erodes the purchasing power of their earnings.

Social legislation permits companies to hire workers on short-term, three-month contracts. Under these conditions, wages are usually below the poverty line and employers are not obliged to contribute to any social benefits. In order to continue avoiding paying the social payments, Iranian companies regularly fire workers within the three-month period and then rehire them. This situation, which the government is content to leave untouched, is compounded by the fact that workers have no recourse. They are denied the right to organise independent unions to defend and promote their interests. Their sole means of representation are the so-called Islamic unions. These unions, in fact, represent the interests of the regime and its state-owned companies, not the working people.

Workers have so far responded either through strikes or through the creation, in defiance of the state, of independent unions. In 2008, workers struck (in spite of government threats) at the Khodro car factory and at the Haftapeh sugar mills. To the Western ear, their demands might not appear extravagant. They sought the right to establish independent unions, to forbid security forces from storming the plants, to halt compulsory overtime, to be entitled to benefits linked to productivity, and to have their wages linked to the cost of living. And they demanded an end to the iniquitous three-month contract, combined with an end to the practice of running employees through revolving doors, in order to avoid having to make social welfare payments. In addition, the workers sought basic social benefits, including a salary that was above the poverty line, a reduction of pressures on workers through the expansion of the workforce, worker participation in factory committees, and improved measures to protect them from work accidents.

The regime's response was to further repress manifestations of organised labour. Mansour Osanloo, the leader of the bus drivers' union, was repeatedly arrested and abused in prison. He is still in jail, and he was denied treatment for a serious heart condition. Osanloo is not the only victim, but his personal experience and that of other Iranian unionists reveal that, even in the field of social justice, repression remains the prevailing theme of the Islamic Revolutionary Republic.

The death penalty is not reserved for the worst possible crimes, but is extended and rigorously applied in cases of rape, armed robbery, drug trafficking, homosexuality (both male and female), sodomy, adultery, incest, fornication (if the convict is caught four times), alcohol consumption (three times) and many other ill-defined crimes, such as apostasy and blasphemy, which is described in Iran's penal code as 'insulting the Prophet'.

A recent reform of the penal code introduced further categories of crimes for which the death penalty is possible. These crimes are defined as posing 'a danger to the psychological security of society'. This includes the management of brothels, human trafficking with the goal of sexual enslavement, kidnapping and the management of Internet sites that promote prostitution. The new legislative package, which was under review in late 2008, would also extend the death penalty to those public officials who obstruct the application of the sentence or who 'allow the criminals [to] escape'.

In cases of crimes against religion, which in Persian are referred to as *hodoud*, punishment cannot be suspended or modified as it derives from Koranic law. Punishing the crime is, of course, problematic. Being an 'enemy of God' or among the 'corrupt of the earth' lends itself to myriad interpretations and, in the hands of religious courts, abuse. In cases where blood is spilled but where punishment does not directly derive from Islamic law, it is possible to avoid the death penalty if the victim's family agrees to accept compensation. But this is often negated by the speed and zeal with which summary trials are completed and the sentences executed. In February 2008, for example, a member of the Baluchi minority, Nasrollah Shanbeh-zehi, was arrested following a terrorist attack against a bus carrying Revolutionary Guards. He was tried and executed five days later in a public square.

A particularly troubling feature of the death penalty in Iran is that it is applied to minors, in spite of Iran's signature on international covenants that prohibit the execution of minors (below the age of eighteen). Iran is, for example, a signatory to the UN Covenant on Civil and Political Rights, which stipulates (Article 6, section 5) that 'sentence of death shall not be imposed for crimes committed by persons below eighteen years of age and shall not be carried out on pregnant women'. Iran has also signed the Covenant for the Rights of the Child, which stipulates (Article 37, section a) that 'no child shall be subjected to torture or other cruel, inhuman or degrading treatment or punishment. Neither capital punishment nor life imprisonment without possibility of release shall be imposed for offences committed by persons below eighteen years of age'. Article 49 of Iran's own criminal code states that a minor who is guilty of a crime does not bear criminal liability. The rehabilitation of minors is the responsibility of a legal guardian or a juvenile detention centre. Nevertheless, Iranian law considers only boys under fifteen and girls under nine to be minors, in contrast to the international covenants Iran has signed; children older than this are considered to bear criminal liabililty.

Iran has repeatedly sent to the gallows children who qualified as minors even under its own criteria. Amnesty International, in a special report on the application of the death penalty in the case of minors in Iran, published in June 2007, noted that Iran holds the dubious record of having executed the highest number of minors in the world – three in 2004, eight in 2005, four in 2006 and one prior to the report's release in June 2007. At the time the report was published, Amnesty noted, 75 minors were on death row in Iran.

In most cases – whether of minors or adults – there is an absolute lack of transparency in the judicial process. Suspects do not enjoy even the theoretical right to a fair trial and they are routinely denied basic rights, such as the right to a public counsel if they cannot afford a lawyer. In criminal proceedings, one person often combines the role of investigator, prosecutor and judge. Such circumstances hardly accord with the separation of functions that is considered to be essential to a fair trial. Women's testimony, if any further evidence were needed of the distance between Iran and democracy, holds half the value of a man's testimony, with potentially devastating consequences in trials where the crime in question may lead to the death penalty. And evidence obtained under torture is considered acceptable.

One category of punishment deserves a special place in this review. The judicial consequence of adultery is death – not by hanging but by stoning. At the time of writing, eight people in Iran are awaiting execution by stoning, a particularly cruel form of punishment, not only because it is intrinsically barbaric, but also because entire communities are involved in carrying it out. According to Islamic law, the stones must be large enough to inflict pain, but not so large as to cause instant death. Death, in the case of stoning, must be a slow, painful affair, with all citizens complicit through their active participation. Iran prides itself on its great civilisation and it expects its magnificent historical heritage to be recognised and respected. There is, however, little evidence of civilisation in a society that stones adulterers, routinely tortures suspects and executes minors.

Offences against public morality permit 'minor' corporal punishments. Lashing and amputations are the most commonly documented. In a recent speech, Iran's ambassador to Madrid, Seyed Davoud Salehi, defended the practice of amputating the limbs of offenders and compared it to 'a surgeon cutting off a limb to avoid the spread of gangrene'. Explaining some Islamic practices Iran adopted in its criminal code, the envoy declared, as reported in the Spanish daily *El Mundo*, that 'our laws permit the amputation of the hand that steals. This is not accepted in the West', he acknowledged, 'but the human rights camp should take into account the customs, traditions, religion and economic development of Iran when passing judgement'. This logic can presumably be extended to justify such brutal practices as female genital mutilation, which is prevalent in the Islamic world and parts of Africa. If human rights are what they are meant to be – inviolable and inalienable – local culture is no excuse for their suspension.

And although torture is formally forbidden in Iran, it is regularly practised. In many reported cases, individuals arrested for such crimes as holding dissenting views or breaching the modesty code end up dying in captivity. Examples abound. One involved a medical student, Zahra Bani Yaghoub, who was arrested in October 2007 while strolling in a public park with her fiancé. This was considered by the Iranian judiciary to be a breach of the modesty rules because the two were not yet married. Zahra died in a prison cell the following day. The authorities claimed the young woman had committed suicide.

It is not the ambition of this short chapter to exhaustively document all human and political rights violations that occur in Iran. Rather, this brief overview aims to describe how the notion of a 'democratic' Iran is both false and deceptive. A country that systematically violates the rights of its citizens and denies them the right to free speech and free association, denies workers their labour rights and denies equality on the basis of religion, ethnicity, language, gender or sexual preference is not a country that, in the 21st century, deserves to be called a democracy. Especially if political power is concentrated in the hands of unelected, supposedly divine political leaders who oversee political and administrative structures that rule the country in the name of a revolutionary and aggressive interpretation of religion.

How does this domestically repressive environment threaten its neighbours and broader Western interests? The most obvious example comes from Iran's legislation forbidding insults against Islam and punishing blasphemy and apostasy with the death penalty. These norms, in the revolutionary context of the Islamic Republic, do not apply exclusively within the national frontiers of Iran, causing distress to Iranians only. They are applied on a global scale to anyone who offends against the Iranian criminal code.

The most famous case involved the Indian-Muslim novelist Sir Salman Rushdie. On 14 February 1989, he was the victim of a fatwa issued by Ayatollah Khomeini, who proclaimed: 'The author of the *Satanic Verses* book, which the Ayatollah deemed to be an insult to Islam, the Prophet and the Koran, as well as all those involved in its publication, are sentenced to death.' Rushdie's Japanese translator was subsequently assassinated; his Italian and Norwegian colleagues narrowly escaped assassination. Rushdie himself lived in hiding for many years under the protection of Britain's MI5 security service – even after Iran's declaration, in 1998, that the fatwa was no longer relevant.

Doubts indeed remain about whether Iran really meant that Khomeini's fatwa had been suspended. These doubts were fuelled in 2005 when the IRGC reiterated the threat against Rushdie. Khomeini's successor, Ayatollah Khamenei, has not repudiated the fatwa, but rather has designated Rushdie an apostate and, as such, deserving of death.

To declare that killing Rushdie is fair game is not the same as sending a hit squad (a substantial bounty on his head achieved the same intimidating effect). But it is nevertheless a mandate for the murder of an intellectual issued by the highest authority of a sovereign state.

This mandate, incidentally, also applies to the Danish cartoonists who drew the Muhammad cartoons, published in a Danish newspaper in 2005, and to the Dutch director of the movie *Submission*, Theo van Gogh, who was slaughtered by a Muslim fanatic in an Amsterdam street in November 2004, and to the French philosopher Robert Redeker, who criticised Islam in the Paris daily *Le Figaro* and now lives under police protection, and to Ayaan Hirsi Ali, the Somali-born former Dutch parliamentarian who dared to criticise the status of women in Islam and who wrote the script for *Submission*. She now lives under constant police protection.

Iran aspires to overtake such competitors as Saudi Arabia and al-Qaeda as the defender-in-chief of Islam. It aspires to extend its writ far beyond Iran's borders, acting on a global scale to demand respect for its dogmas, interpretations and rulings, which may be challenged only at colossal risk. It does not hesitate to send hit squads, sponsor subversive activities and take responsibility, often via its terror proxies, for multiple mass murders as far away as South America. All this in the name of upholding the Islamic principles that underpin the Islamic Republic.

Far from being a democracy, Iran is an oppressive theocracy

which has its place in the seventh rather than the 21st century. Meanwhile, its revolutionary zeal, its religious absolutism and its ambition continue to grow. And, in the process, it continues to oppress its citizens, threaten its neighbours and spread its tentacles of terror throughout the world.

4

Iran's deceptive practices

When news broke of a confrontation involving five Iranian Revolutionary Guard speedboats and two US Navy frigates at the entrance to the Gulf on 9 January 2008, oil prices soared by $10 a barrel. Media reports focused on the mechanics of the incident – the who, why, where, when, how. But the experts asked a different question: who sold those vessels – the world's fastest patrol boats – to the Iranians? Were they the ones Iran bought from the Swedish company Boghammar in the early 1980s? Were they Chinese vessels that had been delivered by Beijing? Did they come from the Italian company FB Design, which had reportedly sold the frames and blueprints to Tehran? Or were they made in Iran?

According to sources at the Pentagon, the vessels were made in Iran, but bore an uncanny resemblance to the Italian designs. The same sources emphasised that after Iran obtained an original version of the Levriero speedboat, produced by Italy's FB Design on Lake Como, they reverse-engineered the vessel and embarked on production of their own version. An investigative report by Gianluca Di Feo and Stefania Maurizi, published in the Italian weekly *L'Espresso* in October 2007, indicated that in 1998 Iranian emissaries bought 'designs, prototypes, materials and whatever is necessary to produce the entire catalogue of record-breaking super-boats, including the frame, back in Iran'.

This should be a cautionary tale for European companies. It is not a unique example of a Western product being bought, and then copied, by the Iranians. This has, in fact, been a common feature in commercial relations between Iran and Europe: Iranian buyers posing as representatives of legitimate front companies seek European technology for apparently benign, in some cases even humanitarian, purposes. The European producers duly obtain the necessary export licences from their governments, as was the case with FB Design, and then proceed to sell their technology to their Iranian clients. Their actions are honest and transparent.

Once the sale has been made, however, the reality is often quite different. More often than not, the Iranian buyers proceed to change the purpose for which those products were designed and divert them to uses that their inventors and producers never imagined in their wildest dreams. Swedish speedboats are an example of this practice. The Boghammar, named after the Swedish family that owns the company, was designed in the 1980s exclusively for civilian purposes. But the size, speed and manoeuvrability of the vessels attracted the attention of the Iranian authorities, who bought them, ostensibly for use by Iran's maritime police. Once they were in Iranian hands, the IRGC modified them – they mounted rocket-launchers and machine guns – for purely military purposes. The Boghammars were first used as military vessels during the Tanker War, in the last phase of the Iran–Iraq War, when IRGC crews launched daring sabotage missions against vessels they suspected of carrying Iraqi merchandise. As a result, the name 'Boghammar' is now associated with naval fighting vessels, regardless of their make. And to this day, the light, versatile speedboats are kept on Abu Musa and other Gulf islands, such as Qaeshm and the Tunbs, near the Strait of Hormuz.

The Boghammar, which was designed and built as a fast civilian vessel, is now commonly regarded as a deadly military weapon. It is the ultimate asymmetric instrument of war, capable of neutralising the advantages of much heavier conventional military vessels. It was a Boghammar which was used by Islamist terrorists in the 2000 suicide bombing of the USS *Cole* in Yemen's Sana'a harbour (seventeen killed), and the 2000 attack on the French oil supertanker MV *Limburg* (one casualty and 90,000 tons of crude spilled). The Tamil Tigers have used similar tactics to hit military vessels of the Sri Lanka navy. The combination of these small speedboats, high explosives and suicide commandos has wreaked havoc on large ships, even sophisticated US warships. As for Iran, the IRGC have turned the speedboat into the centrepiece of their military strategy in the narrow sea lanes of the crowded Strait of Hormuz. In the event of war, these small boats could not only become deadly weapons but could also be used to block commercial traffic in the world's most strategic and sensitive waterway.

The sale of the Italian speedboats was initially reported by the London-based *Daily Mail* in May 2007, following the capture of fifteen British sailors by Iranian speedboats on the Shat al'Arab waterway, which divides Iran and Iraq. British officials were understandably puzzled that the Iranian speedboats could be so fast. The long investigative piece in *L'Espresso* partially answered this question. According to the

Daily Mail, FB Design sold twenty boats to Iran; *L'Espresso* puts the number at twelve. Fabio Buzzi, the founder and owner of the Italian company, in an interview with the local paper, *La Provincia di Lecco*, on 19 October 2007, said he had, in fact, sold only one vessel, before the Italian government revoked the licence and suspended further deliveries. There was nothing illegal about this, because, as Buzzi noted, he had sold 'boats, not weapons' with a regular export licence.

There is no reason to doubt his word. The vast majority of European companies are not run by unscrupulous, dishonest people who engage in shady deals and evade the law. Their natural, default position is to comply with the legal requirements of their governments. And state regulatory regimes are well established, particularly when it comes to exporting goods and services to problematic or rogue regimes. That means that European companies export goods to Iran only after they receive official approval from their governments. Buzzi, like many other entrepreneurs, was duped by Iranian emissaries who, over the years, have become masters of deception. This type of deception is not uncommon. Nor is the reaction of European companies and governments every time Iran seeks to purchase a boat, a crane, earth-moving equipment or some other advanced technological merchandise. They sell boats, not water-borne weapons; lorries, not mobile missile launchers; cranes, not gallows; tunnel-boring machines for the metro, not for underground clandestine nuclear and missile facilities.

In spite of Iranian duplicity, there is considerable evidence that European merchandise often ends up being used – and misused – for illegitimate purposes in utter disregard of the licensing system that is intended to regulate exports beyond the borders of the European Union. European companies operate on the assumption that they are dealing with credible, reliable interlocutors who function according to the sort of principles and practices they themselves apply. In fact, the façade of legality and legitimacy often masks the hand of the IRGC, who engage in a range of deeply malevolent activities, from terrorism and money-laundering to the procurement of technologies for Iran's nuclear and missile programmes. Their function is not to build hydroelectric plants and roads and bridges, but to serve the paranoid interests of the Islamic Revolutionary Republic.

While the vast majority of business leaders scrupulously adhere to the code of conduct and legal requirements of their governments, they do not go further than the law obliges. In the light of Iran's duplicitous behaviour, it is necessary for governments to revise their codes and adopt new rules that protect the good name of their companies by shielding them from deals that might, quite unwittingly, make them complicit in the illegal and immoral activities of their business partners. When potentially dual-use equipment and technologies are used for nefarious purposes, this may directly contradict Europe's vital strategic interests. And this, in turn, could significantly affect its diplomatic capacity.

There are, regrettably, examples of entrepreneurs and middlemen who have been lured into lucrative deals involving transfers to Iran of components and sensitive technology that have been proscribed by sanctions and dual-use regulations. These illegal activities are usually revealed to public scrutiny when the transactions are uncovered and those involved are prosecuted. But they are very much the exception rather than the rule.

Such situations occur when unscrupulous European business people succumb to Iran's procurement efforts or when the Iranians find loopholes or weak points in Europe's control systems. In order to fully exploit the weaknesses, Iran has established front companies in Europe to hide the true Iranian identity and purpose of its activities. These companies are then used to slip goods through cracks in the export-control systems of certain countries.

One example was an elaborate scheme to export sensitive nuclear technology to Iran. The scheme was documented by Benjamin Weinthal in a lengthy investigative report published by the Israeli daily *Ha'aretz* in April 2008. In this case, technology was supplied by 50 German companies ostensibly for a nuclear power plant in the Russian city of Rostov. It is unlikely that the German companies knew that the buyer was acting for Iran or that the goods were intended for anywhere but the Rostov plant. The goods, of course, never arrived in Rostov. They were never intended to. Instead, they were carried along the River Volga to the Kazakh border, then across the Caspian Sea into Iran.

Russia has become an important transit point for prohibited merchandise because it is relatively easy to obtain a European export licence if the end-user is listed as Russian. The Russian compliance systems appear to be weak, as are those of countries like Turkey and the United Arab Emirates, which are also used by Iran to circumvent restrictions and sanctions. But these aspects of Iran's procurement efforts are not the most urgent issues when it comes to trading with Iran. They are illegal traffics and nobody contests that they are forbidden. The solution is to be found in tightening the application and implementation of existing rules, not in formulating new ones. What deserves attention instead, as the case of the speedboats illustrates, is the issue of legal trade with Iran.

Europe's flourishing trade relations with Iran, underpinned by its extensive network of business relations and investments in the country, constitutes a potential conflict of interest in the context of the nuclear crisis. At the same time, Iran's dependence on European technology and know-how offers Europe an opportunity to exercise significant pressure on Iran over the nuclear issue without the need to resort to military force. Europe's soft power, if wisely deployed, could yield the kind of results that have so far eluded Western diplomatic efforts. In the light of Iran's solid record of deception in its trade relations – from forging end-user certificates to converting dual-use civilian products to military applications – Europe would be perfectly justified in the vigorous application of its soft power.

Relations between Iran and Europe are driven by mutual business interests. Iran is a market of 70 million people with the second-largest reserves of natural gas in the world and the fourth-largest reserves of oil. Balance-of-trade figures speak for themselves: the European Union is Iran's largest trade partner. Among EU member states, Germany and Italy are in the lead, followed closely by France and other western European countries. Some 80 per cent of Europe's imports from Iran consist of oil products – crude oil, gas and other hydrocarbons. European energy giants hold contracts in Iran's energy sector. Italy's ENI, France's Total, Spain's Repsol, Anglo-Dutch Shell, Norway's Hydro-Statoil, Austria's OMV and Switzerland's EGL all have important stakes in the areas of exploration, extraction and reservoir management. Europe also plays a critical role in the petrochemical sector, where important downstream projects are developed by such European companies as Italy's Snamprogetti, Technimont and TPL, alongside other prominent European conglomerates such as France's Technip.

Europe's interest in the energy sector is understandable, and not only because of the burgeoning demand for afford-able energy which pushes energy companies to constantly seek new sources of supply. There is also a clear political issue at stake: Europe's desire to reduce its energy dependence on Russia.

Unlike other countries in the area, Iran encourages foreign companies to invest in its energy sector with offers of lucrative contracts, including long-term buy-back schemes. These deals enable companies to enter joint ventures with Iranian state companies with an ideal trade-off for both sides. European companies bring their know-how and technology to the table, which ensures that levels of committed supplies can be sustained once production starts. This ability gives European companies an edge over their Russian counterparts, whose technology is not as advanced.

Everyone involved in the deal wins. Once production is under way, the buy-back scheme ensures that European companies have steady supplies of oil and gas for their own markets over long periods at favourable prices. Small wonder that European companies compete to gain a foothold in Iran's energy sector. Iran gains, too. With Europe as a strategic partner, Iran is able to ramp up its extraction capacity, its reservoir management skills, its technological expertise and its knowledge of construction. Terminals and plants are then geared to fully exploit the extraction, refining and export of Iran's natural resources.

Trade between Iran and Europe goes well beyond energy. As Iran's principal commercial partner, Europe is the source of two-fifths of Iran's imports, with most European sales to the country consisting of advanced technology, and the relationship seems destined to grow. Iran's population is youthful – 70 per cent are below the age of 30 – and the society is characterised by economic dynamism, innovation and creativity.

European countries like Italy and Germany have had a continuous and conspicuous business presence in Iran for decades, in some cases for more than a century. Such economic relations are robust, often resting on personal and family connections that have been developed over many years. European tenacity in penetrating extremely difficult markets has yielded important and lasting results in Iran, winning confidence in an environment where it takes a long time for trust to be established and business to flourish. Iran remains an attractive market and it is understandable that Europeans perceive a strong incentive to invest, in spite of Iran's over-regulated business, the political uncertainties and the risks they pose to foreign investment.

A study of Europe's balance of trade with Iran illustrates the importance of bilateral economic relations, particularly during economic crisis in Europe. This heightens the political dilemma that faces diplomats in the current nuclear stand-off.

On the one hand, Iran is an important energy source, at a time when Europe needs to diversify its sources of supply and reduce its dependence on Russia. Then there are the entrepreneurs, who have invested heavily in Iran. Thousands of jobs depend on the smooth functioning of this vital and profitable trade.

On the other hand there are the risks of doing business with Iranians who can potentially cause significant damage to the reputation of their European trading partners. There is the danger of a CEO becoming aware that his company's products are being diverted to illegal uses. There is the risk of embarrassment at home and, perhaps more important, incurring the wrath of the US administration. And then there are Europe's own strategic interests in the region, which will inevitably clash with those of Iran. It is an uncomfortable balancing act.

Iran is an emerging market. In 1990, two years after the end of the Iran–Iraq War, only 28.6 per cent of Iran's GDP was generated by the industrial sector; agriculture accounted for 23.5 per cent and the remaining 47.9 per cent came from the service industry. Fifteen years later, agriculture had fallen to just 9.6 per cent of Iran's GDP, while industrial output had advanced by 16 per cent, accounting for 44.2 per cent of Iran's GDP. Europe has an important market share in Iran's industrial sector and there is a significant presence of foreign investors.

Available statistics about bilateral trade with the European Union – updated to 2006 and, therefore, not including Bulgaria and Romania, which joined in 2007 – describe a growing relationship which, in spite of political tensions and the recent impact of sanctions, has continued to expand. In 2002, when Iran's clandestine nuclear programme was exposed, imports from Europe amounted to 41.86 per cent of total Iranian imports. Over the next three years, European exports to Iran remained steady at 41.14 per cent, 42.67 per cent and 41.04 per cent respectively. But in 2006, there was a substantial drop – to 33.45 per cent. This probably reflected a change in the political climate.

Sanctions, which were first introduced in December 2006, further affected the trade volume. Regardless of this, the absolute value of Europe's exports to Iran remains impressive – €12,259 million in 2006 against €14,252 million the year before and €9,801 million in 2002. Europe's exports have declined, but its market share remains an important element, with one third of Iran's total imports coming from Europe. By contrast, European imports from Iran are growing steadily, no doubt because of the rise in oil prices. Figures for the period 2002–06 indicate a percentage growth from 22.76 per cent to 23.94 per cent. In absolute terms, though, the figures have doubled: Iran exported €5,150 million worth of goods to Europe in 2002. By 2006, the value of Iranian exports had reached €12,815 million, the first time that the trade balance favoured Iran (by €556 million). All in all, the volume of trade grew from €14,951 million in 2002 to €25,074 million in 2006.

These are important figures which explain why, over the years, Iran has become an increasingly attractive market for European exporters. All this is relative, of course. European exports to Iran amount to about 1 per cent of total European exports throughout the world. Iran accounted for 0.91 per cent of Europe's exports to the world in 2002; 1.14 per cent in 2003; 1.23 per cent in 2004; 1.21 per cent in 2005; and 0.96 per cent in 2006. Meanwhile, Iranian exports to Europe relative to European total imports from the rest of the world also reflected a significant diminution in Iran's importance. Even if strategically important oil is added to the equation, Iran's contribution is small: 0.6 per cent in 2002; 0.74 per cent in 2003;

0.8 per cent in 2004; 0.97 per cent in 2005; and 1.05 per cent in 2006.

In 2006, Iran was Europe's 22nd-largest partner for imports, 25th-largest partner for exports and 26th-largest commercial partner. By contrast, Europe is a vital partner for Iran. In 2006, Europe was Iran's first partner for imports, exports and trade, with a share of, respectively, 33.4 per cent, 23.9 per cent and 27.8 per cent.

To place this data into context and explain the importance of the commercial partnership for Iran, one need only compare them with Iran's trade figures with its second-most significant commercial partner. China trails Europe at 10.7 per cent for imports and 12.3 per cent for trade, while Japan is the second-largest export partner, at 14.7 per cent. This means that trade with Europe is worth more than twice the volume of trade with either China or Japan and more than the aggregate trade with the two Asian giants.

The importance of this relationship becomes even more evident once its qualitative nature is explored. Europe imports mainly raw materials from Iran – 88.3 per cent of Europe's imports from Iran are hydrocarbon fossils and derivatives – which accounts for 3.7 per cent of Europe's total energy imports. The rest is made up of manufactured goods (6.3 per cent); food and livestock (1.8 per cent); other raw materials (1.5 per cent); chemical products (1.2 per cent); machinery and transport equipment (0.4 per cent); other manufacturing goods (0.3 per cent); services (0.1 per cent); and tobacco (less than 0.1 per cent).

The quality of Europe's sales to Iran is very different. Industrial and transport machinery accounts for fully 56.8 per cent of Europe's exports to Iran, followed by finished products

(17.8 per cent); chemical products (11.3 per cent); hydrocarbon products, lubricants and fuel (4.4 per cent); other manufactured products (4.4 per cent); raw materials (1.5 per cent); livestock (1.5 per cent); services (1.3 per cent); tobacco and beverages (0.1 per cent); and wax, animal and vegetable oils (0.1 per cent). In other words, 93 per cent of European imports from Iran are raw materials; 89.9 per cent of Iranian imports from Europe consist of refined products, especially industrial products.

Iran is a developing economy which is undergoing modernisation on a huge scale. It is, therefore, highly dependent on imported know-how for its success. Without Europe's contribution, Iranian industry would not grow as fast as it must to create the thousands of new jobs every year to satisfy the influx of young people on to the job market. This can be done only if there is robust economic growth driven by industrial development. Not only prosperity but also political stability depends on it.

Trade relations with Europe are much more critical for Iran than for Europe. To understand this, it is worth taking a closer look at the energy sector, where, despite fierce competition from mainly Asian and to a much lesser extent Russian companies, Europe is still the dominant market.

There is no doubt that EU member states depend on Iran for their energy needs. In 2006, for example, Italy was the fifth-largest importer of Iranian oil. At 191,000 barrels a day, which amounts to about 9.5 million tons of crude a year, Iran's oil constitutes one eighth of Italy's total domestic consumption. Italy is not alone. France is seventh-largest and Greece ninth-largest importer of Iranian oil in absolute values. In relative terms, Iranian oil constitutes one quarter of Greece's total domestic consumption, twice as much as Italy's, which may explain why Athens is reluctant to support tougher sanctions against Iran.

But dependency is not a one-way street. Iran depends on Europe more than Europe depends on Iran. In order to clarify why this is so, it is necessary to look more closely at three elements of the energy sector: oil extraction, gas extraction and refinement.

Oil – upstream projects

Iran is the fourth-largest oil producer in the world and its oil exports amount to 5 per cent of global oil production. Reserves are estimated to be 136 billion barrels, or about 10 per cent of the world's known reserves. These reserves are to be found mainly in the Khuzestan region, which is mostly inhabited by Iran's ethnic Arab minority, along the Gulf coast near the Iran–Iraq border.

Iran also has the largest fleet of oil carriers in the Middle East, with 29 carriers, including Very Large Crude Carriers (VLCCs), and several more in the pipeline. According to reports published in 2007, the National Iranian Tanker Company (NITC) commissioned seventeen new oil carriers, including four VLCCs, which are being financed through loans from several international financial institutions, including European banks. Some of the carriers already owned by NITC – the VLCCs *Noor*, *Noah*, *Nabi*, *Nejm* and *Nesa* – are powered by engines patented by the Finnish company Wärtsilä and have been built under licence by the Korean company Daewoo. The *Delvar* VLCC, which was delivered in 2002, was built in the Chinese shipyards of Dalian, also with Wärtsilä engines, as was the *Darab*, which was delivered in

2004 and runs on Korean-made Hanjung engines, which were also produced under licence for Wärtsilä. It is an imposing fleet, which projects power and wealth on the high seas.

But at least part of the reason for the impressive appearance of Iran's fleet is far more prosaic. Iran uses its carriers as storage depots because it is able to extract oil – some of low quality – far more quickly than it is able to refine the raw product. As a result, many of its VLCCs are reported to spend much of their time tied up near Iran's largest oil terminal off the coast of Kharg Island loaded with oil that is either earmarked for local refinement and domestic consumption, or is awaiting a foreign buyer.

Crude oil transits through various terminals, including Kharg Island (which has a storage capacity of 16 million barrels and a loading capacity up to 5 million barrels a day), Lavan Island (5 million and 200,000 respectively) and various other Gulf coast terminals, including Kish, Abadan, Bandar Mahshar and one Caspian Sea terminal at Neka.

In 2006, Iran extracted an average of 3.8 million barrels a day, of which about 1.6 million barrels were earmarked for domestic consumption. At current levels, Iran remains the second-largest producer within the OPEC cartel, but it is operating at well below its maximum production capacity and at about half a million barrels below its OPEC quota. In 1974, following the 1973 oil crisis, Iran achieved its highest output in history: 6 million barrels a day. Since the 1979 Islamic Revolution, production has steadily declined owing to a combination of factors, among which are damage to the energy infrastructure by the Iran–Iraq War, sanctions and a natural decline in the productivity of mature oilfields. It follows that Iran needs to invest heavily to modernise its oil sector in order to maintain at least current production levels, if not increase them to their higher 1970s levels. According to the Energy Information Administration, a US government agency,

> Iran's oil fields need structural upgrades, including enhanced oil recovery (EOR) efforts such as natural gas injection. Iran's fields have a natural annual decline rate estimated at 8 percent onshore and 10 percent offshore, while current Iranian recovery estimates are 24–27 percent, 10 percent less than the world average. It is estimated that 400,000–500,000 bbl/d of crude production is lost annually due to reservoir damage and decreases in existing oil deposits.

Iran's sclerotic oil facilities, combined with a growing thirst for energy, mean that the country is losing out as a result of its crumbling infrastructure. It follows that Iran would benefit enormously if it repaired and replaced its run-down facilities. But it cannot do this on its own. In a recent study of Iran's energy sector by the Washington-based Institute for the Analysis of Global Security, co-director Gal Luft estimated that a return to the production levels of the seventies would involve an investment of $80 billion.

Iran has set production targets of 5 million barrels a day by 2010 and 5.8 million by 2015. The current political constellation makes even those objectives unrealistic because a number of upstream projects that are intended to contribute to the increased production are unlikely to meet expectations. Among these are the fields of Salman, Foroozan and Daroud, which are being developed by a consortium of Total and Petro Iran; phases two and three of the Darkhovin field, which is being developed by ENI; and the Yadavaran field, which is being developed by a consortium of five Chinese companies (among them Sinopec) and the National Iranian Oil Company (NIOC).

In spite of problems here, the exploitation of oilfields is a complex matter that requires a great deal of experience and advanced technology. Iran thus needs foreign expertise to achieve its production goals. Oilfields are nationally owned and, not unlike other regional oil producers, Iran does not permit foreign companies to take ownership of its resources. But unlike many other oil producers, Iran welcomes the participation of Western energy giants to develop its fields through lucrative joint ventures, with Western partners gaining access to energy at favourable prices through buy-back schemes. Such schemes often involve payment, or part payment, in kind for exploration and development work. In other words, payment is made – or partially made – through supplies of oil and gas.

Such arrangements are particularly attractive at a time when the global economy is expanding and there is a consequent reduction of supply on the market. Those who secure contracts with Iran's main oil company, NIOC, and its subsidiaries, gain access to critical resources which can be then used to supply national markets or resold at high prices on the international markets.

Iran's energy market is, therefore, highly attractive to Western oil companies. The availability of oil in Iran, the current level of oilfield exploitation, the need to modernise the oil industry infrastructure, Iran's willingness to negotiate buy-back arrangements with foreign companies, and the potential for future expansion and future development combine to offer foreign investors a golden opportunity. No

surprise, then, that European companies are competing fero-
ciously for a share in both the oil and gas markets.

Natural gas – upstream, gas pipelines and liquid natural gas

Natural gas is the coming energy sector. It is readily available
in large quantities, it is clean, and it is reasonably cheap. The
only obstacle – and the great challenge – is transport. Oil can
be transported relatively easily in its natural state by pipeline
or in containers on ships. It is not so simple to transport gas
from fields of extraction to kitchen stoves thousands of miles
away. Gas in its natural state can be delivered only by pipeline,
and this poses a serious logistical problem for both producers
and consumers. Gas fields are often situated in remote
locations and the gas can be extracted only for local consumption. To transport it to distant markets requires complex and
expensive technologies for converting natural gas into liquid
form for transport and then reversing the process before gas
is distributed to consumers.

Liquefied gas drastically shrinks in volume – it is 1,600
times smaller than in its natural condition – and it can be
easily carried in large, purpose-built spherical containers that
will keep it in a liquid state until it is delivered to terminals,
where it will be converted back into gas before distribution.
Converting gas to a liquid state involves cooling it to very
low temperatures (–161°C, or –260°F). To return it to a gaseous
state, the liquid must undergo a reverse process, which is
equally expensive. Costs aside, both procedures are complex,
complicated and risky. If the cooling and reheating processes
occur too quickly, the gas can explode, causing serious injury
and damage on a vast scale. It does not follow that liquid

natural gas (LNG) is unsafe; simply that it requires experience, technical knowledge and the technology needed to build both the freezing and the heating terminals, what are known as the LNG 'trains'.

Iran sits on vast deposits of natural gas. After Russia, it has the second-largest known reserves in the world at 28.3 trillion cubic metres, according to official estimates in 2005. But the lack of technology for extraction and, crucially, distribution means that 62 per cent of Iran's reserves are not being exploited. Worse, it means that Iran is a net importer of natural gas. In the future, Iran could connect to the vast grid that supplies Europe through the Nabucco pipeline project. It could also send its gas to the Indian Ocean, through a planned pipeline that would link it to India through Pakistan. Currently, it is able to supply only Turkey by pipeline, but lacks the entry points into existing or future pipelines that would enable Iranian gas to reach distant markets, but principally European markets.

Of the gas that Iran extracts, 65 per cent is consumed by the domestic market or exported, via pipeline, to Turkey, 18 per cent is reinjected into the oilfields to improve extraction and 17 per cent is lost in combustion and gas reduction during oil extraction. Given these data, there is obviously enormous potential for development. But this is hampered by a lack of technology and political obstacles. According to M. A. Sarmadi-Rad, the director for regional economic cooperation at Iran's Ministry of Foreign Affairs,

> Iran, endowed with the second largest natural gas reserve in the world, should have already been the main exporter of natural gas to the global markets. This has yet to happen.

The reasons for not yet achieving such a status in the world markets are many. They include insufficient investment resources, strong demand at the domestic market for fuel, rapid re-pressurising of some oil reservoirs, domestic environmental policies pertaining to substitution of fuel oil and gas-oil with natural gas and the inability of some potential buyers to separate politics from business or resolve long-festering disputes, such as the India–Pakistan dispute over the status of Kashmir.

Clearly, the simmering Indo-Pakistan dispute has delayed the pipeline that would have enabled Iranian gas to reach the Indian Ocean. Iran lacks the technology to build its own LNG terminals and those European companies involved in the early stages of LNG projects in Iran are nervous. They are in no rush to deliver.

Alongside the political problems alluded to by the Iranian diplomat, there are other problems in the gas sector which mirror the difficulties facing the oil sector. Iran needs infrastructure investments of about $85 billion over the next twenty years (until 2030) in order to realise its natural gas potential. Without Western assistance, Iran has no chance of meeting its targets.

Two steps are essential to revive Iran's gas sector. The first is the exploitation of the country's principal gas field, South Pars. This is the northern extension of Qatar's North Field. South Pars contains, according to official estimates, over 14 trillion cubic metres of gas, which equates to 40 per cent of Iran's total gas reserves. The second is the establishment of four LNG liquefaction terminals – Iran LNG, Pars LNG, Persian LNG and NIOC LNG. This development is almost entirely aimed at the foreign market and, if achieved, would turn Iran into the leading producer and supplier of natural gas in the world. But to develop its field and build its LNG terminals, Iran needs both foreign investment and direct foreign technical involvement in the projects. In particular, it needs European involvement.

A bird's-eye view of the current status of South Pars confirms Iran's dependence on European companies and highlights the current lack of progress due to political uncertainties. South Pars is divided into 30 development phases, each of which requires an initial investment of about $1 billion to become operational. The first phase is operated by Petropars, an Iranian subsidiary of NIOC, which has contracts with Korea's Samsung and Iran's Sadra. The second and third phases, which include two offshore platforms, are managed by France's TotalFinaElf, with the participation of Malaysia's Petronas and Russia's Gazprom. Phases four and five are allocated to Italy's ENI under a buy-back scheme, in partnership with Petropars. Phases six, seven and eight are managed by Norway's Hydro-Statoil for the offshore work and Petropars for the onshore work.

Gas production in this project is destined for reinjection in the oilfield of Agha Jari to maintain its oil output at current levels. Phases nine and ten were won by Lucky Goldstar Construction, which is owned by the South Korean branch of BP, while phases eleven and twelve were assigned to TotalFinaElf and ENI. Phases thirteen and fourteen went to a consortium of Shell and Repsol. More recently, Austria's OMV and Switzerland's EGL signed the two biggest contracts to date with Iran for Western companies. OMV's deal, signed in April 2007, is worth some $22 billion, while the EGL deal, signed in April 2008, is said to be worth between $28 and $42 billion.

Implementation of the various phases of the South Pars work is taking longer than expected. There is worse news for Iran: several European companies are having second thoughts about the political wisdom of investing in Iran owing to current circumstances – Shell and Total, for example, have recently signalled their uncertainty about future investments. Without their crucial contribution, Chinese, Russian and Indian competition can only partially alleviate Iran's requirement to expand its gas production to satisfy not only its own pressing domestic needs but also international demand.

There are not many LNG stations in the world. As of February 2008, there were just 22 operational liquefaction trains globally. A further thirteen are being planned, including the Iranian trains. There are slightly more regasification terminals: 55 are already operational, 21 are under construction and 42 are on the drawing boards. Once completed, this vast network of terminals would revolutionise the energy market, making an otherwise inaccessible resource available and affordable, in spite of the great geographic distances and technological impediments. China, for example, cannot import gas from Iran at present as no pipeline exists that can overcome the imposing heights of the Himalayan and the Hindu Kush mountain ranges. If gas could be turned to liquid, however, it could be easily transported to China from the Gulf.

The impediment is of course that only a few companies have the know-how to build LNG trains. And even if the technology were more readily available, the combined costs of a project demand that all its phases must be planned coherently in order to persuade companies to take the financial risks involved. In other words, attracting investment requires more than a contract between producer and energy companies to transform natural gas into LNG. For an investment to be secured also requires a guarantee that sufficient quantities of gas will be extracted to make the investment profitable. Even that is not enough. It is also necessary to factor into the equation the LNG carriers, the existence (and availability) of a regasification terminal, a contract with the local energy company to ensure there is a market for the product, and an efficient means of distribution to its final destination: the domestic stove and gas heater.

A project must therefore take account of the entire 'chain' and ensure that all the links are in place, are functioning well and are synchronised to make the investment feasible. This was emphasised in a 1999 study by Philip R. Weems, of the Texas firm King & Spalding, which appeared in the *International Energy Law and Taxation Review*:

> For LNG projects to come to fruition, all project activities and facilities must be coordinated through joint, long-range planning. Contractual agreements setting forth the integrated duties and responsibilities of each of the participants in the chain are necessary, as is the flexibility on the participant's part to resolve problems through long-term solutions that maintain the strength of the project as a whole.

According to estimates calculated by Weems, the average costs of an LNG project with an output of approximately five million tons of gas per year in 1999 were as follows: $2 billion to develop the fields; $2 billion for liquefaction; between

$1 billion and $2 billion for maritime transport; between $1 billion and $2 billion for the regasification terminal; and at least $4 billion for marketing and distribution. These costs were estimates at the end of the nineties and were based on a hypothetical example reflecting the realities of profitable LNG deals under very different circumstances, namely with the price of gas and oil at much lower levels.

Regardless of the current price tag, such high costs mean that each participant in the LNG chain is taking a huge risk unless all the other elements are guaranteed to deliver. If one of the links is weak – if it does not perform efficiently and on time – the entire project is jeopardised. Given the costs and risks, no project is likely to succeed unless, in addition to a guaranteed supply of fuel, the entire chain is fully coordinated and interdependent. This includes the liquefaction and regasification terminals, transport and the buyers. As Weems notes, 'where the investment is in billions of dollars, buyers must have a reliable supply and sellers must have stable buyers'. It follows that there are considerable risks in the business, continues Weems:

> If LNG cannot be delivered by the seller and/or received by the buyer, the seller may be unable to secure immediate sales to 'cover' itself and the buyer may be unable to find alternative supplies on short notice. Failure to properly coordinate activities could have severe commercial effects throughout the remaining parts of the chain. This interdependency results in all parties being exposed to all risks in the LNG chain since failure in any part of the chain affects all other parts.

The considerable risks involved in such projects, along with the potential damage caused by delay or a weak link in the chain, can be illustrated by one recent Iranian deal. The Swiss company EGL signed an agreement with Iran for the supply of natural gas. The value of the contract was significant. At €22 billion it was the largest-ever deal between a Western company and the Islamic Republic. The signing ceremony took place in Tehran in March 2008 in the presence of Swiss foreign minister Micheline Calmy-Rey and Iran's President Mahmoud Ahmadinejad. In spite of the great political significance of the event – the ceremony occurred just two weeks after the UN Security Council approved Resolution 1803, introducing a new round of sanctions against Tehran – implementation is crucially dependent on a number of additional projects.

Gas cannot be easily delivered to European markets. There are currently no LNG terminals in Iran to liquefy it and there are currently no pipelines to carry it in its natural state. Time is needed to construct both. Naturally, the guarantee of long-term supply obtained through a deal with Iran is the first step. And EGL can rely on a market and distribution network in Europe. The challenge remains how to transport it from Iran to Europe.

EGL is a partner in a consortium with Norway's Hydro-Statoil for the construction of the Trans-Adriatic Pipeline, which would connect Thessaloniki, in northern Greece, with Brindisi, in southern Italy, after cutting across Albania. By linking this new pipeline to already existing pipelines or future pipelines in Turkey, it would be possible to transport Iran's natural gas all the way to Brindisi and then distribute it, via the Italian grid, throughout Europe. If LNG terminals were ever to be built in Iran, however, gas could be readily transported to various regasification terminals along the Mediterranean cost.

The fragile interconnections of the project with the costs illustrate its vulnerability to several factors, not least political pressure. If delivery were to be made by pipeline (and there are several competing projects that could undermine the viability of the EGL–Hydro-Statoil project), it will be years before the project is completed and the Turkish link established. Then, there are questions about the governments through whose territories the pipeline must transit. And these governments may be vulnerable to political pressures regarding the wisdom of facilitating such a project.

If delivery were to rely on the issue of LNG, the situation might be considerably more complex, given that all of Iran's potential partners in the construction of the LNG terminals are European. The first of three major LNG projects in South Pars was meant to be developed through a joint venture between Shell and Repsol; the second was similarly a co-production involving TotalFinaElf and Malaysia's Petronas; the third involved BP and India's Reliance. In all three projects, the development of the liquefaction plants was to be done by Western companies. But the European partners have in the meantime reconsidered their involvement in Iran and have expressed uncertainty about future investment. So did Petronas and Reliance. Compounding the problem for Iran is that there are not many companies outside Europe, North America, South Korea, Japan and Australia that are capable of producing LNG liquefaction terminals. The main contenders are companies like E.On and Linde (Germany), Woodside Petroleum (Australia), Technip (France), JGC (Japan), Whessoe Oil and Gas Ltd, Shell and M. W. Kellogg

Ltd (United Kingdom). The harsh reality is that non-Western companies lack the necessary know-how and experience to complete the projects on their own. Western partnerships are essential. In short, pressure points are considerable and weak spots, political and economic, abound.

Refineries and fuel imports

Iran owns abundant raw materials and exports fossil fuels in substantial quantities. It lacks, however, the refining capacity to meet its growing domestic needs. This means that Iran is a net importer of refined fuels. Existing refineries cannot produce enough, and current upgrade and expansion projects largely depend on foreign companies. Even with the additional capacity, Iran will still not be able to satisfy its domestic demand.

Iran is currently working on modernising and upgrading a number of its refineries. The refinery at Bandar Abbas will increase daily production to 300,000 barrels a day by 2012; upgrading the Abadan refinery will increase output to 140,000 barrels a day by 2009; upgrading is also under way at the Arak, Tehran and Tabriz refineries and at the second Bandar Abbas refinery, with completion dates ranging from 2009 to 2012. Taken together, the upgrades will increase refined output to 215,000 barrels a day (it should be noted that the production targets and completion dates are not yet a done deal).

Finally, Iran is building new refineries – one near Bushehr through a consortium that according to Iranian sources includes the Austrian company Poerner, and at Bandar Assaluyeh. The schedule here is unclear, although their refining capacity should, theoretically, be increased to 250,000 barrels a day. In total, once these projects are complete, Iran will be producing an additional 1 million barrels a day of gasoline – thereby nearly doubling its refining capacity.

At today's consumption levels, this means that Iran would be able to independently manufacture and refine its entire domestic consumption, though not necessarily at the projected levels of 2012, when the last of these projects should come on stream. It is therefore safe to presume that Iran's energy dependence will continue, unless internal consumption is reduced. For the time being, Iran is purchasing heavily abroad, in some cases by offering attractive deals to friendly countries – low-priced crude in exchange for refined gasoline – or by subsidising the construction of refineries abroad that can then sell part of their product back to Iran.

In the natural gas sector, the problems remain just as acute, given the domestic sector's dependence on gas for heating. This is compounded by the fact that future expansion of the domestic market will depend on natural gas and this will require Iran to improve its ability to extract the gas. The problem with gas became evident in January 2008 when Turkmenistan, a supplier of natural gas to Iran, decided to suspend supplies, officially over a price dispute. In the midst of a particularly harsh winter, residents of northern Iran were left, quite literally, in the cold for several days. To head off a crisis, the Iranian regime was compelled to turn off supplies to Turkey. It took three weeks to restore supplies.

The development of the natural gas sector is a strategic imperative for Iran in view of the accelerating rate of population growth – from 40 million to 70 million since 1980 – and the consequent increase in demand for gas by both industry and the domestic sector. Iran currently produces 10.5 million gallons of gasoline per day and needs 18.5 million. It must, therefore, import 43 per cent of its refined fuels. The regime's strategy to end the shortfall is threefold. It needs to:

- build new refineries and upgrade existing ones;
- guarantee the supply of refined products from friendly countries, such as Venezuela, that would help Iran circumvent potential future embargoes; and
- introduce measures to reduce consumption, such as rationing gasoline, price controls and transforming the economy to rely on alternative energy sources.

In particular, the regime aspires to transform the country's entire car fleet from gasoline and diesel to compressed natural gas (CNG). A deal recently signed with the German company SPG (Steiner-Permatechnik-Gastec), reportedly worth more than €100 million, is intended to supply three producing stations for CNG. According to a recently published study by Gal Luft, of the Institute for the Analysis of Global Security, the conversion plan has four distinct phases:

1. conversion of most existing vehicles from gasoline and diesel to CNG within the next five years, at a rate of 1.2 million vehicles a year, starting with 600,000 government cars;
2. withdrawal from the market of the oldest vehicles by 2010 (approximately 1.2 million);
3. production of new cars, starting July in 2007, with CNG-run engines; and
4. conversion of the existing 10,000 petrol stations within the next five years to CNG-enabled status.

The goal is to have a fleet of vehicles that run entirely on gas by 2015. Iran is aggressively pursuing this objective with a number of measures that include subsidies to the local car industry (Iran is the biggest car producer in the Middle East), high taxes on imported vehicles and generous subsidies for petrol stations to upgrade their pumps to supply CNG. If successful, this policy offers advantages which, in the long term, are enormous on all fronts. They include a drastic reduction in dependence on imported gasoline and other refined products, and an increase in available crude and refined products for export.

Luft notes that 'a daily saving of nine million gallons of gasoline would provide Iran with an extra 450,000 barrels of oil per day for export, which, at $60 per barrel, could generate over $9 billion a year'. With oil at $130 a barrel, Iran's revenues would increase by more than $21 billion a year. With oil at $100 a barrel, the additional revenue would still amount to more than $16 billion a year. Naturally, all this is interconnected with other developments. Iran's energy sector resembles a dog attempting to bite its own tail.

Lack of modernisation in the oil sector makes it difficult to increase production, let alone sustain it at current levels. Delays in the construction of new refineries or in the upgrading of existing ones keep Iran dependent on imports of fuel. Lack of development and full exploitation of Iran's rich gas fields further compounds the problem, delaying the effectiveness of the modernisation programmes in the car industry and in its transition from gasoline to CNG.

Iran's strategy depends on, and is therefore vulnerable to, technological assistance from foreign companies, mainly European. Without this assistance Iran cannot compensate for its shortcomings in the energy sector and, in the long term, reduce its dependence on imports, foreign assistance and foreign investment.

Iran aspires to move from energy dependence to full independence. It wants to be capable of fully developing and exploiting its potential. If successful, Iran's vast fossil-fuel reserves would turn into mighty instruments which would make countries dependent on its supplies and, therefore, on its political goodwill. At present, though, Iran is highly vulnerable to external pressure. And there are many hurdles to be overcome on the path to energy independence. These include:

- lack of foreign investment;
- inability to access advanced foreign technology;
- denial of financing and contracts for proposed LNG terminals;
- denial of connection rights to existing gas pipeline grids in the Caspian area;
- failure of the proposed Pars pipeline to come online (Iran concluded a memorandum of understanding for a feasibility study with Italy's Edison in October 2007);
- failure of the Iran–Pakistan–India pipeline due to political obstacles;
- reluctance of foreign companies to invest in Iran, owing to the uncertain political climate.

Any one of these scenarios could inflame Iran's internal predicament and compound the general dissatisfaction of ordinary Iranians with their regime. Iran's energy sector could make the country a political and economic giant in the future. As it is, it is the regime's soft underbelly.

*

Europe's presence in Iran is not limited to the energy sector. As the data shows, most of Europe's exports to Iran relate to the industrial and petrochemical sectors. A short and non-exhaustive list of European companies and their areas of expertise indicates how significant, diversified and broad Europe's presence in Iran is.

Axiom (Austria), B2A (Austria), Siemens (Germany) and UNIHA (Austria) supply technologies for the industrial treatment of water. UNIHA has had representation offices in Tehran since 2006, through a local partner, Wahang Saran Ltd. UNIHA is involved in important projects, such as the building of a desalination plant for the city of Hendijan. This project is worth 25 billion Iranian rials; it is being carried out by Iran's Noor Vijeh Co., and financed by the Export Development Bank of Iran (recently designated by the US Treasury as a proliferator), and it relies on UNIHA and Axiom technology.

Reynaers Aluminium (Belgium) sells aluminium for doors, windows and winter gardens. It has also maintained an office in Tehran since 2006.

Britain's Terram, a company that specialises in geo-textiles, geo-synthetics and other technical textiles with industrial applications, has a presence in Tehran through its local distributor, Mokarrar Ltd, as do the French companies Alstom (energy sector), Legrand (electrical installations) and Société Générale (financing for the energy sector).

France's car industry is present in Iran, having sold a licence to locally produce an Iranian version of some of its models. This practice is also employed by Mercedes. Iveco, the Italian truck maker, has licensed Iran's automaker, Zamyad, for the production of some of its lorries and buses – including some CNG-fuelled minivans such as the A60.

The presence of German companies is dominant, as one would expect of a country that enjoys primacy among Iran's European trading partners. For example, Daimler Chrysler has a 30 per cent stake in Iran's IDEM, which produces diesel automobile engines. It has also licensed Iran's Khodro to produce Mercedes trucks. The fuse producer Efen GmbH has representation offices in Iran, along with other German companies, such as Endress and Hauser (instruments for industrial measurements and automation), Jumo (measurement and control of physical parameters), Rohde & Schwarz (radio telecommunications) and Uhde (management technology in the petrochemical sector).

Italy is Iran's second-largest European trading partner and, not surprisingly, Italian companies also have a major presence. These include several energy companies, among them ENI and some of its subsidiaries, Snamprogetti, Technimont, Edison, and TPL, (which is itself a subsidiary of France's Technip). Italy's presence is also impressive in other sectors. Cortem Spa exports electrical equipment that is resistant to extreme weather and explosions. It is ideal for construction sites and projects that are conducted under risky conditions. Cortem was awarded a contract for the ninth olefine ethane cracking plant in Nargan, in 2002. Italkrane exports cranes for industrial use and explosion-proof equipment for work sites, refineries, LNG terminals and other dangerous working environments. Basell is involved in important energy projects. Seli Spa sells tunnel-boring machinery and other earth-moving equipment for civil infrastructure and major public works.

Many other European companies are active in Iran even

without having a presence on the ground. They regularly participate, however, in Iran's industrial fairs on the island of Kish (CIBEX for civil engineering and construction, ENEX for the energy industry). According to the fairs' website, the following European firms attended one or both fairs in 2007: Efco, Eltherm GmbH, Frako, Karcher (Futuretech), Leutert, Membran-Filtrations-Technik GmbH, MMZ Technische Abdichtungsprodukte, Novopress, Seba KMT, Wachendorff, Wampfler Group and Witte Pumps and Technology (Germany), Hibon (France), Italkrane, OBL Srl and Rivit (Italy), Saia Burgess (Switzerland), S-Products BV (Netherlands) and UNIHA (Austria).

There are two fundamental problems with Europe's trade relations with Iran. The first relates to the identity of the Iranian business partner. This was evident in the case of the sale of speedboats by Italy's FB Design, described earlier in this chapter. While the Iranian buyer of the speedboats may have appeared to be a businessman seeking the vessels for civilian purposes, he was, in all likelihood, an agent of the IRGC who was procuring the vessels for its military-industrial complex. Unknown to the Italian firm, the boats were thus acquired through an IRGC front company and, although they were sold for civilian use, they were quickly modified and assigned a military role. Any company that engages in business with Iran must be aware that their Iranian business partner might not represent a conventional commercial interest and that the products sold might not be used for innocent purposes.

The second problem derives to some extent from the first. A lack of transparency on the part of Iranian companies poses a risk to the reputation of European companies. European entrepreneurs who deal with Iran are faced with the constant risk that they might, unwittingly, be breaching official rules and their own business codes. These elements alone had a significant impact on the decision of the main European banks to withdraw from Iranian projects and from Iran's financial market. After all, no company or financial institution wishes to harm its reputation through complicity in illicit trade. Equally, the lack of transparency on the part of Iran's financial institutions, including the country's Central Bank and main commercial banks, led to a drastic reduction in relations and transactions between European credit institutions and their Iranian counterparts. It also caused a steep increase in costs for financial activities in Iran. But Iran's financial sector, which is critical to the efficient functioning of the economy, is not unique among Iranian business organisations in its lack of transparency and unethical behaviour.

Two European companies, Italy's Seli Tunnel and Germany's Wirth, provide yet another example of Iran's deception in seeking to divert European technology to the IRGC and their nefarious activities. The two companies are world leaders in the production of earth-moving equipment. Their machines are used in several important civilian infrastructure projects in Iran, including the construction of a water tunnel in the mountains near Isfahan, the Dez Ghomroud tunnel.

According to a promotional brochure produced by Germany's Heinsberg county, where Wirth is based, 'when Barcelona receives a new metro system, a bridge is built over the Orinoco in Venezuela or a new water-supply system is created in the Iranian mountains of Isfahan, Wirth machines are used'. As this promotional brochure boasts, Wirth machines are employed in some of the most ambitious civil engineering projects. But the reality of the Ghomroud tunnel reflects another, more sinister, side to commercial relations between Iran and the West. European companies rely on government licences to ensure the transparency and legality of their trade in a lucrative but difficult market. In the event, however, they are often robbed, not of money, but of their reputation.

Wirth's website indeed lists Ghomroud as one of its projects – it gives the client company, Ghaem, as a reference to prospective buyers. Ghaem is one of a number of Iranian companies that the US Treasury Department has designated as front companies of the IRGC. Wirth undertook the project through its subsidiary company in Iran, which features images of the Ghomroud construction site on its website. The pictures are from phase five of the project (phases three and four were developed through a consortium of which Seli Tunnel was a partner). Among the pictures on the website is a 'welcome' sign at the worksite. In Persian, it reads, 'Phase 5, Ghomroud Tunnel'. The sign bears the symbol of the IRGC. That symbol also appeared on another picture, above the entrance to the tunnel and next to a tunnel-boring machine made by Wirth. In spite of repeated enquiries, the company declined to respond to a request for more information about the identity of its commercial partners in this project.

Independent research revealed, however, that the Iranian company that was responsible for phase five of the Ghomroud project was called Sahel Consulting Engineers, which was also designated by the US Treasury Department in October 2007 as a subsidiary of the IRGC. According to information published on Seli's website, the client for phases three and four was Ghaem, another wholly owned subsidiary of the IRGC. It also emerged that the tunnel project was contracted to another Iranian company, Pars Geometry, which claims to be a private, independent company. But an examination of the Pars Geometry board reveals that almost all its members were associated with Sahel Consulting Engineers in the past. One – the CEO – was employed as an engineer at Iran's Ministry of Jihad during the eighties.

Further enquiries produced a research paper on the use of the Wirth tunnel-boring machine at Ghomroud, which was presented in June 2007 by Professor Jamal Rostami, of Penn State University, and his former master student, Ebrahim Farrokh, at the annual conference of the International Tunnelling Association in Toronto. According to the conference programme, Farrokh worked for Sahel Consulting Engineers. As for Rostami, he has, since 2002, taught in the USA and has participated in important civil engineering projects in mining and tunnelling. His CV, which is available on the Penn State website, indicates that he is still working, presumably as a consultant, for Sahel Consulting Engineers. Despite Wirth's refusal to comment on the matter, it is hard to deny a connection between the project, where its machines are being used, and the IRGC.

There is no doubt that Seli and Wirth operated in good faith. BAFA, Germany's export-control agency, confirmed that the sale of tunnel-boring machines, such as those used at Ghomroud, was not forbidden. As for Seli, its president, Remo Grandori, personally confirmed that its sales to an IRGC company were made under a regular government export licence. Grandori said Seli sold only auxiliary equipment to the Guards (ventilation, moulds and wagons). He also added that such equipment could be used only in the Ghomroud project.

Such machines, sold to an ostensibly legitimate, civilian company, are expected to be used for legitimate, civilian purposes – a water tunnel in Ghomroud, an underground tunnel in Tabriz, and galleries for the Shomal highway are some of the projects in which the two companies are active in Iran. Not nuclear bunkers and missile silos. There is no guarantee, however, that the Iranian 'workers' who were instructed in how to operate the equipment have not also applied their expertise to creating a network of underground tunnels and galleries, built by the Revolutionary Guards Engineering Corps, for Hezbollah terrorists in south Lebanon.

Nuclear bunkers, missile silos, underground military bases … Such projects are a glaring example of how the line can be crossed from legitimate civilian projects to illegitimate military projects using politically neutral technology and morally neutral machinery from European companies that believe they are doing the right thing. A tunnel-boring machine can be used to build both a freshwater facility and a nuclear bunker. However carefully entrepreneurs and governments seek to draw the line, it is porous, malleable and ambiguous in the hands of Iranian partners, who are more likely than not to be agents of the IRGC.

What one can say of the Ghomroud project also applies to other deals. Initially, the European technology that is acquired by front companies for the IRGC is used for legitimate projects. The problem, as the example of the tunnel-boring machines illustrates, is what happens when the legitimate project is completed. Images made available online by the Institute for Science and International Security (www.isis-online.org), headed by nuclear expert David Albright, provide an abundance of evidence indicating that Iran is building tunnels for likely clandestine nuclear sites in the mountainous areas adjacent to the site of the Natanz uranium enrichment plant. The technology and the technical expertise, unwittingly provided by Wirth and Seli to IRGC companies, are ideal for this type of works.

Wirth and Seli are not alone in being duped. Other European companies are, or have been, unwittingly in business with IRGC front companies whose affiliation has been duly exposed by the US Treasury Department in recent years. According to information provided by the companies themselves through their websites, VA Tech Hydropower, a company owned by the Austrian Andritz group, is involved in the construction of the Kharkeh Dam on behalf of Iran's Sepazad Engineering, the engineering branch of the IRGC. Finland's Poyry is building the hydroelectric dam and power plant at Rudbar-e-Lorestan, in the Zagros mountains, also on behalf of Sepazad. Germany's KTI-Plersch has supplied cement-cooling systems for important projects, such as the Jaghin and Saveh dams. Among its clients, the company's website lists Ghorb Nooh and Garangahe Sazandeghi Khatam. Both belong to the IRGC. Canada's Hatch Energy was also a partner in a joint venture with Sepazad in the Karun IV dam project on the Karun river in Khuzestan province. Dams are, of course, important for the development of alternative energy in Iran: hydroelectric energy accounts for only 2 per cent of domestic production. It is thus understandable that the regime wishes to expand its share.

No matter how innocuous or legitimate these projects may appear to be, the wealth they generate enriches the IRGC, whose activities do not stop at building dams and water tunnels. They are also heavily engaged in a variety of activities linked to Iran's nuclear and ballistic-missile programmes, the training of Hezbollah and Hamas, the shipment of weapons and technology to both groups, and the training and financing of terrorists in the Middle East and beyond. What is certain in this murky world is that the money they earn from ostensibly peaceful projects is not money well spent.

The problematic nature of joint ventures and trade relations with Iranian companies is not limited to cases such as those described here, where it is relatively easy to prove that the Iranian partner is an integral part of the IRGC. In many cases, business people deal with apparently legitimate interlocutors, sometimes public companies that are 100 per cent government owned. Even in such instances, the Iranian counterpart frequently diverts material it bought from European suppliers to illegitimate projects, including, crucially, Iran's nuclear and ballistic missile projects.

The British Department for Business, Enterprise and Regulatory Reform (BERR) is the agency in charge of licensing and dual-use items. BERR is unlike some of its far more secretive European counterparts. They have, for example, published a list of Iranian companies which are named as 'blacklisted end-users'. In other words, they have been the supposed final recipients of British-manufactured goods or raw materials, but then violated the terms of their licence and transferred their purchase to other companies, usually with links to proliferation activities.

Again, this does not mean that all their actions are illegal, just as the building of a water tunnel by a Revolutionary Guard affiliate is, in itself, a perfectly innocent, even noble, endeavour. What it does mean is that dual-use items were transferred to individuals or entities who, if they themselves had applied for a licence, would have been denied. The legitimate Iranian client has become a front for illegitimate Iranian proliferators. And European companies, along with the licensing authorities that approve their exports, can be duped into believing that there is nothing untoward about the deal.

A cross-check of the BERR-blacklisted Iranian companies with other European companies reveals a thriving business. In some cases, BERR's blacklisted end-users claim to be distributors of European products from companies like Ebner (Austria), a producer of steel furnaces; Luputherm GmbH (Germany), a supplier of fireproof moulds; and Parsytech GmbH (Germany), a maker of hot rolled strips (an intermediate material in steel production) – all supplied Iran's Mobarakeh Steel Corporation, which is blacklisted by BERR. According to its Internet site, Iran's Samamicro claims to be distributing products for Austrian Grabner Instruments (laboratory equipment), Germany's Mahr GmbH (measuring equipment), Gonotech GmbH (odometers for medical and biochemical purposes) and Sartorius (laboratory equipment). It also claims to be representing the American Agilent company (measuring equipment). Iran's Noavar Hava claims to be Iran's distributor for Germany's Becker und Soehne, while Iran's Talash Sanat advertises itself as the Iranian distributor for Swiss ABB (automation technology), and two US companies, WIKA and Emerson Electric.

There are also strong links between Mobarakeh Steel Co. and IRASCO, an Italian-registered company in Genoa, which was established in 1994 as a joint venture between Germany's Ascotech and Iran's Iritec, which holds 49 per cent of the company's shares. Mobarakeh Steel Co., one of the principal clients of IRASCO, is in turn one of the principal shareholders of IRITEC, alongside other Iranian metallurgy interests such as National Iranian Steel Company, Khuzestan Steel Company and Mine and Industry Development Bank.

Germany's Stahlbau Schauenberg GmbH created a similar joint venture in Iran with the Iranian company Ircast for the construction of a factory producing furnaces for the petrochemical sector. Its clients are Arak and Jam Petrochemical, both blacklisted by BERR. Another joint venture involves the German Biotest AG and the Iranian company Darou Pakhsh. Together they created Biodarou PJS, which holds 49 per cent of the company's shares. Biotest AG is a leading pharmaceutical company in the field of immunology and diagnostics. Darou Pakhsh is on the BERR blacklist. Bilfinger und Berger supplied technical analyses to Arak Petrochemical for the production of high-density polyethylene in labs owned by Arak Petrochemical.

Finally, Italy's Technimont participates in the construction of Iran's petrochemical complex on behalf of the Arak and Jam Petrochemical companies, both of which feature on BERR's blacklist. There is no way of knowing, at least through open sources, whether any of the sales and activities involving European partners has been diverted. European companies themselves may have established their partnership before BERR's details were made public. The presence of Iranian companies on the BERR blacklist does not mean that trade with them is barred – it means only that they have been denied a licence in the past on account of violations of end-user terms. Clearly, then, there is nothing illegal in European companies relying on such Iranian partners for the sale of their products on the Iranian market or in partnering up with them for joint ventures in Iran. But the presence of these companies on a public blacklist for manifestly illegal behaviour in the past should sound a warning for all European companies.

European assistance not only introduces technology and know-how to Iran, but European partnerships with Iranian front companies acting for the IRGC, in the most benign circumstances, have produced profits for the Guards. This fact highlights another problem with Iran's markets, and, by extension, doing business with Iran. According to unofficial estimates, as much as 70 per cent of Iran's economy is in the hands of the IRGC. If European companies wish to do business there, it is almost inevitable that they will do so with the IRGC. This is also true when the Guards are not directly involved. In strategic sectors of Iran's economy, such as energy or metallurgy, links with actors with a record of diversion and deception are frequent.

An additional example, involving authorised sales of military equipment to Iranian police forces, highlights the lessons that must be drawn from the patterns that emerge from an in-depth study of trade relations with Iran. Frequently, European companies do not deal with honest and transparent partners. The opaqueness of their interlocutors has to do both with their identity and with their ultimate purpose. A government licence offers a guarantee – and legitimacy – to European companies that a particular transaction is perfectly legal. But the consequences of such transactions should require governments to pause and rethink the logic behind the norms that regulate Europe's trade relations with Iran.

No matter how innocuous a deal may appear to European companies, it acquires a more sinister aspect when viewed from the Iranian perspective. The abuse of European products is so widespread and knows no limits. Iveco trucks, for example, are pictured in military parades carrying short- and medium-range ballistic missiles. Austrian KTM and Japanese Honda motorcycles also feature in military parades. They are used by the IRGC as mobile field units bearing shoulder-held rocket launchers. Then there are SUVs, such as the Toyota Land Cruisers used by Iranian forces, which are adapted to military use by having machine guns and rocket launchers fixed to them.

Alongside such examples of improper and presumably unauthorised adaptation of civilian products for military use, there are a few instances when Iran could legally buy weapons from European suppliers for very specific uses. These are exceptions, naturally, given the existing arms embargo against the Islamic Republic. The problem is that even in such exceptional instances, the regime ends up diverting equipment to illicit purposes which were never envisioned by the suppliers or the governments who authorised the sales.

This pattern is indeed as old as the Islamic Revolution. German Heckler and Koch G3 assault rifles were licensed for local production in Iran under the Shah (the license was revoked only in the late nineties). But the website of the Iranian defence industries (www.diomil.ir) still features the G3-A3 and G3-A4 Iranian versions of the rifle. And according to Amnesty International, Iran sold tens of thousands of them to the Sudanese government in the early nineties, when it was engaged in a barbaric repression of the non-Muslim south, resulting in the deaths of nearly two million people and the displacement of twice as many southern Sudanese.

Iran pursues self-sufficiency in all sectors. Whatever

technology Tehran can acquire, it will. It will then be reverse-engineered, copied and perhaps even re-exported. This is what seems to have been the fate of an Austrian high-precision sniper rifle produced by Steyr-Mannlicher. Austria sold Iran 800 HS50 12.7mm (.50 calibre) Steyr-Mannlicher sniper rifles to help Iran's drug-fighting police units win their war against smugglers from Pakistan and Afghanistan (Iran has a huge drug problem, with an estimated 3 million addicts). When the USA sanctioned the sale by Steyr-Mannlicher, the Austrian Defence Ministry defended the licensed sale as 'unimpeachable'. That was in December 2005. By February 2007, US troops had seized more than one hundred such rifles during raids against insurgents in Iraq. Steyr-Mannlicher denied the guns came from the stock it sold Iran. They all bore licence numbers, after all, and were accompanied by end-user certificates. Given its high precision, this rifle does not lend itself to tampering. The simple act of scraping the licence numbers would deprive the weapon of a critical few milligrams of weight, altering its balance and affecting its performance.

If the Americans were sure of the origins of such guns, they should have been able to produce some evidence, either of the licence numbers or of attempts to tamper with the numbers on the guns themselves. According to Austrian Foreign Ministry officials, the Pentagon did not provide such evidence, and the trail went cold. But soon after Iran's purchase, an exact copy of the HS50, produced by Iran's defence industries, emerged at an arms fare in Iran.

Other reports have suggested that China's South Defence Industries replicated the weapon. Their AMR-2 12.7mm looks suspiciously like a replica of the Austrian rifle that was sold to Iran. Whatever the licensing issue, it is plausible that

Iran, having acquired a high-precision weapon from Austria, proceeded to ensure it could be replicated in large quantities to suit its needs, including the supply to Iraqi insurgents of the replica, which could be used to kill US troops in Iraq. The likelihood that the weapons found in Iraq were an Iranian-made replica of the Austrian rifle has now been confirmed by a Pentagon source.

Even when military equipment is supplied to Iran under tight controls, for specific purposes and with UN Drug Control Office authorisation, things go wrong. In 2003, Britain and Italy supplied night-imaging equipment to Iran's anti-drug units, also to fight drug smugglers in Iran's eastern provinces. Israeli troops reportedly found some of these inside Hezbollah's headquarters in south Lebanon during the July 2006 hostilities between Israel and Hezbollah.

The Austrian sniper rifle case resembles that of the Italian speedboat Levriero made by FB Design. Set alongside all other evidence of Iranian deception, diversion, opaqueness and subterfuge, it should persuade European companies and governments to rethink their relations with Tehran. Is it really worth handing over Europe's know-how for such abuses by Iranian business interlocutors, who have shown themselves to be masters of deception, abusing trust and good faith in the name of the Islamic Revolution?

This brief overview of trade relations between Europe and Iran not only illustrates the potential for growth and the opportunities that exist for European companies. It also highlights the problematic nature of European relations with Iran and the risks that European companies are asked to take in order to do business with the Islamic Republic. It has also highlighted weak points in Iran's economy, especially but not exclusively in the energy sector. This offers a basis for assessing the type of pressure Europe may exert on Tehran to induce a change of behaviour on the nuclear issue.

5

What is to be done?

Iran's nuclear programme poses a direct threat to the strategic interests of Europe and the West. A nuclear Iran will dramatically change the geo-strategic landscape for the worse. The shadow of its nuclear bomb will extend across the Gulf, the entire Middle East and the Caspian Basin. The consequences will be severe and the possibility of conflict cannot be excluded. Abandoning the option of military action now will not necessarily avoid military action in the future. The difference, of course, is that the balance of power will be infinitely less favourable to Western forces and their regional allies after Iran acquires nuclear capability.

War now or later is not a desirable alternative. Nor is the formulation of the French president, Nicolas Sarkozy, who posed the choice of 'bombing Iran or living with Iran's bomb'. Living with Iran's bomb may mean war eventually, but under different and more challenging circumstances than at present. If diplomacy does not work and war is considered to carry an unacceptably high risk, simply sitting back and allowing Iran to develop a nuclear arsenal poses even greater dangers for the future.

Over the years, Iran has appeared to display flexibility – sometimes more, sometimes less – in its negotiations with the international community. But for all the talk there has been no progress on the crucial issue of persuading Tehran to cease its uranium-enrichment programme. According to diplomatic accounts, informal talks involving American and Iranian diplomats in Paris in 2003 almost yielded a breakthrough in the tortuous bilateral relations. If successful, they might have had an important effect on the nuclear issue. Ultimately, they failed. Nevertheless, Iran briefly agreed to suspend enrichment between 2004 and 2006, though many attribute this to technical difficulties, which Iran eventually overcame, rather than Iran's political readiness to display flexibility in exchange for economic concessions, diplomatic openings and a return to a semblance of rational behaviour.

Finally, Iran initialled an Additional Protocol on Nuclear Safeguards with the International Atomic Energy Agency in December 2003, but it has still not ratified the protocol. The bottom line is that over six painful years of negotiations, Iran has repeatedly stalled, procrastinated and reneged on agreements, while it has relentlessly shifted Europe's 'red lines'.

The dynamics of these protracted negotiations are a testament to Iranian diplomacy and its exceptional skill in exploiting Western doubts and divisions to its own advantage. There is no real evidence that Tehran was ever really serious about reaching a negotiated settlement with its Western interlocutors.

In June 2008, they presented Tehran with still more generous incentives to stop suspending enrichment, but Iran's reception was cool. Then the offer was further sweetened by the offer of direct involvement by a high-ranking US diplomat at the July 2008 Geneva talks. Iran ignored the deadlines that were set for its response. Meanwhile, its enrichment work continued apace. Scorning the Western overtures, President

Ahmadinejad cocked a snook at the international community when he announced, just one week after the Geneva talks, that 6,000 centrifuges were operational in Iran's enrichment factories.

Not much time is left, as David Albright, Jacqueline Shire and Paul Brannan recently reported in a paper for the Institute for Science and International Security following the publication of yet another IAEA report on 15 September 2008. The trio noted: 'A key benchmark of enrichment progress is when Iran accumulates enough low-enriched uranium to have the capability to produce quickly enough weapon-grade uranium for a nuclear weapon. In this case, Iran would use the LEU as feed into its cascades, dramatically shortening the time to produce weapon-grade uranium ...'

Given Iran's reported improved efficiency at running its enhanced bank of centrifuges, its stockpile of low enriched uranium (LEU) is increasing exponentially. Consequently, the paper's authors added, 'whatever the actual amount of LEU, Iran is progressing towards this capability and can be expected to reach it in six months to two years'. A US-based non-proliferation watchdog, the Wisconsin Project for Arms Control, confirmed this assessment in a recent timetable it published about Iran's nuclear progress. According to the Wisconsin Project, Iran was on course to have enough LEU to reprocess and produce weapons-grade uranium for one Hiroshima-type nuclear bomb by Inauguration Day on 20 January 2009. It will be able to then build a bomb within a few months. Every passing day brings Iran closer to its goal. The more time diplomacy offers Iran, the more time the country has to narrow the technological gap, and at little political cost.

*

There is a third option, which occupies a space in international relations between the exhausted diplomatic process and a potentially high-risk, high-cost military engagement. This involves a dramatic escalation of pressure on Tehran with a dual aim: first, to strike at the most strategically sensitive sectors of Iran's economy; and, second, to effectively shut off all Iranian entry points to the global economy. Admittedly, there is not a rich history of success in using sanctions to change the policies of repugnant regimes. The case of Iraq is but one among many failed attempts at using sanctions when diplomacy proves futile. But if diplomacy fails and there is no stomach for the use of force, the only serious option left is the swift, effective use of smart sanctions.

A 'target assessment' indicates that Iran's most vulnerable areas are human rights and trade. It is precisely in these areas that a combination of symbolic and substantive action could inflict enough pain on Iran to deny it access to the resources necessary to pursue its nuclear ambitions – or, at least, dramatically raise the cost of continuing to defy UN Security Council resolutions.

Human rights sanctions are particularly important. Tehran will not be disposed to change policy and liberate its society, but it may well interpret external pressure on the human rights issue as a deliberate push for regime change. If this message is delivered with sufficient seriousness and vigour, Tehran might sense that no less than the survival of the revolution is at stake and may just consider that protecting the revolution is paramount. The bomb can wait.

The first critical step in the process is to learn from past mistakes and understand that, as it has done with 'smart' weapons, the West must devise a system of 'smart' sanctions.

They must be carefully calibrated, surgically directed and geared to cause maximum hurt to the regime with as little collateral civilian damage as possible. In the case of Iraq, sanctions achieved no tangible political results. Indeed, the cynicism and callousness of Saddam Hussein meant that sanctions contributed to a disastrous deterioration in the plight of Iraq's civilian population. The result was not only to add to the burden of an already oppressed society, but also to create a humanitarian crisis in Iraq and fuel anger among Western publics at what they perceived as heartless actions by their governments. They also inflamed the passions of Islamic communities throughout the world.

There are other objections: with the current crisis in the global economy, it might seem too fanciful to expect governments to accept higher energy prices – one inevitable consequence of sanctions – and too optimistic to expect Western companies to pass up potentially lucrative business. This, it could be argued, would hurt Western economies at a time when they can ill afford to absorb further pain. It might further be argued that the acquisition of nuclear weapons has been an Iranian ambition since the days of the Shah and that it might well be impossible to dissuade Tehran from pursuing this path, whoever is in charge. Rather, the West should seek an accommodation with Iran instead of engaging in costly, potentially futile, sanctions.

The fact remains that a nuclear arsenal in the hands of the Islamic revolutionaries is a matter of particular concern because of the nature of the regime and the goals it seeks to achieve. If Iran were a functioning, accountable, transparent democracy which treated its citizens and its neighbours with respect, its hegemonic aspirations would be an uncomfortable reality but would worry its neighbours far less. Under such circumstances, Israel and the West might privately welcome an ascendant Iran, which could conceivably become a trusted friend and ally. Proliferation is something to be avoided, but if Iran were committed to genuine democracy, its nuclear ambitions would evoke far fewer anxieties.

It is necessary also to address other objections: that sanctions will hurt the ordinary people rather than the regime and that the state of the global economy poses a hindrance to sanctions.

There is little doubt that the price of oil would be affected by the successful application of sanctions against Iran's energy sector, particularly if sanctions were reinforced by a naval blockade of oil exports from and refined fuel imports to Iran. This would lead to disruptions in supply and an atmosphere of uncertainty about post-sanctions supplies. In addition, sanctions would adversely affect Western companies, exacerbating the global economic turmoil.

But the reality is that the price of crude could rise even without sanctions. A pre-emptive military strike would undoubtedly cause a rise in prices, though only in the short term. If there is no action, either military or economic, and events are allowed to take their course, a nuclear-capable Iran would drive up oil prices for the long term, possibly permanently. From this perspective, sanctions are preferable to both a military strike and complete inaction because there is ample evidence that the market adjusts to short-term spikes. That was the experience in Iraq during the nineties, when the oil sector suffered greatly and output was significantly reduced, and it was the case during an oil embargo of Iran in the eighties, which also failed to make a long-term dent in oil prices. The consequence for oil prices of sanctions now, however, would be driven more by short-term political uncertainty than long-term issues of supply and demand. Finally, a total embargo is the most extreme of a long list of measures that can target Iran's energy sector, and it may be contemplated as a last resort – short of military action.

It may be argued that Iran will retaliate against such sanctions by cutting off oil supplies to the West. One cannot rule it out, but such an act would be an Iranian own goal. Iran's economy, in spite of the all-time high price of oil over the past two years, is in the midst of a grave crisis. Iran's then oil minister, Gholamhossin Nozari, announced at the beginning of August 2008 that the government would have to draw $8 billion from its foreign currency reserves to avoid any disruption of supplies of refined imports until the end of that fiscal year. With the global economic crisis in the second half of 2008, oil prices fell and Minister Nozari declared that Iran was seeking a significant cut in OPEC's production levels, commenting that 'if OPEC does not take a major decision to confront falling oil prices, investment conditions in the oil industry would be faced with a serious danger'. Even at $60 a barrel, oil income is not enough to salvage Iran's economy and its ailing energy sector.

Meanwhile, Iran is rationing petrol, house prices have risen steeply and inflation is running at 30 per cent, while unemployment has crept above 20 per cent. With such a bleak domestic economic outlook, Iran desperately needs hard currency from its sales of crude. Suspending supplies to the West may cause prices to rise. But it could also boomerang, leaving Iran without desperately needed hard-currency revenues. Such a response can therefore be discounted. Unless the West decides to blockade Iran's oil exports, Iranian oil will continue to flow, even as sanctions are tightened. True, sanctions will add to the economic woes of the West and companies, enduring a bitter economic climate, will not react kindly to demands that they renounce lucrative trade opportunities.

Media reports in 2007 estimated that the German economy could lose as many as ten thousand jobs if Berlin were to impose harsher sanctions on Iran. Politicians are correctly sensitive to such assessments, and they should not be lightly dismissed. But the grim reality is that sanctions represent the 'least worst' of bad options. Sanctions, like the military option, will involve short-term pain for the West; continuing the current round of futile diplomacy – the most favoured option in the West – will lead inevitably to a nuclear Iran. And this will have a catastrophic long-term effect on oil prices. Not only will a nuclear Iran raise prices, but it will compel its newly vulnerable neighbours – Iraq, Saudi Arabia and Kuwait, among others – to follow suit. How many jobs will then be sucked out of the German economy?

There is a serious question about whether a tough sanctions regime can be effective. Precedents are mixed and do not provide a definitive answer. Sanctions were not successful in catalysing change in Iraq (although they probably were responsible for preventing Saddam from resuming his nuclear programme and the construction of other WMD). But Iraq was the exception, not the rule. In the Balkans, sanctions against the former Yugoslavia from 1992 to 1995 and again from 1998 to 2000 achieved important political goals without causing the disintegration of Serbian society. In the case of Libya, sanctions forced the regime to hand over those responsible for the Lockerbie terrorist attack. Eventually, sanctions were instrumental in persuading Libya to abandon its clandestine nuclear programme and negotiate terms for its readmission into the respectable community of nations. In the case of Cambodia and Angola (sanctions were imposed against the UNITA rebels), there were also positive outcomes. For all their shortcomings, sanctions have contributed to the achievement of political goals they were designed to advance. Experience does teach us four important lessons about sanctions:

- To be effective – in other words, to induce a regime to change its harmful policies – sanctions must seek to surgically target areas of the economy that will hurt or destabilise the regime while minimising harm to the general population.
- Sanctions must be coupled with sufficient incentives to persuade the regime that its survival will be threatened unless it changes course.
- To achieve their goals, sanctions must be accompanied by effective enforcement mechanisms. Porous borders, corrupt bureaucrats, the lack of political will or subversion by business leaders will reduce the impact of sanctions.
- Politicians and business leaders must be prepared for a long-term commitment. They must understand that sanctions can take a long time – years rather than weeks or months – to achieve their goals.

Based on these criteria, it would be potentially counterproductive to impose blanket sanctions on Iran. More preferable is the adoption of selective measures – 'smart' sanctions – which cause sufficient discomfort to the regime and discontent across the country to trigger change, but not enough to harm and antagonise that part of the civilian population which is likely to support a change of direction.

It would be pointless to directly target such sectors as agriculture, and products such as leather and carpets. Not all of Iran's business sectors are strategic; not all are indissolubly linked to the regime. Instead, the focus should be on imposing tough sanctions against those in charge of strategic decision-making in Iran and against those sectors from which regime stalwarts draw their wealth, power and influence. This means that sanctions must target activities and businesses directly linked to the IRGC, to the oil sector, the petrochemical complex, free-trade zones, and the vast economic empires of the religious foundations.

It also means that sanctions must exact a high price on those who continue to do business with Iran – even if such business is technically speaking not forbidden. It is not only a matter of using financial obstacles and legal prohibitions to discourage or prevent joint ventures with specific companies or defined sectors. Sanctions must make it profoundly unattractive to do business with Iran, in all sectors and at any time. That means that insurance costs, transport costs and the cost of borrowing money must go up dramatically for companies wishing to do business with Iran.

Iran must know that the West is prepared to exact a steep price and that the sanctions are designed to cause economic damage that will undermine the legitimacy and credibility of the regime. Not least, Tehran should be told that the international community will support regime change from within. It must know that the West will work tirelessly to make Iran poor and internationally isolated unless dramatic changes occur in its approach to the nuclear issue. At the same time, it is also important that the revolutionary leaders know that the pressures would cease if and when they changed course and complied with UN Security Council demands to cease uranium enrichment and fulfil Iran's obligations under the NPT. In those circumstances, sanctions would be lifted, Iran's energy sector would be modernised, and investment would return, along with technical assistance and beneficial commercial deals.

The international community placed a basket of incentives on the table in June 2006. This was enhanced two years later with the support of the five permanent members of the UN Security Council, as well as Germany. Iran was promised that existing sanctions would cease and that Western technological assistance would be forthcoming to develop light-water nuclear reactors. In addition, Iran was informed that its security concerns would be addressed at a regional level. What the international community must do now is to make sure Iran understands the consequences of rejection.

Ultimately, though, the announcement of punitive measures – however harsh and comprehensive – is not enough to deter those in the West who might be tempted to break sanctions. When, for example, sanctions were imposed on Sierra Leone during its civil war, the porous nature of the border between Liberia and Sierra Leone made restrictions against the diamond trade less effective.

The announcement of sanctions against Iran must be accompanied by effective political, legislative, and administrative mechanisms to ensure their full implementation. A strong political will must be accompanied by intrusive national and international rules to monitor compliance and punish those who seek to evade them. Assistance should be awarded to those countries that have the political will but lack the resources and qualified personnel to implement the stringent elements of the sanctions regime. And appropriate penalties must be contemplated for those countries that might be tempted to close an eye to Iran's efforts to evade sanctions.

Sanctions against third parties are already in place. In 2008, the US Treasury Department targeted Bahrain's Future Bank because of its ties to Iran's blacklisted Bank Melli. The department designated Future Bank, among other reasons, because, as its press release stated,

> Future Bank was established in 2004 as a joint venture between two Iranian banks, Bank Melli and Bank Saderat, and a private bank based in Bahrain. Bank Melli and Bank Saderat each hold 33.3 percent of Future Bank's outstanding shares. At the time of designation, Bank Melli and Future Bank publicly identify the same individual as chairman of both institutions. Other information available to the US Government also demonstrates that Future Bank is controlled by Bank Melli.

More recently, the EU has issued a warning against Future Bank and other Iranian-owned financial institutions in third countries, owing to concerns that they may be involved in proliferation activities. Iran, however, continues to evade sanctions, at significant additional costs, as a result of the leniency, support and, in some cases, the active complicity of friendly countries. Others are drawn unwittingly into breaking sanctions because their systems of control, monitoring and implementation of sanctions are inadequate or because they are simply not equipped to neutralise the multiple firewalls Iran erects in the form of front companies to overcome the obstacles. So, even when governments do wish to maintain sanctions against Iran, their limited ability to do so is exploited by Iran. Such is the case in countries like Turkey and the United Arab Emirates, where geographic proximity to Iran and the presence of significant Iranian expatriate communities facilitate Iranian penetration.

It is unrealistic to expect a breakthrough barely two years after the passing of the first UN sanctions resolution against Iran, particularly as the sanctions imposed so far have been reasonably modest and limited in nature. A much more robust regime could yield results more quickly, but even so it would take time. Nevertheless, before the cracks begin to appear in Tehran, sanctions would have had the primary effect of weakening Iran's procurement efforts while undermining the regime from within.

It might already be too late, but it is worth giving sanctions – deep, invasive, rigorously applied and targeted – an opportunity to work. Naturally, the risk remains that Iran may reach the nuclear finishing line before sanctions have had an opportunity to do their work. If David Albright's assessment is correct, Iran may be very close to building its first bomb. Another nuclear expert, David Kay, has suggested that Iran is two to five years away from nuclear capability. Better than Albright's assessment, but not by much.

So sanctions may end up failing because Iran could decide to bear the short-term pain imposed by sanctions in order to win the main prize: a nuclear bomb. It is a significant risk, but given the alternatives – failed diplomacy and a pre-emptive strike – it is a path worth pursuing.

Clearly, sanctions will impose economic hardship on Europe

and there will be political impediments. But that alone should not act as a deterrent against any action. Sanctions need not be embraced or rejected en bloc. They can be approached like dishes on a menu, with a calorie value for each. European diplomats can then assess whether the political 'value' of each measure is worth the cost. But they should at least consider the measures. The more broadly they are accepted, the greater will be the overall impact.

Europe's privileged business relationship with Iran, and Iran's dependence on European trade, means that Europe can deploy a particularly persuasive range of economic measures. Denying its commercial relationship with Tehran could inflict severe damage on the regime's stability and, ultimately, its survival. Consequently, measures specifically designed to make the Islamic revolutionaries believe that Europe is prepared to facilitate regime change may have a sobering effect on Tehran's decision-makers.

Europe can contemplate a long list of measures that will exact a high price on Tehran for its refusal to comply with the NPT and with UN Resolutions 1696, 1737, 1747, 1803 and 1835. Such measures range from the highly symbolic to the painfully substantive. Some measures draw on examples applied elsewhere, such as the embargo Europe has adopted against the Burmese military junta. Others derive from European legislation that has already been approved within the framework of the UN resolutions against Iran. Yet others go beyond sanctions derived from either international or European legislation against Iran and consist of measures that Europe can impose unilaterally on Tehran. One example is the targeting of specific economic sectors where European technology is irreplaceable, at least in the short to medium term. Europe's enormous economic might, even under strain, places it in a powerful position to affect a change of policy in Iran without having to resort to force.

Human rights

During its five years of dialogue with Iran, Europe has never seriously raised the issue of human rights. The European negotiators no doubt have good reason for this. After all, Europe's primary goal has been to persuade Iran to abandon its nuclear ambitions, not to become a liberal social democracy. Putting pressure on Iran's human rights record might have created the impression that Europe was seeking to promote regime change in Tehran. Such an implication, it is argued, would be counterproductive because the regime might feel more justified than ever in seeking to acquire nuclear weapons to protect the revolution and ensure its survival.

According to this logic, negotiations should ensure that Iran understands that Europe does not intend to promote regime change but simply seeks firm, verifiable guarantees from Tehran that it will not seek nuclear weapons. Besides, if a united international front is maintained, insistence on human rights issues might alienate Russia and China, which are important, if reluctant, members of the alliance. Both are permanent members of the UN Security Council and both have supported all five resolutions against Iran, including the three that impose sanctions. Both have lamentable records on human rights and Europe's focus on this issue could put their further support in jeopardy.

There is something to this argument, and it certainly explains Europe's reluctance to adopt this course. But there are at least two reasons why Europe should revisit the issue. First, there is principle at stake. Europe has put human rights at the centre of its value system. By proclaiming human rights to be integral to the human condition, Europe must also regard respect for human rights to be universal. And that requirement includes Iran. Respect for human rights is a prerequisite for joining the European Union, and every association agreement that Europe signs with non-European countries includes a human rights clause. It is a conditionality clause, which, at least in theory, determines the quality of the economic and political relationship.

In Iran's case, the so-called Comprehensive Dialogue between the European Union and Iran was an integral part of their association agreement. Europe chose to suspend this dialogue in 2004 because Tehran systematically refused to discuss its own human rights record. The point is not so much the restoration of that framework for the sake of dialogue. What matters is that Europe should live up to its principles. Human rights are woven into the fabric of Europe, and imposing sanctions, at least partly based on a concern for human rights, is not an artificial contrivance. There are precedents for this and compelling reasons of principle.

There are also compelling grounds on which to reject normal trade relations with Tehran as long as Iranian judges order the stoning of adulterous women, the hanging of homosexuals, the amputation of limbs for thieves, and the persecution of religious and ethnic minorities, such as the Baha'is. European companies should not trade within a legal system that regards the testimony of a woman as being worth half that of a man, which denies due process, engages in summary justice and disregards the most elementary principles of fairness and transparency. Europe's sense of genuine outrage would be justified and understandable. Europe should signal to Tehran that the regime will be held to account for the way it mistreats its citizens and that bilateral relations will be conditioned by such treatment.

The fact is, Iran's human rights record is appalling and deserves to be condemned, with or without the impending nuclear danger. That is not to say Europe should pull up the drawbridge and refuse to engage in any trade with Iran. After all, how many of Europe's trading partners have less-than-perfect human rights records? But Iran's violations of human rights are so egregious that Europe would be justified in raising its voice and backing this with selective, highly strategic, limitations on its trade with the Islamic Republic.

Basing sanctions on the issue of human rights will also send a highly nuanced message: that the West is intent not only on denying Iran a nuclear arsenal, but is also seeking to undermine the revolutionary regime itself. There are serious disagreements among experts about whether the Iranian regime is acting on the basis of a rational calculus when it comes to its nuclear programme. If it adopts a cost–benefit approach, then it will quickly realise that the greater the pressure, the higher the price it will have to pay if it persists with its nuclear programme. By demanding compliance on human rights issues, Europe will be seen to be tacitly threatening the existence of the revolution and the survival of the regime. If Europe ratchets up its demands on human rights at this point, what does it have to lose?

But what if the regime is not operating according to a rational calculus; if its nuclear quest is genuinely inspired by medieval apocalyptic-religious fantasies? In those circumstances, is any price too high? The answer, at least for Supreme Leader Ayatollah Khamenei, seems to be yes. The survival of the regime trumps the nuclear programme. For this reason alone, bringing Iran's human rights record into the spotlight has the undeniable advantage of being both a pressure tool and a signal: unless Iran changes course, Europe will seek to depose the regime.

The European Union can follow a twin-track approach in building pressure on Iran over its human rights record by adopting a series of largely symbolic measures designed to embarrass the regime and highlight its gross human rights abuses. It can also implement EU legislation restricting exports to third countries of equipment that might be used for repression, torture, inhuman treatment, or imposition of the death penalty.

Furthermore, through its institutions and its civil society, Europe can embrace the cause of human rights by focusing on specific themes. Unions can be mobilised to support dissident Iranian workers in their struggle for labour rights; journalists' associations can be drafted to voice solidarity with their belea-guered Iranian colleagues; lawyers and jurists can express their abhorrence of Iran's criminal-justice system; women's associations can embrace the cause of equality, and so on. Such action would raise awareness in Europe about the true nature of Iran's regime, thereby indirectly helping the case for imposing sanctions to keep Iran's nuclear ambitions in check. It would also signal to Iranian reformists, much as it did to dissidents in the old Soviet Union, that the free world was standing with them and cared about their plight no less than its own security.

Action on human rights can be undertaken in phases and

tied to specific events. Europe could, for example, make commercial ties with Tehran conditional on Iran's responsiveness to such issues. And it can consider explicit, verifiable implementation mechanisms and punitive measures if Iran fails to comply with specific human rights standards. By making trade conditional on specific areas of action rather than demanding a grand commitment to the universal principles of human rights, Europe can impose restrictions and add pressure.

Sanctions against human rights abuses: symbolic measures

Even if Europe were to decide not to adopt new economic sanctions beyond those enshrined in UN resolutions, it can at least enact a series of largely symbolic measures that would embarrass Tehran and may have an adverse, if indirect, effect on trade. Human rights lend themselves to such 'higher-ground' diplomacy. Criticising the regime openly would not be useless if it created embarrassment for Tehran, focused public attention on Tehran's true nature and helped to isolate Iran on the international stage. For all these reasons, Europe should consider adopting the following, largely symbolic measures:

- European officials (ministers, parliamentarians, undersecretaries and deputy ministers) rarely travel to Iran any more, but if and when they do, they should make a habit of visiting prominent Iranian human rights dissidents. It should be an official part of their visit so that if Iran tries to block such meetings, visits would be cancelled. And if such events take place, they should be given broad exposure through joint press conferences, perhaps convened inside European embassies.

- When they meet their Iranian counterparts, European dignitaries should insist on raising human rights as the first item on the agenda for bilateral discussion.
- These exchanges should be concrete, specific and practical. And they should be recorded in any statement, communiqué or protocol issued. The discussions on human rights should not be mere gestures or generic condemnations. European officials must provide a detailed list of specific abuses, with requests for action.
- Such issues could include, say, a demand for the reopening of the many daily newspapers and magazines that the regime has closed down in recent years, as well as the freeing of political prisoners. Europeans should come to meetings equipped with lists of names, not a generic demand for more press and political freedom.
- Europe should also provide a timeline for implementation, with a clear statement of the punitive economic and diplomatic measures it will impose for lack of compliance.
- Europe should signal its displeasure to Tehran. First, it could downgrade diplomatic relations by recalling all EU ambassadors in Tehran, leaving chargés d'affaires to represent their countries. There would be little immediate fallout for trade, but it would have significant diplomatic impact.
- Other types of bilateral contacts should be affected.

EU parliamentarians could stop their frequent parliamentary delegations to the Iranian Majlis, while invitations to Iranian parliamentarians should be conditional on improvements on human rights issues. The composition of the Majlis and the way its members are selected are an insult to Europe's democratic standards. Iranian parliamentarians should not be granted equal status with European MPs and MEPs. Denmark recently decided to cancel one such trip, but only because of renewed Iranian incitement over the Muhammad cartoons. All EU national parliaments should follow this example. It does not mean suspending all contacts, but some contacts may not be worth maintaining for the sake of dialogue. Dialogue should continue, but it should not be 'business as usual'.

- When Iranian dignitaries visit Europe – and they still visit often – European hosts should severely limit the scope and extent of their visits. For example, there is no need to roll out the red carpet and offer them high-level meetings; nor is there any reason to grant visas to accompanying business delegations.
- Even if some visits are still allowed in the name of dialogue, Europe should make it clear that specific figures among Iran's ruling elites are not welcome. In the case of the visit by President Ahmadinejad to Rome in June 2008, ostensibly to attend a Food and Agriculture Organisation Summit, there were no meetings with government or opposition officials, or with the Pope. This approach should be extended to other lower-ranking Iranians.

- In addition, Europe should ban travel to or through Europe for all Iranians who are suspected of involvement in the Buenos Aires bombing of 1994. Interpol did not issue an international warrant for all seven Iranians whom Argentina named as suspects, presumably for political reasons. Those who are not on the Interpol wanted list – former president Rafsanjani in particular – should not be granted permission to set foot on European soil under any circumstances.
- The already existing lists produced by UNSCR 1737, 1747 and 1803 of Iranian individuals who are subject to restrictions should be extended to lower levels of the political hierarchy and of the IRGC.
- When visits are unavoidable – for example, when Iran's foreign minister or Iran's nuclear negotiator come to Europe – European cities should mark their arrival with additional high-profile symbolic gestures. They could, for example, rename streets or districts where Islamic Republic embassies are located after prominent Iranian dissidents. The USA, under the late president Ronald Reagan, named the street where the USSR embassy was located after late Soviet dissident Andrei Sakharov. Similarly, the plight of famous dissidents could be highlighted in newspaper campaigns giving a human face to the suffering Iran visits upon its own citizens.

One such initiative was adopted by Rome's municipal authorities in response to Ahmadinejad's June 2008 visit. The street adjacent to Iran's embassy was renamed as '9th of July 1999 Street' to honour the student movement in Iran which rose against the regime in a wave of protests on that date. These demonstrations were put down by bloody repression. Such an initiative should be replicated throughout major cities in Europe, involving civil society and NGOs that would sponsor such actions. Labour unions could, for example, become standard-bearers in efforts to honour their dissident Iranian colleagues who have been imprisoned and tortured by the regime: Mansour Osanloo, for example. The same could be undertaken by women's rights groups or the gay and lesbian community, given that they potentially face the death sentence in Iran. None of these measures has direct trade consequences.

When criticised for its human rights record, Tehran has shown weakness. It is easily embarrassed. European officials should exploit this vulnerability and contemplate a number of symbolic measures to signal their displeasure with Tehran while also demonstrating to the Iranian people that Europe is concerned about their plight no less than about their government's relentless nuclear ambitions. Dialogue can continue, then, but not as it was.

Sanctions against human rights abuses: substantial measures

The purpose of these proposed human rights measures is twofold. As far as Europe is concerned, they are aimed at increasing public knowledge and awareness of Iran's human rights abuses. As far as Iran is concerned, they are intended to embarrass and humiliate Iranian dignitaries as they try to fulfil their official roles while abroad, while also sending a message of solidarity to ordinary Iranians.

The potential for embarrassing senior Iranian officials should not be underestimated. The Italian snub of Ahmadinejad caused the regime to place its anger on full display. The Iranian ambassador to Rome, for example, was immediately replaced for his failure to secure any meetings with Italian officials for his president. Such embarrassments should become the rule, rather than the exception. The regime's loss of face as a result of such events should not be dismissed as gesture politics. A country that holds national honour and pride so high will not be indifferent to regular displays of contempt to their leaders.

Beyond these measures, the EU has the power to impose further economic and trade restrictions on Iran on the basis of existing EU legislation that targets commercial relations with countries with poor records on human rights. EU Council Regulation 1236/2005, for example, specifies that there are 'community rules on trade with third countries in goods which could be used for the purpose of capital punishment and in goods which could be used for the purpose of torture and other cruel, inhuman or degrading punishment'.

Clearly, some goods have the capacity to be used for both good and ill. A tunnel-boring machine can be used to channel clean water and it can be used to make missile silos. With this in mind, EU Regulation 1236/2005 instructs member states considering whether to grant an export license that 'it is also necessary to impose controls on exports of certain goods which could be used not only for the purpose of torture and other cruel, inhuman or degrading punishment, but also for legitimate purposes'.

It sets clear procedures for creating lists of such products. They rely on periodic reports by heads of missions as the basis for deciding when export licences should be granted or denied: 'Such reports should also describe any equipment used in third countries for the purpose of capital punishment or for the purpose of torture and other cruel, inhuman or degrading treatment or punishment.' Member states should then draw conclusions and implement appropriate measures to restrict exports in particular cases.

There is no evidence that Regulation 1236/2005 is being applied to Iran. It would be perfectly appropriate for all 27 EU member states to instruct their ambassadors in Tehran to start drafting such reports to verify whether Iran uses legitimate equipment for illegitimate purposes as spelled out by the regulation. It would not be hard to discover abundant evidence in Iran of Western equipment being used for repression and public executions. Convicts are routinely hung from cranes made by such Western companies as KATO, TADANO and UNIC. Gallows are often built with metal rods produced in Europe. Many items of equipment that result in blatant violation of human rights originate in Europe.

The death penalty is only the most glaring example of Iran's human rights abuses. Iranian paramilitary forces are engaged in almost constant repression – of students, trade unionists and 'immodest' women, among others. Some of the instruments of repression – from water cannon to ordnance pistols – are made in Europe. These should be embargoed, along with a list of other items, in the name of human rights and in accordance with EU legislation. European missions in Tehran should be in a position to quickly identify the types of products that Iran uses for illicit purposes, as defined by Regulation 1236/2005. Europe should then introduce tighter export licensing controls to forbid their export to Iran altogether.

Mobilising civil society
Activism in support of human rights in Iran should neither

begin nor end with government action. It is important, of course, that governments use the instruments of state – diplomatic channels, multilateral forums, international organisations, domestic legislation and other channels – to promote human rights in Iran. Activities aimed at raising public awareness need not always have the official backing of states. Encouraging civil society to become involved may have a significant impact on Iran's domestic condition. First and foremost, such activism could communicate to Iranian dissidents that the free world is aware of their plight and is ready to take concrete steps to express its solidarity. The important point is to let them know they are not alone in their struggle.

The following are examples of initiatives that NGOs and other organisations could initiate, sponsor, undertake and promote:

- mobilising national unions and European federations of unions to support labour rights in Iran by embracing, for example, the plight of individual Iranian dissident unionists;
- mobilising women's rights groups in support of women's rights in Iran;
- mobilising the gay and lesbian community, through their organisations, activists, cultural centres and magazines, to promote gay rights in Iran;
- mobilising professional and trade organisations to promote people-to-people contacts in their particular areas of specialisation;
- organising conferences and workshops on Iran's human rights record under the auspices, and with the sponsorship, of national and local authorities;

- organising awareness campaigns on specific themes through the national media to highlight incidents of ongoing abuses, such as the absence of rights for religious minorities;
- launching media campaigns in support of individual dissidents, for example with newspapers 'adopting' individual dissidents by telling their stories and launching campaigns on their behalf.

Such measures would transcend relations between governments, involving European civil society as a whole in the struggle for human rights in Iran. It is not only a worthy battle in its own right but it also has the advantage of imposing formidable pressure on the regime when it comes to the other contentious issues that divide Europe and Iran, from Iran's support for terrorism to the nuclear issue.

Trade restrictions against publicly owned companies in Iran

An essential component of an effective sanctions regime involves the identification of strategic sectors of the economy. If effective pressure can be surgically directed, the target of sanctions becomes particularly vulnerable. In Iran's case, not only companies may be targeted but also individuals who, owing to their institutional roles, are direct beneficiaries of foreign trade. It is, therefore, possible to contemplate imposing trade restrictions on state-owned companies and businesses that are subsidiaries of the IRGC, as well as existing sanctions that target Iranian companies involved in the nuclear and ballistic-missiles programmes. Introducing additional measures, such as freezing foreign assets and issuing travel bans against senior officials, would be a first step. A second step would be to identify specific areas where punitive and restrictive measures can exert maximum effects on the regime's stability.

The precedent that was set in the Myanmar sanctions regime could be extended to Iran. With regard to Myanmar, the EU's Council Regulation (817/2006 of 29 May 2006) included a new range of restrictions:

> an arms embargo, a ban on technical assistance, financing and financial assistance related to military activities, a ban on the export of equipment which might be used for internal repression, the freezing of funds and economic resources of members of the Government of Burma/Myanmar and of any natural or legal persons, entities or bodies associated with them, a travel ban on such natural persons, and a prohibition on making financial loans or credits available to, and on acquiring or extending participation in, Burmese state-owned enterprises.

The EU thus denied any financial advantage to commercial organisations and individuals involved in the repressive acts of the regime, even if the specified items bore no immediate relation to human rights abuses and denial of freedom in Myanmar. Though companies and governments might object to such a blanket restriction in the case of Iran – because of their long-term dependence on the Iranian energy sector – these measures could be contemplated for other areas, such as Iran's refineries, petrochemical and metallurgy sectors. Most Iranian companies involved in these fields are owned by the state, if not by the IRGC.

There are compelling reasons to impose sweeping trade restrictions on a country whose record of human rights abuses is egregious. And there is ample justification for applying the Myanmar precedent to Iran. EC Regulation 817/2006 states that 'the restrictive measures in this Regulation are instrumental in promoting respect for fundamental human rights and thus serve the purpose of protecting public morals ... The new restrictive measures target sectors which provide sources of revenue for the military regime of Burma/Myanmar' and target practices that are 'incompatible with EU principles'. As the regulation continues,

> These restrictions are designed to prevent those subject to EC jurisdiction from deriving benefits from trade which promotes or otherwise facilitates the implementation of such policies, which are in breach of international law and are incompatible with the principles of liberty, democracy, respect for human rights and fundamental freedoms, and the rule of law, which are common to the Member States.

It is a model worth considering, particularly as so much of the Iranian economy is controlled by the IRGC – up to 70 per cent, according to reports. The massive construction conglomerate Sepazad, for example, has been identified as an integral element in the apparatus of the IRGC – it was designated as such by the US Treasury Department in October 2007. In Myanmar, the same could be said of important companies whose activities are as innocuous as timber and logging operations but whose revenues are used to finance illicit activities.

Even taking account of Europe's strategic interests, the EU

could impose additional burdens on Iran's trade with government-owned companies, subsidiaries of the Revolutionary Guard and companies – mostly monopolies – owned by the major religious foundations. The EU could, for example, impose additional licensing obstacles, such as end-user certification. It could limit trade – in terms of quality and quantity – with blacklisted companies and impose travel restrictions on senior officials associated with such companies. Travel bans involving a denial of visas to European countries, as well as transit through European ports, could be imposed on CEOs, directors and board members of blacklisted companies.

Applying existing sanctions in areas that are likely to affect the nuclear and ballistic-missile programmes

Europe should take urgent steps to implement already existing legislation concerning Iran, elaborating and extrapolating additional sanctions from the text of the laws that the twenty-seven member states have already approved. Such a step could allow the introduction of important additional restrictions on the export of European technology to various sectors of Iran's economy where there are clear applications to the nuclear and ballistic-missile programmes. Equally, Europe should review its visa policy vis-à-vis Iran to target students and academics whose scholarly interests have potential application to the nuclear, ballistic-missile and WMD programmes. According to the EU Common Position on implementing UN Resolutions concerning Iran, which was passed on 23 April 2007, and further amended in June and August 2008, the EU could adopt the following additional measures:

- A ban on the export of earth-moving equipment and any other equipment needed in significant civil engineering projects. There is evidence that the purchase of such European technology could be diverted to clandestine underground facilities for Iran's missile and nuclear programmes.
- A ban on visas for Iranian students to study natural and exact sciences, particularly those with possible applications in the nuclear and ballistic-missile areas (nuclear physics, engineering, rocket science, etc.).
- A suspension of visas to students already enrolled in such programmes.
- A ban on visas for the same research fields to Iranian scholars and scientists who take sabbatical leave in Europe.
- The suspension of all exchange and scientific cooperation arrangements in areas with potential applications to Iran's nuclear and ballistic-missile programmes.
- A ban on visas for Iranian delegations seeking to participate in specialised industrial fairs if the focus of the fair is products with potential applications to the nuclear and ballistic-missile programmes (including, for example, the two major civil engineering fairs held in Europe every three years – BAUMA in Germany and SAMOTER in Italy).
- The imposition of fines on European companies whose products and processes are on the sanctions list but who attend specialised industrial fairs in Iran's free-trade zones, such as the island of Kish, which hosts the annual Enex energy fair and the Cibex engineering fair.

Sanctions against strategic economic sectors in Iran

These measures are either symbolic or can be used to target companies and individuals that are linked to either the ballistic-missile or the nuclear programmes. The measures have three goals: first, to increase pressure on Tehran to change course; second, to exact a high price for Iran's procurement efforts; and third, to slow down and complicate Iran's procurement process and the acquisition of scientific knowledge needed to realise its nuclear ambitions.

But the proposals that follow have little to do with the attempt to impede Iranian access to technology and know-how. Rather, the intention is to strike at the most vulnerable aspects of Iran's economy, particularly those areas where the absence of European technology, experience and know-how would seriously hamper Iran's economic development (Iran would have difficulty replacing European suppliers of such technology with Chinese or Russian suppliers who have fewer scruples in their commercial dealings).

The example of commercial airliners best illustrates this point. Before the Islamic Revolution, Iran's commercial fleet consisted of US-made Boeings and the French Airbus. The embargo imposed on the sale of spare parts and new aircraft has caused a serious downgrading of Iran's commercial fleet, which cannot be overcome by the purchase of alternative products from other sources. The erosion is so significant that some of Iran's planes may constitute a safety hazard. Europe could, therefore, consider denying landing rights and ground services – maintenance, refuelling and insurance – to Iranian airliners. European foreign ministries could issue travel warnings and insurance companies could introduce exemption clauses in life insurance policies if policy-holders were to perish in the crash of an Iranian airliner. Companies could also discourage their representatives from travelling to and from Iran on Iranian airliners.

Certainly, Iran's other commercial partners – notably Russia and China – would attempt to fill the void created by the withdrawal of European companies. Thus, sanctions might cause economic damage without necessarily achieving a political gain. But European exports to Iran are a relatively small percentage of Europe's total exports, and they are relevant to only a small number of European countries. By contrast, Iran's dependence on European imports is enormous. In some sectors, including spare parts and equipment for everything European companies have sold to, and built in, Iran over the past 30 years, imports are so critical that the sudden cessation of European supplies would have a devastating impact on the Iranian economy, at least in the short to medium term. Even where China and Russia can step into the breach and supply substitutes, it will take time for Iran's infrastructure to adapt and adjust. And the time and cost of making the conversion from a European to a non-European specification would, in some cases, be daunting.

The following sectors are particularly susceptible to this type of European pressure:

- refineries and refined oil products;
- liquid natural gas;
- extraction technology for oil and natural gas;
- spare parts for the energy industry and the petrochemical complex.

Iranian attempts to achieve self-sufficiency in these sectors indicate that Tehran is aware of its vulnerability to European technology – and the lack of appropriate substitutes. Before Iran manages to copy, reverse-engineer and master the embargoed technology, Europe has time to withhold it. Without it, the Iranian economy would cease functioning effectively. Some of it would be brought to a halt.

Refineries

Iran's ability to reduce the gap between its refining capacity and domestic consumption depends on a number of projects which were discussed earlier. Meanwhile, Iran must purchase petrol and other oil derivatives from abroad. Some of its suppliers are European. Targeted sanctions against the refining sector would take several distinct paths:

- an embargo on the supply of technology for the construction of refineries, a ban on European companies bidding for new Iranian refineries or upgrading existing ones, the withdrawal of European participation in existing projects;
- an embargo, including a naval blockade, on the sale of refined products to Iran;
- sanctions against those countries that break the embargo and incentives to habitual Iran suppliers to sell elsewhere;
- a ban on sales to Iran on the international market.

Such sanctions would have a dramatic impact. True, many contractors involved in the construction of refineries are Iranian companies, but in some cases they have key European partners. In fact, the expansion of Iran's refining potential is a distant possibility. Only in 2012 will Iran be capable of refining enough petrol to meet *current* needs. Consequently, even expansion projects will not be sufficient to meet the growing demand in years to come. Iran will continue to be vulnerable, certainly until all existing and planned projects are completed.

When it comes to imports, Iran's major suppliers are the United Arab Emirates, which sold $2.57 billion worth of petrol to Iran in 2006. That equates to 62 per cent of total Iranian imports. Part of this is the result of the UAE's ability and willingness to play the role of middleman, with trans-shipments accounting for much of the trade. The UAE's robust and expanding downstream sector – five operational refineries and a sixth in the works – is due largely to the active participation of European and North American companies in upgrading existing refineries and building new ones. Clearly, these present significant additional pressure points if Europe chose to use them.

The second-largest supplier of refined products to Iran is India, with sales worth about $558 million in 2006, followed by the Netherlands and France, with a total of $560 million in 2006. These two European countries take the view that increased pressure on Iran is both desirable and possible – even if the price proves to be high. Other suppliers are former Soviet republics and countries from South-East Asia. There is no guarantee that all these countries can be persuaded to join an embargo against Iran, even if such a measure were backed by a new UN Security Council resolution. The problem of implementation remains, and sanctions would no doubt create enormous incentives for smugglers to circumvent the embargo.

Even so, if France and the Netherlands stopped their exports of refined products to Iran, there would a significant impact. Add the fact that part of Iran's supplies comes from purchases on the international market – from such companies as BP, Shell, Lukoil, Vittol, Reliance and other international wholesalers, such as Trafigura – it is clear that an embargo on petrol would cause serious damage to the regime. Within a few days, Iran would be unable to supply petrol at the pump to its population.

Iran implicitly signalled this vulnerability when it declared that such a step would be considered a declaration of war. The country recently introduced a rationing regime for subsidised petrol which caused protests and unrest at petrol stations, including assaults and riots, particularly among poorer sections of the population. An effective embargo would rapidly bring the country to its knees and trigger a wave of popular protests that would be difficult to quell.

Liquid natural gas

Liquefying gas is the most cost-effective way of transporting this commodity from its source to marketplaces around the world. For Iran, this is clearly a strategic priority. There are currently fewer than twenty exporters of LNG in the world, and the few companies that are capable of building LNG 'trains' for liquefaction – a total of about thirty – are in high demand. Some of these companies are in Asia and North America. And the principal actors in this sector – alongside such energy giants as Shell and BP – are mainly located in Europe.

As in the case of refining, sanctions against LNG technology might not necessarily be foolproof, but the embargo of such technology could delay for some years Iran's goal of developing the gas sector for domestic as well as foreign consumption.

It would also deny vital revenue to Iran in the short term. An article in *Global Insight* in December 2007 noted,

> Reports that Iran is suffering more and more from the financial squeeze caused by increasingly harsh sanctions are now being reported through all kinds of channels. Meanwhile, its large LNG export projects, involving foreign majors such as Total and Shell, as well as Malaysia's Petronas and Spain's Repsol, have fallen years behind schedule and look increasingly impossible to start up with less than a total resolution to Iran's nuclear crisis and a lifting of the international sanctions affecting its economy. The inertia surrounding the downstream phases of Iran's Pars and Persian LNG has also spread to the currently wholly Iranian-developed Iran LNG venture, as the Iranian companies involved lack the technology to develop liquefaction facilities and have not been able to learn from the other two projects, which were meant to precede it.

Imposing sanctions on the LNG sector would heighten the difficulties and concentrate minds in Tehran.

Modern extraction technology

Another great weakness of Iran's energy sector is in the management of its own resources, both oil and gas. Reservoir management to guarantee a constant level of extraction is best undertaken by Western companies, using technologies and know-how that they have developed over more than a century. Their withdrawal from Iran, a slowdown in their activities and the drying up of their investments are all possible steps to be encouraged.

Delays in negotiating contracts based on already concluded memoranda of understanding would aggravate the situation further. Governments could signal to companies involved that they consider investments in Iran's energy sector to be contrary to their strategic interests. Naturally, this type of intervention applies first and foremost to contracts signed by major companies that deal with Iran, notably the Swiss EGL gas deal for 155 million cubic metres of natural gas for Europe.

Such deals, and the complexities involved in their execution, explain how governments can exercise pressure. Gas pipelines still need to be built and states must agree to allow pipelines to transit their territory. LNG projects in Iran and at destination points have yet to be built, which permits the lack of political will to thwart the deal – and all the economic benefits Iran might have hoped to derive. Restrictions could extend to smaller subcontractors that are still active in Iran's energy sector.

These are difficult projects to execute. They rely for their success on careful preparation, sophisticated technology and know-how derived from decades of study and experience. Without the participation of Western contractors, all of these ingredients would be missing. We have already seen that the majority of companies involved in the development of South Pars are European. If they were to slow down their activities, retard new investments, suspend pending projects or withdraw altogether, this would involve enormous delays in the ability of all the other phases of the project to function. This is true even if Russian and Chinese companies (such as Sinopec, which recently signed a multibillion-dollar preliminary agreement with Iran) are able to quickly step into the breach.

A quick survey of current projects indicates how vulnerable the natural gas sector is to Western pressure. Of the liquefaction trains currently being built around the world, Nordic LNG in Norway (owned by Nordic Energy Solutions) involves the active participation of Norwegian companies, among which is Norway's Lyse. Australia's Pluto LNG, owned by Woodside Petrol, relies on Shell technology and has been contracted to Foster Wheeler Worley Parsons, a joint venture between the American Foster Wheeler and the Australian Worley Parsons. The Peru train (owned by America's Hunt Oil, Spain's Repsol, South Korea's SK Energy and Japan's Marubeni) is contracted to the US company CB&I. The Qatari projects, LNG QatargasII, QatargasIII and RasGas III of Qatar Petroleum (majority shareholder), have the ownership participation of Conoco Phillips, ExxonMobil, Mitsui, Shell and Total, and are contracted to France's Technip SA, Italy's Snamprogetti and Japan's Chiyoda. With few exceptions, the main contracting companies are Western. Once the US companies are removed, as a result of the US embargo, the remaining main players are mostly European or Japanese. The same is true, more or less, of the oil sector. The reason? Superior technology.

Financial sanctions

Financial sanctions also offer a potentially fruitful opportunity to capture the attention of the Iranian regime and isolate it from a critical entry point to the global economy. The USA long ago imposed financial restrictions on Iran and its banking sector. With a number of executive orders (the most recent of which were signed in October 2007 and in the spring and summer of 2008), the US Treasury has designated a number of entities and individuals, including several Iranian commercial banks, as participants in proliferation activities, terrorism and money-laundering. Such action has been supported by an intensive and meticulous lobbying campaign conducted by members of the Treasury with European companies, enterprises and banking institutions. All this has heightened awareness among the business and financial communities about the enormous risks involved in doing business with Iran. Those risks, quite simply, involve being considered accomplices, unwitting or not, of Iran's illicit activities.

Europe can adopt similar measures. To some extent, this has already been done. According to recent statements by the 34 members of the Financial Action Task Force, a group of countries and international organisations devoted to combating money-laundering and terror financing, Iranian involvement in these activities as well as in missile and nuclear proliferation is grossly inconsistent with its membership of the international community. Some parts of Iran's banking sector are suspected of providing a transit point for illicit funds that may contribute to financing Iran's nefarious activities. In application of UN resolutions, the EU has already shut down two Iranian banks that the US Treasury had previously designated – Bank Sepah and Bank Melli. In a recent revision of its common position on Iran, it has also issued a warning against all banks domiciled in Iran and their branches and subsidiaries operating abroad – making their banking coordinates public. It remains to be seen whether Europe will decide to ban all Iranian banks from operating in Europe.

But regardless of possible links to Iran's proliferation endeavours, its banking sector should be targeted, if only to inhibit the Iranian economy. Pressure on lending is having the desired effect. Iran has been largely excluded from dollar transactions. If Europe chose to exclude Iran from the Eurozone, that would be another harsh blow to the regime.

The US Treasury campaign, alongside UN resolutions and an uncertain political climate, has served to persuade important European banking institutions to withdraw from Iranian markets. Now is the time for the remaining banks and financial institutions to leave the Iranian theatre. The reduction of available credit should be the result of two parallel phenomena: government sanctions, which close down Iranian banks that operate on European soil; and a decision by European banks, as a matter of self-interest and self-preservation, to stop financing economic and financial operations in Iran. These measures, though only partially successful so far, have nevertheless wreaked havoc on Iran's economy and strongly discouraged foreign investment.

The effect of the credit squeeze can be heightened still further by raising the costs of commercial transactions with Iran by increasing the risk factors that determine lending rates to finance projects in Iran. Lending rates are, in part, a function of Iran's credit rating by Europe's export credit-rating agencies, which are used to assess insolvency risks for investors in third countries. Such agencies vary from country to country, but all are semi-public if not actually government owned. Ratings can, therefore, be affected by political fiat, not simply macroeconomic indicators. Iran's rating is already high, but not the highest. A decision by European governments to coordinate a further increase in the risk factor for Iran would raise the cost of loans and depress investment by European companies still further.

Can sanctions be effective?

The sanctions menu available to Europe is broad and offers a variety of choices – from the largely symbolic to the most severe and hostile actions short of military force. None of them offers a guarantee of success. Iran might, after all, be prepared to pay a very high price to acquire nuclear capability and thereby succeed in its ambition to become the hegemonic power in the region. Even so, these measures can immensely complicate matters for Tehran. And this, in turn, could heighten internal tension between the regime and the Iranian public, with unpredictable consequences for the future of the Islamic Revolution. Such a spectre might cause senior Iranian officials to adopt a more conciliatory course.

Regardless of the risks involved, this is a path worth taking by Europe, given its principled aversion to the use of force as a legitimate tool of policy, its abhorrence of human rights violations and its recognition of the mortal dangers posed by a nuclear Iran. These measures will stand no chance of success, however, if they are not accompanied by more muscular enforcement mechanisms to ensure that the entire edifice of restrictions and sanctions is not just a house of cards.

A simple way to improve the operational aspect of a sanctions regime against Iran is to strengthen the agencies that are in charge of monitoring Europe's trade links with Iran. And the obvious way of achieving this is through export licences. Export control agencies could immediately undermine the effectiveness of EU measures by capricious decisions on whether to grant or deny export licences. Europe does not have a single export-control agency. Rather, it has 27 different national agencies. And there is significant variance in these agencies with regard to personnel and technical competence. Not all agencies volunteer information on their internal structure. Representatives of export-control agencies in Austria, Italy and France refused to inform the author about the overall numbers of employees, and how many of them were specialised technicians who were competent to evaluate the possible military uses of supposedly civilian technology.

Nevertheless, a brief survey offers a detailed picture of the present state of affairs. Of the nineteen members of the EU that eventually provided the author with accurate and current data, the following results emerged: Belgium has eighteen officials (three for the Brussels region, six for Wallonia and nine for Flanders); Cyprus has four; the Czech Republic has 35; Denmark has five for dual-use controls; Estonia has three; Finland has five; Germany has 250; Britain has 90; Hungary has five; Ireland, Lithuania and Luxembourg have four each; Malta has one; the Netherlands has ten; Poland has twenty; Romania has 45; Spain has fifteen; and Sweden has eight.

The disparity in numbers (to say nothing of competence) means that the tools for compliance vary greatly from country to country. This will presumably lead to disparate performances and will also make the entire export-control regime vulnerable to exploitation by shrewd procurement efforts. Europe can adopt provisions that have nothing to do with harsher sanctions but which would enable member states to improve their ability to implement export-control measures more coherently. These include:

- additional personnel with enhanced technical skills at national export-control agencies;
- unified control processes among member states, leading perhaps to a single, centralised EU agency that

coordinates and harmonises procedures and criteria;

- a harmonised range of products and technologies that are prohibited for export;
- a harmonised, shared list of blacklisted foreign entities at a European level.

The creation of these controls is a function of political will as much as anything else. Strengthening the compliance mechanisms can only be beneficial for Europe and its ability to implement both UN resolutions and its own regulations, which should include an extended and expanded regime of sanctions against the Islamic Revolutionary Republic. Such a regime would also, incidentally, make life more difficult for Iranian agents operating in Europe in their constant efforts to procure technology that is so vital for Iran's nuclear ambitions and which poses such immense dangers to the security of Europe.

Conclusion

On 8 August 2008 the tenuous post-Soviet world order suffered a seismic change. With Russian tanks rolling into Georgia, the spectre of a new cold war cast a shadow over Europe. One of the consequences of the invasion was Russia's withdrawal of its grudging support for pressure on Tehran. It should not have been so. Russia, after all, perceives Iran's nuclear quest as a strategic threat to its own security. Georgia should not matter.

Why should Moscow seek to thwart UN Security Council efforts to increase pressure on Iran? Russia fears Iran's nuclear ambitions, but the Kremlin's calculus on a nuclear Iran clearly is not the same as that of Washington, London or Paris, let alone Beijing. Perhaps, after all, the Russians do not believe that Iran can be stopped. They might prefer instead to ingratiate themselves with what they believe to be the inevitability of a future nuclear power on their doorstep. Perhaps Russia sees the region as a zero-sum game, in which every American loss is a Russian gain. That might explain why Moscow appears to be rather sanguine about Tehran's push for power.

There is also another possible explanation. Seen from the Kremlin, Iran's quest for regional hegemony may threaten Russia, too. But how far? In the list of Iran's enemies, Russia cannot rank very high; it is probably quite low. The Gulf Sunni monarchies, Israel, Europe and the United States have much more cause for concern than Russia. Moscow was an impediment to pressure on Iran even before the crisis in the Caucasus. Now it must be discounted altogether.

The other casualty of the invasion of Georgia was Europe's quest for alternative sources of energy. In the hope of reducing its dependence on Russia and on the Middle East for energy supplies, Europe could choose between the Caspian Basin and Iran. Now, with the Caucasus option severely hampered by Russia's imperial ambitions, Iran could become the default option. Even before the Georgia crisis, the prospect of tough new sanctions was receding in the face of limited Russian support and a diminishing appetite for such measures at a time of economic and financial crisis. Now the desire by many European governments to reduce their own dependence on Russian oil and gas, and the global financial turmoil of late 2008, has further reduced any lingering enthusiasm for new sanctions. Even as oil prices plummet, exposing the structural weaknesses and Ahmadinejad's incompetent mismanagement of Iran's economy, Iran knows that the current constellation is hardly hostile to its goals.

This development came after a summer of promises when the five permanent members of the UN Security Council, plus Germany, agreed on a more substantive incentive package than that given to Iran in June 2006. Then the USA announced it was sending a high-profile diplomat, Undersecretary of State William Burns, to meet Iran's nuclear negotiator, Saeed Jalili, when the incentive package would be up for discussion.

Iran's nuclear negotiator travelled to Geneva in mid-July to meet with the EU High Representative for Common Foreign and Security Policy, Javier Solana, at talks aimed at defusing the impending crisis and exploring Iran's willingness to accept the enhanced incentives in exchange for halting its enrichment.

But Iranian president Mahmoud Ahmadinejad quickly doused the embers of optimism. Barely a week after the Geneva talks, he informed the world that thousands of new centrifuges had just been installed at the Natanz pilot fuel-enrichment plant. Then came the Iranian response to the proposal: Tehran would study it, but it would neither reject nor accept it out of hand. More negotiations might be necessary. Meanwhile, Iran's ambassador to the IAEA, Ali Asghar Soltaniyeh, insisted that Iran would not suspend uranium enrichment, pouring more fuel on to the fire.

After six years, it is hard not to see Iran's negotiating strategy as a skilful effort at playing for time. And with Russia unwilling to contemplate new sanctions after its Georgia adventure, there is a consensus that a new UN Security Council resolution introducing new punitive measures against Iran is out of the question. The Security Council actually passed a new resolution – 1835 – which was quickly drafted and approved on the margins of the General Assembly's inaugural session in New York, in late September 2008. But at the time of writing there is no sign that Russia is willing to consider a change of policy. Without Russian support for new sanctions, the Security Council is paralysed. Washington, too, was beset not only by an economic crisis but also a presidential campaign. The prospect of a dramatic tightening of the screw by the new administration is considered unlikely, at least in its early days.

As the global financial system became engulfed in turmoil and the markets plunged, Europe also had little appetite for further burdens on a deeply unsettled business community. It would prefer the Security Council to maintain a united front, but it is realistic about its chances of success. New sanctions are being considered as of this writing, but divisions still exist in Europe about both the extent of their reach and their overall effectiveness.

Meanwhile, Western diplomacies are readying themselves for a new round of negotiations with Tehran and are busy discussing the meaning of the 'freeze-for-freeze' initiative. This idea would involve Iran's suspension of enrichment in exchange for a suspension of sanctions. There is agreement that this would apply to new sanctions, but not much beyond that. And no doubt, Tehran might embark on an interminable negotiation on precisely such meaning, exploiting as it did in the past the divisions and disagreements that exist among allies to its own advantage.

Iran is also entering a presidential election campaign and some Europeans are hoping that President Ahmadinejad will be unseated, opening the way for a more palatable and pliable Iranian leader, like former president Khatami or his predecessor Rafsanjani. But given the time it will take Iran to reach the 'point of no return', even when assessed by such specialists as David Albright and David Kay, it might be too late. Besides, Khatami and Rafsanjani might differ on tactics and style over the nuclear issue, but not on substance. Khatami and Rafsanjani might be more sophisticated and worldly, but not on the issue of disarmament.

The combination of the Caucasus war, UN diplomatic deadlock and a global financial crisis seems to offer a formula for inaction on the question of a new round of UN sanctions. Instead, given the paralysis of international forums, an argument could – and should – be made for European sanctions now. Only Europe, with its economic leverage over

Iran, its diplomatic clout and its closeness to the USA can take the lead on this challenge now.

America will not act until the new administration is firmly in control of the executive branch. The Security Council will not act as long as Russia is a stumbling block. And the Middle East, itself fearful of the consequences of a nuclear Iran, will side with the West only if it perceives that the West is impelled by a strong and determined political will. This is the hour of Europe. European negotiators have tried the paths of compromise, concession and conciliation, dialogue (both critical and constructive) and accommodation for long enough.

Now, before the capitals of Europe learn the earth-shattering news of a successful nuclear test in Iran, is the time to demonstrate that Europe's soft power can be transformative. It is, after all, a vital European interest to ensure that Iran remains a non-nuclear state.

Bibliography

Books

Afary, Janet and Kevin B. Anderson, *Foucault and the Iranian Revolution: Gender and the Seductions of Islamism*, University of Chicago Press, 2005

Cortright, D. and G. A. Lopez, *Smart Sanctions: Targeting Economic Statecraft*, Rowman & Littlefield, 2002

Heisbourg, F., *Iran, le choix des armes*, Stock, Paris, 2007

Jafarzadeh, Alireza, *The Iran Threat*, Palgrave Macmillan, 2008

Ledeen, Michael, *The Iranian Time Bomb*, Truman Talley Books, 2007

Parsi, T., *Treacherous Alliance. The Secret Dealing of Israel, Iran and the US*, Yale University Press, New Haven, 2007

Pollack, K. M., *The Persian Puzzle. The Conflict between Iran and America*, Random House, New York, 2005

Takeyh, R., *Hidden Iran. Paradox and Power in the Islamic Republic*, Times Books, New York, 2006

Tertrais, B., *Iran la prochaine guerre*, Collection Actu, Le Cherche Midi, La Rochelle, 2007

Short publications

Adams, J. and T. Downing, *We Should Not Attack Iran*, Campaign against Sanctions and Military Intervention in Iran, www.campaigniran.org/casmii/index.php?q=node/4544/print

Arasli, J., *Obsolete Weapons, Unconventional Tactics, and Martyrdom Zeal. How Iran Would Apply Its Asymmetric Naval Warfare Doctrine in a Future Conflict*, Research Project, George C. Marshall European Centre for Security Studies, Garmisch-Partenkirchen, Germany, December 2006

Bialer, U., 'Fuel bridge across the Middle East: Israel, Iran, and the Eilat–Ashkelon oil pipeline', *Israel Studies*, 12(3)

Chossudovsky, M., *Planned US–Israeli Attack on Iran*, Centre for Research on Globalization, 1 May 2005, www.globalresearch.ca/articles/CH0505A.html

Clawson, P., 'Could sanctions work against Tehran?', *Middle East Quarterly*, Winter 2007, www.meforum.org/article/1068

Clawson, P., 'How much does weaponization matter?', *Policy Watch*, Washington Institute for Near East Policy, 4 December 2007

Clawson, P. and M. Jacobson, *How Europe Can Pressure Iran*, Henry Jackson Society Project for Democratic Geopolitics, http://hjs.byheart.com

Estelami, H., 'The evolution of Iran's reactive measures to US economic sanctions', *Journal of Business in Developing Nations*, 2, 1998

Estelami, H., 'A study of Iran's responses to US economic sanctions', *Middle East Review of International Affairs*, 3(3), September 1999

Forden, G., B. Ramberg and J. Thomson, 'Iran and the bomb: an exchange', *New York Review of Books*, 55(6), 17 April 2008, www.nybooks.com/articles/21268

Fridman, A. and M. Kaye, *Human Rights in Iran 2007*, American Jewish Committee, New York, March 2007

Hoover Institution, *Policy Review*, 142, Stanford University, April/May 2007

Inbar, E., 'The need to block a nuclear Iran', *Mideast Security and Policy Studies*, 67, Begin–Sadat Centre for Strategic Studies, Bar Ilan University, Ramat Gan, Israel, April 2006

International Crisis Group, 'Dealing with Iran's nuclear program', *Middle East Report*, 18, 27 October 2003, www.crisisgroup.org

International Institute for Strategic Studies, *Nuclear Programmes in the Middle East. In the shadow of Iran*, London, 20 May 2008

Heller, M. A. (ed.), *The Middle East Strategic Balance 2007–2008*, Institute for National Security Studies, Tel Aviv University, Ramat Aviv, November 2006

Jones, T., *Iran Military Options Open*, Interview with M. S. Indyk, Brookings Institution, www.brookings.edu/interviews/2006/0309iran_indyk.aspx?p=1

Kagan, F. W., D. Pietka and K. Kagan, *Iranian Influence in the Levant, Iraq, and Afghanistan*, American Enterprise Institute for Public Policy Research, 19 February 2008

Kalman, M., 'Hezbollah night-vision gear was from Britain, Israel says. It's believed to be an export to Iran in drug-fighting effort', SFgate online, 20 August 2006, www.sfgate.com

Kam, E., *A Nuclear Iran: What Does It Mean, and What Can Be Done*, Memorandum 88, Institute for National Security Studies, Tel Aviv University, Ramat Aviv, February 2007

Karmon, E., 'Israel and the Iranian nuclear bomb: daunting choices', *Aspenia*, 39, Aspen Institute, www.aspeninstitute.it

Kemp, G., *US and Iran, the Nuclear Dilemma: Next Steps*, Nixon Center, April 2004

Khalaji, M., 'Apocalyptic politics. On the rationality of Iranian policy', *Agenda Iran*, Washington Institute for Near East Policy, Washington, DC, 2008

Koch, A. and J. Wolf, *Iran's Nuclear Facilities: A Profile*, Center for Nonproliferation Studies, Monterey, CA, 2008

Kroupenev, A., *Russia's Policy vis-à-vis Iran and Hezbollah*, International Institute for Counter Terrorism

Luers, W., T. R. Pickering and J. Walsh, 'A solution for the US–Iran nuclear standoff', *New York Review of Books*, 55(4), 20 March 2008

Luft, G., *Iran's Oil Industry: A House of Cards?*, Jewish Policy Center, www.jewishpolicycenter.org/article/25

Luft, G. and A. Korin, *Ahmadinejad's Gas Revolution: A Plan to Defeat Economic Sanctions*, Institute for the Analysis of Global Security (IAGS), December 2006

Mekelberg, Y., *Israel and Iran. From War of Words to Words of War?*, Chatham House and Webster University, London, March 2007

Middle East Economic Survey, 'Kuwaiti opposition MPs push for transparency on oil reserves', *Marketing*, XLIX(31), 31 July 2006

Miller, R. R., *Possible Polish–Iranian energy cooperation puts US policy makers between a rock and a hard place, as America finds itself committed both to isolating the Islamic Republic and supporting Polish efforts to outflank Russia's Gazprom*, Atlantic Community website, www.atlantic-community.org

Ministry of Foreign Affairs, *Elements of a revised proposal to Iran made by E3+3*, Paris, www.diplomatie.gouv.fr/en/article-imprim.php3?id_article=5314

Rostami, J., *Research*, Energy and Mineral Engineering Department, Penn State University, 2007

Rubin, U., *The Global Reach of Iran's Ballistic Missiles*, Memorandum 86, Institute for National Security Studies, Tel Aviv University, Ramat Aviv, November 2006

Sadjiadpour, K., 'Guidelines for approaching Iran', *Policy Outlook*, Carnegie Endowment for International Peace, June 2007

Salama, S. and K. Ruster, *A Preemptive Attack on Iran's Nuclear Facilities: Possible Consequences*, James Martin Center for Nonproliferation Studies, September 2004

Salama, S. and E. Salch, *Iran's Nuclear Impasse: Give Negotiations a Chance*, James Martin Center for Nonproliferation Studies, 2 June 2006, http://cns.miis.edu

Weems, P. R., *Overview of issues common to structuring, negotiating and documenting LNG projects*, King & Spalding, Houston, TX, 29 June 2000

Zambelis, C., 'Insurrection in Iran Balochistan', *Global Terrorism Analysis*, 6(1), Jamestown Foundation, Washington, DC, 11 June 2008

Documents

Al-Rodhan, K., *Iranian Nuclear Weapons? The Options if Diplomacy Fails*, Centre for Strategic and International Studies, 7 April 2006

American Enterprise Institute for Public Policy Research, Analysis of foreign investments to Iran, updated 21 May 2007, www.aei.org

American Israel Public Affairs Committee, *National Intelligence Estimate: Continued Pressure Could Prevent Nuclear Iran*, Memo, 5 December 2007

Arbitrio, R., K. Moradi, M. Rezaeian, G. Motashari and M. Kato, *I.R. of Iran. Strategic Programme Framework*

2006–2008, United Nations Office for Drugs and Crime, Vienna, October 2005

ASP Engineering Company Roma SpA, *Oil and Gas*, www.apsengineering.it/oil_gas.htm

Energy Information Administration, *The Global Liquefied Natural Gas Market: Status and Outlook*, US Government official energy statistics, December 2003

Energy Information Administration, *Iran*, Country Analysis Briefs, October 2007

Energy Information Administration, *Oil*, US Government official energy statistics, October 2007

EU, 'Concerning trade in certain goods which could be used for capital punishment, torture or other cruel, inhuman or degrading treatment or punishment', *Official Journal of the European Union*, Council Regulations (EC) No. 1236/2005, 27 June 2005

EU, 'Amending Council Regulations concerning trade in certain goods which could be used for capital punishment, torture or other cruel, inhuman or degrading treatment or punishment', *Official Journal of the European Union*, Commission Regulation (EC) No. 1377/2006, Brussels, 18 September 2006

EU, 'Council Regulations (EC) No. 423/2007 concerning restrictive measures against Iran', *Official Journal of the European Union*, 19 April 2007

EU, 'Amending Council Regulations (EC) No. 423/2007 concerning restrictive measures against Iran', *Official Journal of the European Union*, Commission Regulation (EC) No. 116/2008, Brussels, 28 January 2008

Financial Action Task Force on Money Laundering, *Guidance regarding the implementation of activity-based financial* prohibitions of United Nations Security Council Resolution 1737, 12 October 2007, www.fatf-gafi.org

Foundation for Defence of Democracies, *Understanding the New National Intelligence Estimate*, 4 December 2007

Fox, J., 'Expert assails intel assessment of Iran's nuclear ambitions', *Global Security Newswire*, Nuclear Threat Initiative, 31 January 2008, www.nti.org/d_newswire/ issues/print.asp?story_id=05937BD, accessed 2 February 2008

Government of Australia, *First Chinese built LNG carrier arrives in Western Australia*, Department of Industry and Resources, May 2008, www.doir.wa.gov.au/4868_5581. aspx

IAEA, *The text of the agreement between Iran and the agency for the application of safeguards in connections with the treaty on the non-proliferation of nuclear weapons*, Information Circular INFCIRC/214, 13 December 1974

IAEA, *Non-Proliferation of Nuclear Weapons and Nuclear Security*, IAEA Safeguards, Agreements and Additional Protocols, September 2002

IAEA, *Islamic Republic of Iran Profile*, December 2002

IAEA, *Implementation of the NPT Safeguards Agreement in the Islamic Republic of Iran*, Report by director-general, GOV/2003/40, 6 June 2003

IAEA, *Director General Dr Mohamed ElBaradei's intervention on Iran during the IAEA Board of Governors Meeting*, 18 June 2003

IAEA, *Statement by the Board*, Media Advisories, 19 June 2003

IAEA, *Implementation of the NPT Safeguards Agreement in the Islamic Republic of Iran*, Report by the director general, 26 August 2003, GOV/2003/63

IAEA, *Statement to the Board of Governors*, Report by Director General Dr Mohamed ElBaradei, 8 September 2003, Vienna, www.ieae.org.NewsCenter/Statement/2004/ebsp2004n019.html

IAEA, *Remarks to the IAEA Board of Governors during its meeting on 9 September 2003*, Report by Director General Dr Mohamed ElBaradei

IAEA, *Implementation of the NPT Safeguards Agreement in the Islamic Republic of Iran*, Resolution adopted on 12 September 2003, GOV/2003/69

IAEA, *Implementation of the NPT Safeguards Agreement in the Islamic Republic of Iran*, Report by the director general, 10 November 2003, GOV/2003/75

IAEA, *Implementation of the NPT Safeguards Agreement in the Islamic Republic of Iran*, Resolution adopted on 26 November 2003, GOV/2003/81

IAEA, *Statement to the Board of Governors*, Report by Director General Dr Mohamed ElBaradei, 8 March 2004, Vienna, www.ieae.org.NewsCenter/Statement/2004/ebsp2004n002.html

IAEA, *Note by the Secretariat, Secretariat response to Comments and Explanatory Notes provided by Iran in INFCIRC/628 on the Director General's report on 'Implementation of the NPT Safeguards Agreement in the Islamic Republic of Iran'*, GOV/2004/11

IAEA, *Implementation of the NPT Safeguards Agreement in the Islamic Republic of Iran*, Resolution adopted on 13 March 2004, GOV/2004/21

IAEA, *Implementation of the NPT Safeguards Agreement in the Islamic Republic of Iran*, Report by the director general, 1 June 2004, GOV/2004/34

IAEA, *Implementation of the NPT Safeguards Agreement in the Islamic Republic of Iran*, Corrigendum,18 June 2004, GOV/2004/34/Corr.1

IAEA, *Statement to the Board of Governors*, Report by Director General Dr Mohamed ElBaradei, 14 June 2004, Vienna, www.ieae.org.NewsCenter/Statement/2004/ebsp2004n003.html

IAEA, *Implementation of the NPT Safeguards Agreement in the Islamic Republic of Iran*, Resolution adopted on 18 June 2004, GOV/2004/49

IAEA, *Implementation of the NPT Safeguards Agreement in the Islamic Republic of Iran*, report by the director general, 1 September 2004, GOV/2004/60

IAEA, *Implementation of the NPT Safeguards Agreement in the Islamic Republic of Iran, proposed amendments by Malaysia, Chairman of the Non-Aligned Movement, to the draft resolution submitted by France, Germany and United Kingdom*, 17 September 2004, GOV/2004/78

IAEA, *Implementation of the NPT Safeguards Agreement in the Islamic Republic of Iran*, Resolution adopted on 18 September 2004, GOV/2004/79

IAEA, *List of locations relevant to the implementation of safeguards in Iran*, Annex 1, November 2004, GOV/2004/83

IAEA, *Implementation of the NPT Safeguards Agreement in the Islamic Republic of Iran*, Report by the director general, 15 November 2004, GOV/2004/83

IAEA, *Statement to the Board of Governors*, Report by Director General Dr Mohamed ElBaradei, 25 November 2004, Vienna, www.ieae.org.NewsCenter/Statement/2004/ebsp2004n017.html

IAEA, *Statement to the Board of Governors*, Report by Director General Dr Mohamed ElBaradei, 29 November 2004, Vienna, www.ieae.org.NewsCenter/Statement/2004/ebsp2004n016.html

IAEA, *Implementation of the NPT Safeguards Agreement in the Islamic Republic of Iran*, Resolution adopted on 29 November 2004, GOV/2004/90

IAEA, *Introductory Statement to the Board of Governors*, Report by Director General Dr Mohamed ElBaradei, 28 February 2005, Vienna, www.ieae.org.NewsCenter/Statement/2005/ebsp2005n002.html

IAEA, *Introductory Statement to the Board of Governors*, Annual Report by Director General Dr Mohamed ElBaradei, 14 June 2005, Vienna, www.ieae.org.NewsCenter/Statement/2005/ebsp2005n007.html

IAEA, *Implementation of the NPT Safeguards Agreement in the Islamic Republic of Iran and Related Board Resolutions*, Resolution adopted 11 August 2005, GOV/2005/64

IAEA, *Implementation of the NPT Safeguards Agreement in the Islamic Republic of Iran*, Report by the director general, 2 September 2005, GOV/2005/67

IAEA, *Introductory Statement to the Board of Governors*, Report by Director General Dr Mohamed ElBaradei, 19 September 2005, Vienna, www.ieae.org.NewsCenter/Statement/2005/ebsp2005n009.html

IAEA, *Implementation of the NPT Safeguards Agreement in the Islamic Republic of Iran*, Resolution adopted on 24 September 2005, GOV/2005/77

IAEA, *Implementation of the NPT Safeguards Agreement in the Islamic Republic of Iran*, Report by the director general, 18 November 2005, GOV/2005/87

IAEA, *Introductory Statement to the Board of Governors*, Report by Director General Dr Mohamed ElBaradei, 24 November 2005, Vienna, www.ieae.org.NewsCenter/Statement/2005/ebsp2005no18.html

IAEA, *Developments in the Implementation of the NPT Safeguards Agreement in the Islamic Republic of Iran and Agency Verification of Iran's Suspension of Enrichment-related and Reprocessing Activities*, 3 February 2006

IAEA, *Implementation of the NPT Safeguards Agreement in the Islamic Republic of Iran*, Resolution adopted on 4 February 2006, GOV/2006/14

IAEA, *Implementation of the NPT Safeguards Agreement in the Islamic Republic of Iran*, Report by the director general, 27 February 2006, GOV/2006/15

IAEA, *Introductory Statement to the Board of Governors*, Report by Director General Dr Mohamed ElBaradei, 6 March 2006, Vienna

IAEA, *Implementation of the NPT Safeguards Agreement in the Islamic Republic of Iran*, Report by the director general, 28 April 2006, GOV/2006/27

IAEA, *Implementation of the NPT Safeguards Agreement in the Islamic Republic of Iran*, Report by the director general, 8 June 2006, GOV/2006/38

IAEA, *Implementation of the NPT Safeguards Agreement in the Islamic Republic of Iran*, Report by the director general, 31 August 2006, GOV/2006/53

IAEA, *Implementation of the NPT Safeguards Agreement in the Islamic Republic of Iran*, Report by the director general, 14 November 2006, GOV/2006/64

IAEA, *Cooperation between the Islamic Republic of Iran and the Agency in the light of United Nations Security Council*

Resolution 1737 (2006), Report by the director general, 9 February 2007, GOV/2007/7

IAEA, *Implementation of the NPT Safeguards Agreement and Relevant Provisions of Security Council Resolution 1737 (2006) in the Islamic Republic of Iran*, Report by the director general, 22 February 2007, GOV/2007/8

IAEA, *Implementation of the NPT Safeguards Agreement and Relevant Provisions of Security Council Resolutions in the Islamic Republic of Iran*, Report by the director general, 23 May 2007

IAEA, *Report on Possible New Framework for Using Nuclear Energy*, 15 June 2007, www.iaea.org/NewsCenter/News/2007/nuclenframework.html

IAEA, *Understanding of the Islamic Republic of Iran and the IAEA on the Modalities of Resolution of the Outstanding Issues*, Tehran, 21 August 2007, GOV/2007/48 or INFCIRC/711

IAEA, *Communication dated 27 August 2007 from the Permanent Mission of the Islamic Republic of Iran to the Agency concerning the text of the 'Understandings of the Islamic Republic of Iran and the IAEA on the Modalities of Resolution of Outstanding Issues'*, Information Circular, 27 August 2007, INFCIRC/711

IAEA, *Implementation of the NPT Safeguards Agreement in the Islamic Republic of Iran*, Report by the director general, 30 August 2007, GOV/2007/48

IAEA, *Implementation of the NPT Safeguards Agreement and Relevant Provisions of Security Council Resolutions 1737 (2006), 1747 (2007) in the Islamic Republic of Iran*, Report by the director general, 15 November 2007, GOV/2007/58

IAEA, *Strengthened Safeguards System: Status of Additional Protocols*, 23 November 2007, www.iaea.org/OurWorks/SV/Safeguards/sg_protocol.html

IAEA, *Implementation of the NPT Safeguards Agreement and Relevant Provisions of Security Council Resolutions 1737 (2006), 1747 (2007) and 1803 (2008) in the Islamic Republic of Iran*, Report by the director general, 26 May 2008, GOV/2008/15

IAEA, *Implementation of the NPT Safeguards Agreement and Relevant Provisions of Security Council Resolutions 1737 (2006), 1747 (2007), 1803 (2008) in the Islamic Republic of Iran*, Board of Governors report, 15 September 2008

IAEA, *The Technical Cooperation Programme*, Department of Technical Cooperation, http://tc.iaea.org

IAEA, *Safeguards Overview: Comprehensive Safeguards Agreements and Additional Protocols*, www.iaea.org/Publications/factsheets/English/sg_overview.html

IAEA, *Model protocol additional to the agreement(s) between State(s) and the International Atomic Energy Agency for the application of safeguards*, Informative Circular, INFCIRC/540

Intelligence and Terrorism Information Centre, *Senior Hamas operative figure tells London Sunday Times' Gaza Strip correspondent about Iranian and Syria military aid, detailing the training received by hundreds of Hamas terrorist operatives and describing the transmission to Hamas of Iranian technical know-how for the manufacture of rockets and IEDs*, Israel Intelligence Heritage & Commemoration Centre, 17 March 2008

International Security Resources, *Language from November 2007 National Intelligence Estimate on Iran compared with the*

New York Times headlines and opening paragraphs, www.internationalsecurityresources.com/NIE/%20 Language.htm

ISRIA, *Austria to Fund Private Refinery in Bushehr*, www.isria.info/INTRO/alerts/2007/ SEPTEMBER/09282007, accessed 28 September 2007

Jentleson, B. W., *Sanctions against Iran. Key Issues*, Century Foundation Report, Century Foundation, New York

Jewish Policy Centre, *Companies Angered by SEC's Iran List*, Blog, www.jewishpolicycenter.org/blog/2007/7/ companies-by-secs=iran-list.html

Knesset, *Law Prohibiting Investment in Entities Maintaining Commercial Relations with Iran 2008*, Unofficial translation, 2 April 2008

Mates, M., 'Nato Parliamentary Assembly Special Report', Missile Defense Debate, Science and Technology Committee, 7 September 2007, www.nato-pa.int

Nargan Engineers and Constructors, Research, www.nargan. com/projects/index.html

National Geoscience Database of Iran, *Statistic Reports of Earthquake*, www.ngdir.ir/Earthquake/EarthquakeReport. asp

National Intelligence Council, 'National Intelligence Estimate', *Iran: Nuclear Intentions and Capabilities*, November 2007

Nuclear Threat Initiative, *Analysis of Chemical Industry Facilities in Iran*, www.nti.org/e_research/profiles/Iran/ Chemical/2337_2406.html, accessed 18 January 2008

Nuclear Threat Initiative, 'Bush warns Iran on uranium enrichment program', *Global Security Newswire*, 29

January 2008, www.nti.org/d_newswire/issues/print.
asp?story_id=3909553, accessed 2 February 2008

Petropars Ltd, *South Pars, Qatar North Field, Iran*, Industry
projects, www.offshore-technology.com/projects/
southpars

Trade & Forfeiting Review, *Kerman Water Tunnel Project, Iran:
Financing technical excellence*, 8(4), 23 February 2005,
www.tfreview.com

UN (United Nations), *Treaty on the Non-Proliferation of Nuclear
Weapons (NPT)*, 12 June 1968, New York, INFCIRC/140

UN Security Council, *Security Council, in presidential
statement, underlines importance of Iran re-establishing full,
sustained suspensions of uranium-enrichment*, Department of
Public Information, News and Media Division, New York,
29 March 2006

UN Security Council, *Security Council demands that Iran
suspend uranium enrichment by 31 August, or face possible
economic, diplomatic sanctions*, Department of Public
Information, News and Media Division, New York, 31
July 2006

UN Security Council, Resolution 1737, adopted on 23
December 2006, S/res/1737(2006)

UN Security Council, Resolution 1747, adopted on 24 March
2007, S/res/1747(2007)

UN Security Council, Resolution 1803, adopted on 3 March
2008, S/res/1803(2008)

UN Security Council, Resolution 1835, adopted on 27
September 2008, S/res/1835(2008)

United States Treasury, *Designation of Iranian Entities and
Individuals for Proliferation Activities and Support for
Terrorism*, Press release, 25 October 2007

US Senate, *Chain Reaction: Avoiding a nuclear arms race in the middle east*, Report, Committee on Foreign Relations, 110th Congress, 2nd session, Washington, DC, February 2008

Wassenaar Arrangement on Export Control of Conventional Arms and Dual-Use Goods and Technologies, *The Sensitive List of Dual-Use Goods and Technologies*, 3 June 2005, www.wassenaar.org

WIRTH Gmbh, 'WFGm List of enterprises working in the Heinsberg region', www.wfg-heisenberg.de.

Press sources

Adnkronos International, *Iran: International Economic Boycott Bites*, www.adnkronos.com

Albright, D., 'Swiss smugglers had advanced nuclear weapons designs', *ISIS REPORT*, 16 June 2008, www.isis.online.org

Albright, D. and P. Brannan, 'Arak heavy water reactor construction progressing', *ISIS REPORT*, 13 November 2008, www.isis-online.org

Aminmansour, M., 'Iran earthquake: safety of nuclear power plants', 'Opinions', *Persia Journal*, 28 April 2004, www.iranian.ws

Barkin, N., 'Tough Iran sanctions to hit Germany hard', Report, Reuters, 24 November 2007, www.reuters.com/articlePrint?articleId=USL2446337820071124

BBC News, 'Teheran killers hanged in public', 2 August 2007

Becker, M., 'Iran could have enough uranium for a bomb by year's end', *Der Spiegel* online, 21 February 2008, www.spiegel.de/international/world/0,1518,536914,00.html

Berman, I., 'The national intelligence guesstimate', *American Spectator*, 6 December 2007

Bolton, J., 'The flaws in the Iran report', *Washington Post*, 6 December 2007

CBS News, 'Iran report won't slow missile defense', Brussels, 6 December 2007, www.cbsnews.com

Chung, J. and A. Hill, 'Kouchner urges EU for fresh Iran sanctions', *Financial Times* online, 15 October 2007, www.ft.com

Daily Mail, 'Miles tops charts in rock and roll band', www.dailymail.co.uk/pages/live/articles/sport/othersports.html.

Di Feo, G. and S. Maurizi, 'Cosi l'Italia arma Teheran', *L'Espresso*, 18 October 2007, http://espresso.repubblica.it

Dinmore, G. and H. Wetzel, 'Bush changes step on Europe's efforts with Iran', *Financial Times*, 25 February 2005

Erlanger, S. and G. Bowley, 'Israel unconvinced Iran has dropped nuclear program', *New York Times*, 5 December 2007

Gatti, C., 'Intesa sotto la lente dei Pm di new York', *Il Sole 24 Ore*, 3 April 2008

Jerusalem Post, 'Swiss customs seize equipment for Iran nuke plant', 3 August 2007, www.jpost.com

Jerusalem Post online, 'Iran could enrich uranium in Switzerland', 18 November 2007, www. jpost.com

Kagan, R., 'Time to talk to Iran', *Washington Post*, 5 December 2007

Kay, D., 'What's missing from the Iran debate. Building a security framework for a nuclear Tehran', *Washington Post*, 8 September 2008

Levitt, M., 'Contending with Iran's nuclear intentions and capabilities', *San Francisco Chronicle*, 5 December 2007

Lee Myers, S. and H. Cooper, 'Bush insists Iran remains a threat despite arms data', New York Times, 5 December 2007

Lincy, V. and G. Milhollin, 'In Iran we trust?', *New York Times*, 6 December 2007

Maddox, B., 'Relax? Don't. Iran can still build its bomb', *The Times*, 5 December 2007

Maisano, L., 'Corsa al gas dell'Asia centrale. Compagnie americane pronte a investire nella pipeline sotto il mar Caspio', *Il Sole 24 Ore*, 30 March 2008

Mathe, A. U., 'Doch keine Austro-Waffen im Irak', *Wiener Zeitung*, 29 March 2007, www.wienerzeitung.at

Omidvar, H., 'Iran's aggressive natural gas expansion plans – I', *Shana News* online, 19 September 2007, www.shana.ir/newsprint.aspx?lang=en&newsid=114771

Persian Journal, 'Iran, Italy to sign gas export agreement', 19 December 2007, www.iranian.ws/iran_news/publish/article_23728.shtml

Press TV, 'No decline in German exports to Iran', 20 November 2007

Province of Lecco, *Produco Superbarche non armi per ayatollah*, www.laprovinciadilecco.it/PolComo/20071019/pdf.LE1910-ATTU03.pdf

Reuters, 'Iran hangs judge's killers in public', 2 August 2007, www.reuters.com/article/newsOne/idUSHOS22472320070802

Reuters UK, 'Iran hopes to sign gas field deal with China soon', 2 February 2008

Rocard, M., 'Européens, empêchons la guerre contre l'Iran', *Libération*, 16 November 2007, www.liberation.fr/rebonds/291732.FR.php

Samii, A. W., 'Ahmadinejad's ravings are part of his plan', *New York Daily News*, 14 December 2006, www.nydailynews.com

Sands, D., 'Analysis: Iran gas to Europe a problem', United Press International, 13 August 2007, www.upi.com

Scarborough, R., 'Intelligence officials downplay Iran report', *Washington Times*, 4 April 2008

Sciolino, E., 'On nuclear seesaw, the balance seems to shift to Iran', *New York Times* online, 30 November 2007, www.nytimes.com

Sciolino, E., 'Monitoring agency praises US Report, but keeps wary eye on Iran', *New York Times*, 5 December 2007

Slavin, B., *Hyping the Threat from Iran*, SFGate online, 20 May 2008, www.sfgate.com

Stark, H., 'Will a German crane be used by the mullahs to make missiles?', *Der Spiegel*, 25 April 2005

Stephens, B., 'The road to Teheran: polite society helped pave the way for Iran's Holocaust conference', Dow Jones & Company, 16 December 2006

Stern, Y. and A. Uni, 'Israeli gov't "very happy with success" of IAF strike on Syria', *Ha'aretz*, 11 September 2007

Takeyh, R., 'Shaping a nuclear Iran. The West's diplomatic goal needs to move from "suspension" to "transparency"', *Washington post* online, 18 May 2008, www.washingtonpost.com, accessed 19 May 2008

Tehran Times, 'Iran acts as an East–West bridge: Italian MP', 16 January 2008, www.teherantimes.com

Wall Street Journal online, 'High confidence game', 5 December 2007

Wasserman, A., 'German technology ends up in Iranian nuclear plant', *Der Spiegel*, 4 September 2007

Weinthal, B., 'Germany probes 50 firms that sold nuclear equipment to Iran', *Ha'aretz* online, 22 November 2007

World Tribune, '50 German firms under investigation for helping Iran's nuke program', 20 July 2007, www.worldtribune.com/worldtribune/WTARC/2007/eu_germany

Zecchini, L., 'Iran: document shows Tehran pursued a military nuclear program after 2003', *Le Monde*, 27 March 2008

Index

Abadan oil terminal 166
Abadan refinery 178
Abdullah II, king of Jordan 110
adultery 147
Ahmadinejad, Mahmoud 58,
    88, 91–2, 127, 138, 176, 219,
    245
    alternatives to 127–8
Ahwazi Arabs 141–2
Alani, Mustafa 59, 117
Albright, David 51, 189, 201
Ali, Ayaan Hirsi 150
amputations, as punishment
    147–8
Andritz VA Tech Hydro 190
Angola, sanctions 207
Arafat, Yasser 90
Arak heavy water production
    facility 5, 24
Asghari, Ahmad Reza 64
Azeris 141–2

Baha'i Faith members 139–41
Bahrain, threats from nuclear-
    armed Iran 103–4
Baluchis 141–2
Bandar Abbas refinery 178

Bandar Assaluyeh refinery 178
Bandar oil terminal 166
Bani Yaghoub, Zahra 148
Bank Melli 210, 238
Bank Sepah 238
Bayh, Evan 47
BERR (Department for
    Business, Enterprise and
    Regulatory Reform) 191
Boghammar speedboats 152–4
Bolton, John 46
'bomb in the basement'
    approach 10–11
Botimar, Abdolvahed 136
BP 172, 177, 234
Brannan, Paul 201
Brzezinski, Mark 48
Burns, William 244
Bushehr nuclear reactors 19–20
Bushehr refinery 178
buy-back schemes 159, 168
Buzzi, Fabio 155

Calmy-Rey, Micheline 176
Cambodia, sanctions 207
cars, conversion to CNG 180–1
Castro, Fidel 109

Centre for Nuclear Research
(Tehran) 20
Centre for Nuclear Research
and Enrichment (Isfahan) 28
Chávez, Hugo 109
China
    under Mao 84
    supply of reactors to Iran 23
    trade relationship with Iran
    163
Christians 130, 139
civil society, in Iran 125–6
    see also sanctions against
        Iran, supporting
        mobilisation of civil
        society
'civil work', in NIE report 6
Clawson, Patrick 46
commercial airliners 230–1
Cordesman, Anthony 94, 98
corruption 134
Cortem Spa 184
Council of Expediency 130
Council of Guardians 129–30
cranes, used for executions
    123–4, 155, 223
Cuba, under Castro 84–5

Daewoo 165
Daimler Chrysler 184
D'Alema, Massimo 79
Darab VLCC 165–6
death penalty, use by Iran
    123–6, 144–7, 149–50

deception, as tool of statecraft 2
Delvar VLCC 165
democracy
    in Iran 125–7, 130–4
    in Middle East 133
deterrence
    and Iran 77
    and rationality 77–80
    see also mutually assured
        destruction
Dez Ghomroud tunnel 186–8
Di Feo, Gianluca 152
dirty bombs 11, 68

EGL (Elektrizitäts-Gesellschaft
    Laufenburg AG) 176
Egypt, under Nasser 84–5, 121
ElBaradei, Mohammad 29,
    35–6, 38–42, 44–5, 50–3, 86
Europe, trade relationship with
    Iran 2, 158–64
executions, public 123–5, 223
export control agencies 240–1
extremism, increase resulting
    from nuclear-armed Iran
    106–8

Fallahian, Ali 64
Farahbakhsh, Ali 136
Farrokh, Ebrahim 188
FB Design 152–5, 185
Federation of American
    Scientists 34
Financial Action Task Force 238

Fiore, Roberto 107–8
Foucault, Michel 85–6
France
    in 1789 83, 121
    oil imports from Iran 164
Frattini, Franco 79
Freedom House, rating Iran for
    freedom 134–5
freedom of the press/
    expression 135–7
French companies' presence in
    Iran 183–4
Future Bank 210

Garangahe Sazandeghi Khatam
    190
Gazprom 172
Georgia, invasion of 243–4
German companies' presence
    in Iran 184
Germany, under Hitler 84, 121
Ghaem 187
Ghorb Nooh 190
Glucksmann, André 88
Grandori, Remo 188
Greece, oil imports from Iran
    164–5

Hadad, Adel Gholam 93
Haftapeh sugar mills 144
Hamas 11, 88–9, 106, 116, 133,
    191
Hamilton, Lee 48
hangings, public 123–4

Hanjung 165
Hassanpour, Adnan 136
Hatch Energy 190
Heisbourg, François, *Iran, le
    choix des armes* 2
Hezbollah 63–4, 87–8, 115–16,
    191
    strengthening by Iranian
        nuclear arsenal 11, 105–6
hodoud 145
homosexuals 138–9
human rights
    abuses in Iran 223
    see also death penalty, use
        by Iran; Iran, personal
        freedoms
    as objective of sanctions 202,
        213–17
    substantial 221–3
    symbolic 217–21
Hussein, Saddam 119
Hydro-Statoil 172, 176

IAEA (International Atomic
    Energy Agency)
    inspections 4–5
    and NPT obligations 19
    reports on Iran 8–9, 23,
        28–30, 44–5, 50–3
    reports on Iraq 32–3
    unanswered questions
        54–5
    see also ElBaradei,
        Mohammad

IAP (Institute for Applied
    Physics) 42
Ignatius, David 80–1, 121
India, and NPT 65–9
Internet, Iranian restriction of
    137
Interpol, warrants for Iranian
    officials 64
Iran
    airforce 113
    circumvention of European
        export controls 156–8
    comparison to Iraq WMD
        28–38, 54–5
    corporal punishments 147–8
    death penalty 123–6, 144–7,
        149–50
    democracy 125–7, 130–4
    duplicity in trade relations
        152–6, 158, 185–7, 191–3,
        197
    enrichment programme 4,
        6, 24, 39, 40–1, 43, 56–7,
        200–1
    see also Centre for
        Nuclear Research and
        Enrichment; Natanz
        uranium-enrichment
        plant
    ethnic minorities 141–2
    European companies
        present in 183–5
    freedom of the press/
        expression 135–7

gas
    conversion of cars to
        CNG 180–1
    dependence on fuel
        imports 179
    international partnerships
        172, 176–7
    investment required to
        realise potential 170–2,
        177–8
    pipeline connections 170
    reserves 170
    sanctions against 234–5
    South Pars gas field 171–3,
        177
    judicial system 125–6
    labour conditions 142–4
    leaders' mindset 62–3, 74–5
    military capabilities 114
    missile programme 43–4
    ballistic missiles 6, 11, 23,
        33, 36
    Shahab-3 missiles 42, 52–4
    nationalism 118–19
    negotiations with 9, 78–9,
        199–201
    as never having threatened
        anyone 63–4
    non-Shi'a religious
        communities 139–41
    nuclear programme
    2003 suspension 4–6, 200
    capability 7, 36, 39
    as defensive 17–18

history 19–24
momentum 3
motives for 1
outcomes of acquiring
    nuclear arsenal 10–13,
    100–6
possession of bomb plans
    50–1
sites 24–7
nuclear strike on Israel
Hezbollah delivered 95–8
likelihood 60–2, 87–93
missile-delivered 93–5
oil
dependence on fuel imports
    179, 181–2
need for facilities upgrade
    167–9
production capacity 166–7
refineries 178–9
reserves 165
tanker fleet 165–6
personal freedoms 137–9
political power structure
    128–31
problems trading with
    185–95
refineries and fuel imports
    178–98
sanctions against 232–4
response to pre-emptive
    military strike 112–22
as a revolutionary power
    74–6, 80–2

trade relationship with
    Europe 2, 158–64
unanswered IAEA questions
    54–5
Iran–Iraq War (1980–88) 20–2
Iran, la prochaine guerre
    (Tertrais) 32–3
Iran, le choix des armes
    (Heisbourg) 2
Iraq
    nuclear weapons
        programme 33–5
    sanctions 120, 206
Iraq War (2003–)
    impact on Iran nuclear
        programme 4
    and scepticism regarding
        Iran's nuclear aspirations 8
IRGC (Iranian Revolutionary
    Guard Corps) 132, 190–1,
    194, *passim*
Islamic unions 143
Israel
    and NPT 65–7
    nuclear strike by Iran
    Hezbollah delivered 95–8
    likelihood 60–2, 87–93
    missile-delivered 93–5
    peace prospects and Iranian
        nuclear capability 11
    possibility of military action
        against Iran 10, 112
    usage of nuclear capability
        70–1

Italian companies' presence in
Iran 184
Italkrane 184
Italy, oil imports from Iran 164
Iveco 195

Jalili, Saeed 48, 244
Japan, trade relationship with
Iran 163
Jazayeri, Seyyed Massoud 92
Jews 130, 139
Jordan, threat from nuclear-
armed Iran 110
journalists 135–6

Kagan, Robert 48
Kavoosifar, Hossein 123
Kavoosifar, Majid 123
Kay, David 29, 30, 47, 55, 57,
211
Kazemi, Mehdi 139
Kazemi, Zahra 135
Khamenei, Ayatollah Ali 74,
88–9, 128–9, 130–1
Khan, Abdul Qadeer 23, 32, 37,
51, 70
Kharg Island oil terminal 166
Kharkeh Dam 190
Khatami, Mohammad 58, 88,
90, 127–8
Khobar Towers Bombing
(Dhahran, Saudi Arabia,
1996) 63
Khodro car factory 144

Khomeini, Ayatollah Ruhollah
75, 129
closure of nuclear activities
20
revival of nuclear
programme 22
Kish oil terminal 166
Kissinger, Henry 46, 81
KTI-Plersch 190
Kurds 141–2

Larijani, Ali 128
Larijani, Mohammad 93
Lavan Island oil terminal 166
Leverett, Flint 49
Leverett, Hillary 49
Levriero speedboat 152
Libya, sanctions 206–7
Lincy, Valerie 46
LNG (Liquefied Natural Gas)
169–70, 173–5
sanctions against 234–5
LNG trains 170, 173–4
Lockerbie (Pan Am flight 103
bombing) 63
Lucky Goldstar Construction
172
Luft, Gal 167, 180–1

Mahshar oil terminal 166
Majlis 130
Maurizi, Stefania 152
McConnell, Michael 47
Milhollin, Gary 46–7

Milosevic, Slobodan 119
minors, subject to death
    penalty in Iran 145–6
Mirnehad, Yaghoob 136
missiles *see* Iran, missile
    programme; sanctions
    against Iran, missile
    programmes related;
    Shahab-3 missiles
Mofaz, Shaul 101
Moghadas, Hassan 123
Mottaki, Manouchehr 92
Mughniyeh, 'Imad 64, 93,
    116
Musharraf, Pervez 23
mutually assured destruction
    (MAD)
    India–Pakistan 69–70
    in Middle East 61–2, 99–100
Myanmar, sanctions 226–7

Nabi VLCC 165
Natanz uranium-enrichment
    plant 5, 24, 26, 37
National Council of Resistance,
    revelation of clandestine
    nuclear sites 4–5, 24
National Intelligence Estimate
    (NIE, December 2007) 3–4,
    6–7, 8, 45–50
NATO, impact of nuclear-
    armed Iran 111
Nejm VLCC 165
Neka oil terminal 166

Nesa VLCC 165
NITC (National Iranian Tanker
    Company) 165
Noah VLCC 165
non-governmental
    organisations, in Iran 142
Noor VLCC 165
North Korea, acquisition of
    nuclear weapons 72–3
Nozari, Gholamhossin 205
NPT (Nuclear
    Non-Proliferation Treaty)
    breach of obligations by Iran
        5, 18–19, 28–9
    fear of precedent by Iran
        enrichment programme
        65–9
    impact of Iran acquiring
        nuclear arsenal 12, 67–9,
        111
    reliance on integrity of
        signatories 27
nuclear arms race, prospect of
    109–10
nuclear cycle 33
nuclear-free Middle East 69

oil price
    and sanctions 204–6
    threat from nuclear-armed
        Iran 100–3, 105
Organisation for Islamic
    Propaganda 141
Osanloo, Mansour 144, 221

Pakistan
    and NPT 65–9
    threatened by any Iranian
        nuclear arsenal 11
    usage of nuclear capability
        70
Pan Am Flight 103 Bombing
    Incident (1988) 63
Pars Geometry 188
Petronas 172, 177
Petropars 172
PIJ (Palestinian Islamic Jihad)
    88
Pilger, John 31
Platzeck, Matthias 79
Poerner 178
Pollack, Kenneth 75–6, 117–18
Power, Samantha 49
Poyry 190

Rabbani, Mohsen 64
Rafsanjani, Akhbar Hashemi
    64, 88, 90–1, 127–8
Redeker, Robert 150
regime change, impact of
    pre-emptive strike on Iran
    118–19
Reliance 177
Repsol 172, 177
reverse-engineering of Western
    products 152–3
revolutionary powers 82–5
    Iran as 74–6, 80–2
Reynaers Aluminium 183

Rezai, Mohsen 64, 90
rifle production 195–6
Ritter, Scott 31
Rockefeller, John D., IV 47
Ross, Dennis 46
Rostami, Jamal 188
Rushdie, Sir Salman 149–50
Russia, attitude toward Iran
    243–5

Safavi, Rahim 93
Saghand, uranium deposits 24
Sahel Consulting Engineers 187
Salehi, Seyed Davoud 147–8
Samsung 172
sanctions against Iran
    appetite for 8–10
    effectiveness 206–7, 211–12,
        240–2
    extraction technology 235–7
    financial sector 237–9
    human-rights-related
        sanctions 202, 213–17
    substantial 221–3
    symbolic 217–21
    LNG 234–5
    missile programmes related
        228–32
    necessity of 14–16, 242–7
    NIE and 48
    objections to 203–6
    post-1991 Gulf War 33
    post-2006 41, 162
    post-NIE 50

against publicly owned
companies 225–8
refineries 232–4
'smart' sanctions 202–3,
207–11
strategic sectors 230–2
supporting mobilisation of
civil society 223–5
Sarkozy, Nicolas 199
Sarmadi-Rad, M. A. 170–1
satellite dishes, Iranian
restriction of 137
Saudi Arabia
purchase of nuclear-capable
missiles 109–10
threat from nuclear-armed
Iran 13, 104–5
Sawyer, John 30–1
Schlesinger, James 46
Seli Spa 184
Seli Tunnel 186–8, 190
Shah of Iran, nuclear
development under 19–20
Shahab-3 missiles 42, 52–4
Shanbeh-zehi, Nasrollah 145
Shariatmadari, Hossein 103
Shell 172–3, 177
'Shi'a Crescent' 110
Shirazi, Ali 59
Shire, Jacqueline 201
Siemens 19, 23
Solana, Javier 244
Soleimanpour, Hadi 64
Soltaniyeh, Ali Asghar 245

South Africa, deal to supply
yellowcake 19
South Pars gas field 171–3, 177
speedboats 95, 101, 114–15, 185
see also Boghammar
speedboats
SPG (Steiner-Permatechnik-
Gastec) 180
Stalin, Josef 77
Steyr-Mannlicher sniper rifles
196–7
stoning, death by 124, 147
Straw, Jack 79
street names 220–1
Sunni Muslims, in Iran 139–40
Supreme Leader of the
Revolutionary Republic 129
see also Khamenei, Ayatollah
Ali; Khomeini, Ayatollah
Ruhollah
Syria, protected by nuclear-
armed Iran 110

Tabriz refinery 178
Takeyh, Ray 48, 74–5
Technimont 193
Tehran refinery 178
Terram 183
terrorism, increase resulting
from nuclear-armed Iran 105
Tertrais, Bruno 106
Iran, la prochaine guerre 32–3
torture
evidence obtained under 147

practised in Iran 148
  see also Bani Yaghoub, Zahra;
    Kazemi, Mehdi; Kazemi,
    Zahra; Osanloo, Mansour
Total 173
TotalFinaElf 172, 177
Toyota 195
'Trinity test' 42

UNIHA 183
unions of workers, in Iran
  142–4
uranium deposits, in Iran 24
US
  European opposition to
    military intervention in
    Iran 78–9
  past military conflict against
    Iran 114
  pre-emptive military strike
    against Iran 112–22
  likelihood 3, 6–7, 48
USSR
  rebuilding of Bushehr
    nuclear power plant 23

as revolutionary power
  83–4, 121

Vahidi, Ahmad 64
value targeting 78
van Gogh, Theodorus "Theo"
  150
Velayat-el-Fakih doctrine 129
Velayati, Ali Akhbar 64
VLCCs (Very Large Crude
  Carriers) 165

'War of the Cities' 21
Wärtsilä 165–6
Weems, Philip R. 174–5
Weinthal, Benjamin 157
Wirth 186–90
Wisconsin Project for Arms
  Control 36, 201
  see also Milhollin, Gary
women 137–8, 147–8

Zagros mountains tunnels 57
Zoroastrians 130, 139